Indigeneity and Politi

Indigeneity and Political Theory engages some of the profound challenges to traditions of modern political theory that have been posed over the past two decades. Karena Shaw is especially concerned with practices of sovereignty as they are embedded in and shape Indigenous politics, and responses to Indigenous politics.

Drawing on theories of post-coloniality, feminism, globalization, and international politics, and using examples of contemporary political practice including court cases and specific controversies, Shaw seeks to illustrate and argue for a way of doing political theory that is more responsive to the challenges posed by a range of contemporary issues.

An engaging and highly original analysis of Indigenenity and sovereignty, this book enables the reader to develop a more robust consideration of relationships between theory and practice, and thus the politics of theorizing.

Karena Shaw is Assistant Professor in the School of Environmental Studies at the University of Victoria, Canada. A political theorist by training, she is particularly interested in how a range of contemporary political challenges—such as those raised by indigenous, feminist, and environmental movements—are reshaping political space and possibility.

Routledge Issues in Contemporary Political Theory

This series engages with the most significant issues in contemporary political theory. Each text is written by a leading scholar and provides a short, accessible and stimulating overview of the issue for advanced undergraduates and graduate students of political theory. As well as providing a survey of the field, the books contain original and groundbreaking thinking which will drive forward debates on these key issues.

1. **Indigeneity and Political Theory**
Sovereignty and the limits of the
political
Karena Shaw

Indigeneity and Political Theory

Sovereignty and the limits of the political

Karena Shaw

Routledge
Taylor & Francis Group

LONDON AND NEW YORK

First published 2008 by Routledge
2 Park Square, Milton Park, Abingdon, Oxon, OX14 4RN

Simultaneously published in the USA and Canada
by Routledge
270 Madison Avenue, New York, NY 10016

Routledge is an imprint of the Taylor & Francis Group, an informa business

Typeset in Times by RefineCatch Limited, Bungay, Suffolk, UK
Printed and bound in Great Britain by
CPI Antony Rowe, Chippenham, Wiltshire

British Library Cataloguing in Publication Data
A catalogue record for this book is available from the
British Library

Library of Congress Cataloging-in-Publication Data
Shaw, Karena.
Sovereignty and political theory : indigeneity and the limits of the
political / Karena Shaw.
p. cm.—(Routledge issues in contemporary political theory; 1)
Includes bibliographical references and index.
1. Sovereignty.   2. Political science.   I. Title.
JC327.S52 2008
320.1′5—dc22   2008010911

ISBN 10: 0–415–77700–3 (hbk)
ISBN 10: 0–415–77701–1 (pbk)
ISBN 10: 0–203–89114–7 (ebk)

ISBN 13: 978–0–415–77700–1 (hbk)
ISBN 13: 978–0–415–77701–8 (pbk)
ISBN 13: 978–0–203–89114–8 (ebk)

Contents

vi   *Contents*

Acknowledgments

This book had a rather long, if not very exciting, life as a manuscript. Along the way its existence was considerably enriched by the engagement of many readers: Jane Bennett, David Campbell, Bill Chaloupka, Bill Connolly, Virginia Draper, Richard Flathman, John Horton, Thom Kuehls, Tim Luke, James Rowe, Warren Magnusson, Susan Quirk, Michael Shapiro, Gary Shaw, Kathleen Shaw, Rob Walker, and six anonymous reviewers read most if not all of the manuscript, some of them more than once. All have balanced insightful critiques with generous space to find my way through these questions. Many others, including Kennan Ferguson, Carole Patemen, Paul Patton, and Debbie Lisle, gave me feedback on parts of the manuscript. Although I've almost certainly not taken their advice often enough, I owe them all my sincere thanks. Readers do too. Trust me on this.

I have been tremendously fortunate to have been surrounded by excellent colleagues, support staff and students at the University of Victoria and Keele University while working on the manuscript. In both cases, it has been a real pleasure to work with people I enjoy and admire. John Horton and Warren Magnusson in particular have both been astute and generous readers and good friends. Other colleagues—near and far—have intervened at key moments to bolster my belief in this project: Michael Asch, Russel Barsh, Angharad Closs, Costas Constantinou, Barry Hindess, Ronnie Lipschutz, Tim Luke, Kirstie McClure, Mat Paterson, Sanjay Seth, Peter Stephenson, and Hidemi Suganami may not know how vital their contributions have been, but I have appreciated them deeply. My students, including research assistants Adam Barker and Robin Kells, also deserve a special thanks. Although I have never taught the material in this book, my interactions with students have sustained my interest in it, and their curiosity has inspired me to finish it.

Finally, of course, there are those whose diverse contributions extend far beyond the current book, but who are nonetheless also implicated in it. Friends gathered from various places as I've struggled through this project have bolstered my spirit, provided support and distraction, and reminded me what is most important. Didier Bigo, Elspeth Guild, and Philippe Bonditti made crucial writing stints in Paris possible, and provided wonderful company. Likewise all those in the Institute of International Relations (IRI) at

PUC-Rio proved excellent hosts, providing just enough distraction to support a frenzy of writing in Brazil. Philippe Correia, Liam Eady, Margaret Eady, Mark Franke, Caitlin Gordon-Walker, Johanna Gordon-Walker, Julie Heegaard, Gogi Hodder, Thom Kuehls, Valerie Langer, Michelle Miller, and Derek Shaw each deserve much more than thanks for their companionship and varied interventions in my life. Debbie Lisle has consistently offered incomparable humor and sanity. Joanna Gislason has been and reinvented herself, which is more than anyone could ask for and has inspired and grounded me. Rob Walker has provided breakfast, inspiration and distraction almost on demand, and has sustained and enhanced my spirit in myriad ways. All of them, and many others who deserve my thanks, have been themselves in ways that I deeply appreciate.

My parents, Gary and Kathleen Shaw, deserve my greatest thanks and admiration. They have not only supported me in this project, but in all things. They have given me my love of the world, of teaching, and of ideas, and they have tried to keep me from taking it all too seriously. Most importantly, they have been my friends, which has been and will remain a tremendous pleasure.

My thanks also to the editors and publishers who have given permission to use the following material. Parts of Chapter 4 were previously published as "Indigeneity and the International," *Millennium: Journal of International Studies*, 31:1 (May 2002). Parts of Chapter 5 were previously published as "Creating/Negotiating Interstices: Indigenous Sovereignties," in *Sovereign Lives: Power in Global Politics*, Jenny Edkins, Véronique Pin-Fat and Michael J. Shapiro, eds., New York: Routledge, 2004, and are reproduced with permission of Taylor & Francis Group LLC.

1   Introduction
The problem of the political

This book is most centrally about the problem of the political; it is about the conditions under which and the practices through which authority is constituted and legitimated, and what these constitutions and legitimations enable and disable. It is also an argument for and illustration of a way of understanding and approaching this problem, and of conceptualizing what is at stake in considering it. The argument is developed through a specific focus on how this problem has framed the possibilities for Indigenous peoples in Canada, and how their struggles with it have in turn reframed the problem. Nevertheless, the core argument of the book concerns non-Indigenous people, the political ideas and institutions we have inherited and which express our ideals and aspirations for collective life. It is motivated by a desire to understand something of the violences and limitations of these ideas and institutions, and to contribute to a conversation about how, under contemporary circumstances, we might constitute and legitimate forms of authority that address some of them.

These are big themes and claims, and how they fit together will not be immediately obvious. Much of this chapter focuses on unpacking them, exploring first of all what the book seeks to achieve and why, and then explaining how the argument proceeds.

Why the problem of the political?

The 20th century was characterized by a range of important political movements: anti-colonial, nationalist, feminist, and ecological, not least. While the dynamics within and among these movements vary widely, a key aspiration of many of them has been not only to gain access to or representation in political institutions, but to forward a deeper challenge to the character and constitution of these institutions themselves.

In the case of anti-colonial nationalism, for example, there have been those who saw the eviction of colonizers and the formation of their own government as the pinnacle of their political aspirations, while others have been concerned about the dangers inherent in nationalism itself as a discourse of liberation for colonized peoples. The latter have argued that simply seizing control over institutions of governance might not effect a liberation from colonialism, in fact perhaps quite the opposite, suggesting the need for critical reformulations of the institutions and even subjectivities of colonialism in order to achieve the aspirations of movements for national liberation.[1]

Similarly in the case of feminist movements: some feminists have argued that giving women the vote, or equal political representation, would be adequate to remedy the basis of wrongs against them, while many others have raised concerns that the architecture of the oppression of women is much more complex, requiring a redefinition of what counts as political in order for gender-based oppression to be effectively engaged. In fact, feminist theory and politics have consistently reproduced this tension between the strategic necessity of working "within" structures of politics and the realization that these political structures are themselves gendered in such a way as to render such "inclusion" unsatisfactory to address their demands. Many of the crucial texts of early "second wave" feminism, for example, questioned the implications of our inherited accounts of the proper space for and character of politics.[2] These texts argued that women's exclusion from political space was neither accidental nor incidental, but was crucial to the construction of the space for and character of politics. Thus it was not enough only to add women to existing political space; the gendered character of the space of the political itself, and the political concepts and practices through which it was constituted, needed to be reshaped in order for gendered forms of oppression to be engaged.[3] Other feminist theorists have extended this analysis to the political dynamics of forms of subjectivity, practices of knowing, and the implications of emerging political practices.[4] The feminist analysis of politics has, in other words, expressed a complex of different understandings, practices, modes of analysis and interpretation of the political.[5]

As is the case with nationalism and the other movements mentioned above, debates have raged within feminist movements, as well as between movements and the institutions they seek to change, about what should count as properly political, what the strategic aspirations or claims of the movement should be. Although frequently minimized or dismissed as irrelevant, these debates are anything but; they have absorbed significant amounts of energy and been the cause of the spilling of much blood, both metaphorical and literal. They express and stretch the limits of our imagination and our aspirations, as well as our political strategies. As suggested by a range of recent titles, one of the outcomes of these struggles has been the emergence of a debate focused on rethinking the political.[6] But what might it mean to "rethink the political" under contemporary circumstances? There is a consistent lack of clarity in these emerging literatures about what this might involve, or indeed why we might want to do it. That is perhaps the core problem this book seeks to explore. It takes up this question not with an aspiration to discover or define a space of the properly political, but with a desire to better understand what it might mean to take up the question of the political: to examine the historical and intellectual contexts we inherit and must engage when we do so, to consider why we might want to do so, and to explore what such an inquiry might seek to achieve. As such, it especially seeks to contribute to two kinds of ongoing debates: those within and across political movements about what forms and understandings of political action are appropriate—enabling, responsive, progressive—under contemporary circumstances, and likewise those within contemporary political theory about what forms of theorizing are appropriate in these contexts.

Globalization, sovereignty, and the political

One of the reasons for the current vogue of rethinking the political emerges from the relatively recent convergence between the debates described above and another set of debates: those loosely (and frustratingly) clumped under the label of "globalization." There is, of course, more disagreement than agreement about what globalization is, whether it should be characterized as an independent set of processes, if so when it might have begun, and what its broader implications might be. However, from amidst the fury of disagreement a set of shared questions and debates has begun to emerge. One of the most persistent and important questions that has emerged has been that of the implications of contemporary processes for one of the great achievements of modernity: the sovereign state.

Although its expression has varied widely, and its histories are rather uneven, for the past few centuries the sovereign state has been the assumed locus of political community and authority, first in Europe and eventually globally. In fact, sovereignty as an assumption, discourse and practice has been the key ordering principle of political organization since the collapse of ecclesiastical forms of authority. It has defined political community and situated us, sometimes against our will, each as a citizen of a particular bounded territorial state, which in turn has an obligation to provide us with the freedom to live in peace as individuals, and with a locus for the expression of our individual and collective political will. Inside each state is the space for political community, and outside is a space of some kind of anarchy, where states interact on the principle—if not the reality—of equality, in the absence of a global sovereign to keep order. While sovereign states might choose to cede some of that sovereignty through treaties, or the formation of global bodies with specific responsibilities, the ultimate authority always rests with the sovereign state. For us individuals, then, the sovereign state is our home and the boundary of our political community. Or that at least is how the sovereignty story has been told.

However, according to some analysts of processes of globalization, what is new now is that the sovereignty story may no longer be either adequate or appropriate, if indeed it ever was. Perhaps the expansion of international law and global economic institutions means that sovereign states no longer have the capacity to be responsible for governance of the territory within state borders. Perhaps the rise of forms of global communication and political organization means that the sovereign state no longer provides the boundary of political community, as people's identities are now expressed and articulated across very different non-territorially defined spaces. Perhaps, even, with the rise of intra-state violence, sovereignty no longer indicates the legitimate control over violence within a territory. Perhaps the sovereign state, or indeed sovereignty itself, is either on its last legs or in the process of fundamental transformations.

Whether or not this is the case, the rise of the sustained debate about it has reinforced the urgency of considering the question of the political: insofar as state sovereignty has provided the structure and organization of political community for recent history, and sovereignty seems to be under some considerable strains or pressures, what does this mean for the expression of collective political will? What does this mean for the legitimacy of political authority? Who, or what, is or should be responsible, accountable, obliged to respond to individual or collective desires, ambitions, complaints? Anxiety about this question is evident not only in literatures on globalization, but also in the diversity of collective actions expressed in opposition to what are taken to be specific manifestations of increased globalization, such as the World Trade Organization, the International Monetary Fund, the World Economic Forum, Group of 8, the proposed Free Trade Agreement for the Americas, and so on. One of the core complaints expressed in such protests is precisely that of legitimacy and accountability: on whose behalf do these institutions act? To whom are they accountable? Are they in fact making decisions that affect the lives of citizens who have no access to or representation in their decision making processes?

While these specific questions are beyond the scope of this analysis, they are indications of the more general problem to which it speaks, and they have helped to give it form and urgency. The concerns they express are about the problem of the political, about the conditions under which and the practices through which authority is constituted and legitimated, and what these constitutions and legitimations enable and disable. The primary modern answer to this problem has been state sovereignty. If these protesters and some analysts of globalization are correct, this answer may no longer be sufficient, or at least may be in need of more specificity. The problem of the political from this perspective thus takes us to sovereignty, as a discourse and practice, and this provides the focal point of the analysis here.

Sovereignty and indigeneity

This still leaves many questions about my starting point unanswered. If I claim to be interested in the political, in the constitution and legitimation of authority, why begin with Indigenous peoples?[7] I do this not primarily because I take their situation to be particularly desperate, or noble, or just, or righteous; rather, because I find their situation to be especially revealing about the contemporary problem of the political in two ways.

First, although they vary widely, their situations are revealing in that they provide a microcosm in which one can examine crucial elements of situations much of the world faces: struggles against marginal material conditions; very tentative and uneven connections to economic structures, systems, and flows; relatively high levels of social disruption and their attendant problems, including high levels of violence; very politicized and highly ambivalent relationships to dominant practices of knowing; multiple and highly conflictual subjectivities, both internal to selves and expressed across communities in relation to conflicting desires, visions for the future, values in the present, and so on. Put more crudely (and perhaps misleadingly), these are communities constituted partly through the oppositional practices of modernity: they know there are dominant systems and forms of power; they know what it feels like to be victim to them; they know these systems work for others; they know, and have borne, some of their costs. They seem to share a desire to create collective futures for themselves that do not succumb to either side of the oppositional structures they face: to be Indigenous or to be Modern.

Most centrally, they seek to create collective futures: in this they provide a microcosm that is potentially revealing. It is revealing not least because the modern answer to this ambition is sovereignty, but sovereignty on the modern (state) model will not work for Indigenous peoples, or indeed perhaps for anyone else under contemporary circumstances. Thus they are struggling to create legitimate authorities—sovereignties—within and across spatial, temporal and discursive conditions that may be at odds with those that have enabled modern state sovereignty. There are many ways to characterize their ambitions, leading us to a variety of different literatures: they seek to establish sovereignties within sovereignties;[8] they seek to create post-colonial sovereignties;[9] they seek to create economically and ecologically viable "local" sovereignties within and through processes of "globalization,"[10] and so on. Thus, Indigenous peoples provide a microcosm in which one can see elements of struggles faced by a large percentage of the world's population, struggles that tend to appear very marginally in discourses and practices of contemporary political theory. In the details of this microcosm there will be resonances and discontinuities with the situations of other peoples, communities, and locales, both internally and externally, but the conditions are shared or resonate often enough with a broad range of other situations that they are revealing of a range of crucial struggles over the preconditions for, meaning and practices of, the political.

The second reason I find Indigenous peoples' situations especially revealing about the character of modern politics is that because they exist in "our" spatially defined political states, because our own identities are constituted partly in relation to them, because our economies and political communities are enabled by resources colonized from them, their situations reveal most profoundly the violences inflicted by our own modes of life and understanding.[11] Their situations thus pose challenges that I take to be my challenges, in the sense that I have benefited and do benefit from precisely the modes of thought and understanding, social, material and political organization that are primarily responsible for the situation they find themselves in today. To be clear, this is not simply an assertion that it is "our" fault that they are in the situation they find themselves in. It is a more sustained assertion that their situation is a condition of possibility of our own, both historically and in present times. This is true in crude material or economic terms, but also in discursive and subjective terms. So, although the struggles listed above are revealing of a range of key struggles that are often represented as distant from those of us in North America and Europe, they are most centrally our problems, not because "we" should go there and attempt to solve them, but because of the ways in which they implicate our own modes of life and understanding. We must understand these relationships to understand ourselves and politics. Further, they are increasingly being expressed and understood as such: the roots of many of the environmental crises we face today, for example, are embedded in ontologies and expressed in discourses and practices often defined explicitly through opposition to Indigenous ways of life.[12] This has enabled both the successes of these discourses and practices and the constitutive violences of these successes.

As the flip side of my argument that their struggles implicate us, I want to be very clear that I do not wish to speak on behalf of Indigenous peoples, or in the interests of extending (our) justice to them, both of which, however well intentioned and sometimes strategically important, are essentially demeaning and at times disempowering activities. Nor am I especially interested in "them"—their worlds, cosmologies, modes of social and political interaction, and so on. Although such an interest has an important place, for reasons that I hope are becoming clear, that place is not here. I am interested in "us": in how our modes of understanding, practices of knowing and acting, structures of social and political organization, establish and reflect political possibilities, in how these spaces are always both enabling and constraining for Indigenous peoples (as well as many other "marginal" peoples), and in how they might be critically reformulated.

This leads to a further question: if this is why I choose to focus on Indigenous peoples, why in Canada, specifically? Again there are at least two reasons. First, Canada is where I found myself when it came time to do the research, and, as suggested above, part of the motivation for the analysis is an immediate effort to think through the political contexts I have inherited and in which I live. However, this expresses more than a personal preference; it is also a considered response to the challenges posed by a range of literatures about how we might proceed as political theorists under contemporary circumstances. The second reason why the text focuses specifically on Indigenous politics in Canada is that Canada provides a site that both is important on its own terms—it is where some of the most important recent developments around Indigenous issues have arisen and developed—and has key resonances with a range of other contexts of Indigenous politics globally. Although Indigenous politics vary considerably from site to site, not only across international contexts but also within Canada, one of the character-istics of the rise of Indigenous politics has been its international ar-ticulation.[13] Events in one part of the world, whether legal decisions, violent confrontations, or innovative political strategies, tend to be communicated much more widely, adapted and reproduced at other sites, and events in Canada have been important in this regard. This is most obviously the case in relation to legal decisions, where in some cases decisions of the Canadian Supreme Court have been cited in court cases at other sites around the world, influencing the development of Indigenous law and policy in these places. One of the cases I discuss below, *Delgamuukw v. B.C.*, provides a recent and important example of this. In addition to the legal connection, however, Canadian Indigenous peoples have also been at the forefront of inter-national efforts to address Indigenous issues. The first meeting of the World Indigenous Council, for example, took place on Vancouver Island in British Columbia, and Canadian Indigenous groups have provided leadership to many other processes.

Perhaps even more to the point, however, the Canadian state provides an important site because of the characteristics of Canada itself, which have shaped the relationship between the Indigenous peoples and the state in ways that have implications for other sites around the world. Canada, unlike, say, the United States, is a federal system that has had to respond to a serious and sustained nationalist and secessionist movement in Quebec, and this has pro-vided a context for the articulation of Indigenous issues that highlights some of their complexities and uniqueness in important ways. This complexity is consistent with the rise and expression of Indigenous politics in parts of Africa, in particular, where Indigenous and nationalist movements overlap and conflict. Also unlike the United States, but more like a range of other countries struggling with Indigenous issues, the legal status of Indigenous peoples has never been systematically resolved: many groups have never signed treaties and thus have viable claims to large tracts of territory, for example.[14] On some readings their legal claims pose potential challenges to the legal basis of the sovereignty of the states themselves. This leads to some of the tensions that also characterize relationships between Indigenous peoples and states such as Brazil and Australia, for example, where Indigen-ous groups also inhabit large tracts of land that are extremely sparsely popu-lated but are under great pressure from resource extraction industries. In all three cases, the unique legal status of Indigenous groups renders their claims a significant blockage to the respective governments being able to provide access and stability for these industries, which in turn gives Indigenous issues a certain urgency and profile within the state. Perhaps most importantly, in many of these cases the political institutions and imaginaries against and through which Indigenous peoples are struggling are also inherited from the same colonial sources as those that govern Canada.[15] Despite important differences in each context, consistent structural constraints and echoes resonate through political strategies and possibilities at diverse sites around the world, as individuals and communities seek to seize and shape political possibility in contemporary times.

In this way, this book begins with an ancient problem—the problem of the political—that has contemporary expression at and through multiple sites, both empirical and theoretical, perhaps most crucially between the two. It will be occupied with carefully setting out a specific way of conceptualizing this problem, of understanding what is at stake in it, and how we might proceed in relation to it. To do so, it will focus on a particular context in which this problem manifests—the political situation, aspirations, and activities of Indigenous peoples in Canada—a context that is at the same time quite specific and yet also provides an important microcosm through which a broader consideration is possible.

This book is thus about Indigenous politics insofar as it tries to explore the conditions under which these movements have evolved and to argue that these conditions must be critically engaged. It forwards an argument that it is in "on the ground" negotiations that these movements are enacting that crucial renegotiations of state sovereignty and the political are occurring, and that these activities must be engaged with far more rigor by contemporary theorists interested in the problem of the political. More centrally, however, it is an attempt to come to terms with how discourses and practices of sovereignty still set the conditions under which Indigenous—and other forms of "marginal"—politics occur at all. It also seeks to explore how other possibilities can be, and are being, rethought and reconstructed. To this end, it sets out a map of some of the conditions of possibility for Indigenous politics, and most specifically of sovereignty as both an enabling and a limiting discourse. This map implies, in turn, a much broader argument about the status of sovereignty in modern political thought. That the argument leads to such broad ground is not surprising in that "Indians" already make a crucial appearance at key textual moments in which modern political thought was articulated. Perhaps most importantly, then, this map implies the necessity of reconceptualizing the relationship between political theory and the challenges posed by contemporary Indigenous politics, and of progressive or critical politics more generally. This, in turn, requires a critical engagement with the conditions of possibility for the political, a rearticulation of the political, a repoliticization of the political.

I thus argue below that contemporary politics are framed by discourses of sovereignty. These discourses are neither natural nor neutral. They reproduce a space for politics that is enabled by and rests upon the production, naturalization, and marginalization of certain forms of "difference." Indigenous politics illustrate and challenge this in three ways: first, Indigenous peoples are among those both implicitly and explicitly produced and marked as "different" in and through sovereignty discourse, and this is one of the enabling conditions of sovereignty discourse; second, even as these discourses enable Indigenous peoples' political claims, they also continue to be marginalized by and through these same discourses; and, third, through their (necessary) engagement with this paradox, these movements are encountering, challenging, and reshaping the "limits" of contemporary politics. Thus, even as Indigenous politics are framed by these discourses and practices, they also, in part because of their centrality to them, expose, denaturalize, and reformulate them.

The challenges posed to discourses of sovereignty by Indigenous politics are thus important not only because unless these discourses are challenged and the realm of the political reformulated, Indigenous politics will continue to be forced between impossible alternatives, but also because the problems confronted by Indigenous peoples in relation to sovereignty discourses are not only "their" problems, but go to the heart of contemporary understandings and practices of politics. Unless political theorists, as those people most concerned to understand, evaluate and legitimize authoritative political activity, begin to engage with these problems, we will all continue to be stuck with the same unsatisfactory answers to the crucial political questions of the day, and we will continue to reinforce the marginalization of a range of contemporary political movements. This text thus attempts to challenge and loosen the hold of particular ways of thinking about politics, those especially dear to many contemporary political theorists. It also, however, attempts to suggest ways in which a serious engagement with Indigenous politics might disrupt established thinking about politics, and open new political spaces.

Structure of the book

The book is divided into three parts. Part I, "Sovereignty and the political," explores how discourses and practices of sovereignty "work" to construct the space of the political, and—in precisely the same gesture—how they simultaneously effect the exclusion of Indigenous peoples. To this end, my argument begins by unraveling Thomas Hobbes' production of sovereignty in the first book of *Leviathan* (Chapter 2). The structure of sovereignty that Hobbes produces is enabled and authorized through the production of a shared ontological ground, an identity. This identity, in turn, rests upon the necessary exclusion of Indigenous peoples at several different levels, not least through the explicit marking of Indigenous peoples as "different," as "Other." What is more crucial in determining the character of contemporary Indigenous politics, however, is that Hobbes renders the construction of this exclusionary identity, the processes through which authority is produced and guaranteed, as pre-political, as necessary and natural rather than contingent and violent. He does this by subsequently locating the space of the properly political in relations between the sovereign and the citizens. The processes through which sovereignty is produced and secured are in this way rendered apolitical and uncontestable, necessary and inevitable. Although there are many other important theorists of modern sovereignty, Hobbes' account of the architecture of sovereignty, in which the constitution of authority through processes of collective subjectification is effaced and "politics" is produced as relations of governance, is paradigmatic. It remains crucial for understanding how practices of sovereignty work both to construct the space of the properly political and to effect the exclusion of Indigenous peoples (as well as many others), and as such provides the central reference point for much of the analysis that follows.

The two chapters that follow illustrate how this architecture produced by Hobbes works to structure the political much more broadly, first through practices of nation-building in North America, and then through the production and disciplining of knowledge. Chapter 3 traces Hobbes' architecture in Alexis de Tocqueville's description of emerging forms of democracy in America, and in the practices of "Indian policy" in Canada. In both cases the analysis focuses on revealing the resonances across discourses and practices of sovereignty, and on revealing the exclusions they effect. These continuities are important not only for developing an understanding of the past violences effected by and through discourses of sovereignty, but, as is taken up in Part II, in understanding some of the tensions and double-binds contemporary Indigenous movements must negotiate.

Chapter 4 moves on to explore how sovereignty works through a different, although related, set of practices: the contemporary disciplining of knowledge. The chapter focuses specifically on how the disciplinary divide between anthropology and international relations works to reproduce sovereignty as the enabling ground of politics, and on how this in turn impacts the ways in which the contemporary concerns of Indigenous peoples have been apprehended and understood. The analysis concludes with a consideration of how the practices of sovereignty shape strategic possibilities for Indigenous peoples, posing the question of what kinds of analytical as well as political practices must be effected in order to enable their situations to be engaged more productively.

As a whole, then, the first part of the book seeks to introduce the problem of the political through an examination of how sovereignty works, using Hobbes as an example, and of some of the ways we inherit Hobbes' framing of the problem, how it continues to shape our possibilities for engaging the challenges posed by Indigenous politics. It also seeks to illustrate the necessity of addressing the conditions of possibility of claims to authority in contemporary academic work as part and parcel of the struggle to address and reformulate the exclusions effected by modern productions of sovereignty. In the absence of a critical engagement with the structures of authority that enable political work—both "theoretical" and "practical"—we will, I argue, necessarily continue to reproduce an impossibly narrow and marginalized terrain for Indigenous politics, as well as for political theory.

Part II of the book, "Negotiating the limits of the political," explores how Indigenous movements are encountering and negotiating the problem of the political. It examines several contemporary political dilemmas faced by Indigenous political movements in Canada, using the analysis of sovereignty in order to differently frame and better understand what is at stake in them.

Chapter 5 examines a key moment in the rise of Indigenous politics in Canada: the efforts to include a guarantee to the right of self-government for Aboriginal peoples in the Constitutional Referendum of 1992. It focuses specifically on the complex political terrain produced for Indigenous movements by their appropriation of sovereignty discourse and on how reading this terrain through an understanding of sovereignty discourse reveals both important political possibilities and necessities.

Chapter 6 extends this approach to a pair of recent legal decisions in a case posed by the Gitksan and Wet'suwet'en First Nations of British Columbia, *Delgamuukw v. B.C.*, where the forms and effects of sovereignty discourse on contemporary politics emerge more clearly. The analysis emphasizes the ways in which the two apparently very different decisions in relation to the case—the original decision in the Supreme Court of British Columbia and the Supreme Court of Canada's decision on appeal—together illustrate the simultaneously enabling and constraining effects of sovereignty discourse. While the contrast between the two decisions reveals the flexibility and adaptability of sovereignty discourse, even the much more enabling political ground produced by the second decision leaves Indigenous peoples on marginal political terrain.

Chapter 7 then turns the focus back to political theory, examining the responses of contemporary North American political theorists to these challenges. It focuses specifically on what I take to be the most sustained attempt by a contemporary North American theorist to take seriously the challenges posed by Indigenous politics to the history of political thought and contemporary political theory: James Tully's *Strange Multiplicity*. In *Strange Multiplicity*, Tully draws upon the rich histories of political thought in order to provide a blueprint for a constitutional dialogue—a renegotiation of sovereignty—that would address the past violences done in the name of sovereignty. Tully's work is exceptional in that it makes visible the violences and dangers of modern political thought to Indigenous peoples, opening a space within this history for their concerns to enter and be engaged. While his response refigures constitutional processes in a much more sensitive, inclusive and politically enabling way, however, it also poses a range of dangers to contemporary Indigenous politics. These dangers emerge from the ways in which his project remains grounded in, rather than critically engaging, the assumption of sovereignty. This assumption both enables the richness of his analysis and also—of necessity—frames it in such a way that crucial questions raised by Indigenous activism cannot be engaged. Further, the limits Tully reveals and confronts in his struggles to address the challenges posed by contemporary Indigenous movements suggest a larger challenge facing contemporary political theory. Insofar as political theorists continue to assume the discourses and practices of sovereignty to authorize their analyses, insofar—in other words—as they reinscribe Hobbes' production of sovereignty as the necessary precondition for political theory, they will remain unable to address the violences effected by both the past and present reassertion of sovereignty as the necessary precondition for social and political order. Tully's work thus breaks crucial ground, but it also demonstrates the need for further work to reformulate the necessities of sovereignty that continue to frame and constrain contemporary political theory.

The analysis in the first two parts focuses on the role of practices and discourses of sovereignty in shaping the political terrain Indigenous movements face, as well as the challenges they pose to this terrain. The final part, "Emerging politicizations," takes up the question of how these challenges might be more productively met. There is no way to evade the problematic of sovereignty; we need to be able to create and legitimate forms of collective authority, lest we find ourselves in the situation of a war of all against all: Hobbes was right in this regard. However, the discourses and practices of modern, Hobbesian sovereignty are but one response to this problem. They are a response that we must begin from, insofar as they provide a sketch of our inherited forms of legitimate authority, but instead of assuming and building on them, we must reformulate them. This part explores some of the strategies through which these reformulations are being effected, and some of the dangers and possibilities that reside in them.

Chapter 8 turns to *A Thousand Plateaus*, in which Gilles Deleuze and Félix Guattari forward a sustained analysis and critical engagement with sovereignty as the ground for modern politics. Echoing Hobbes' analysis of sovereignty, they insist upon the interconnection between structures and practices of knowledge production and authorization and structures and practices of politics. They argue that any effort to challenge these political institutions must simultaneously challenge how we produce and authorize knowledge: it must be as much concerned with how we think as what we think. They also provide a rich analysis of the processes of sovereignty, one that suggests possibilities for evading some of the violences towards Indigenous peoples that are embedded in the assumptions that ground Hobbes' production of sovereignty. Their work thus provides a perspective on discourses and practices of sovereignty that suggests possibilities for disrupting its operation, for opening different kinds of political spaces. It also, however, insists upon the limits and dangers any such disruption necessarily encounters, limits that require constant and difficult critical interrogation.

Chapter 9 turns to an examination of contemporary analyses of the political by Indigenous scholars, considering how the political terrains they articulate, challenge and reformulate inherited spaces of the political, suggesting modes of engagement for contemporary political theorists. Although—as is to be expected—there is much diversity and contestation in Indigenous articulations of the political, even the relatively limited engagement developed in this chapter reveals an emphasis on themes that, while familiar to many contemporary theorists, are often marginalized in the work of political theorists. The terrain they suggest challenges political theorists beyond the need for "inclusion" or "recognition" and on to a reconsideration of the role, function and modes of authorization for political theory, simultaneously insisting on a more substantial reconsideration of practices of theorizing themselves and offering a rich ground for critical re-engagement. Embedded in the work of Indigenous scholars are thus both resources for and challenges to contemporary political theory.

The book concludes with an argument that although we have yet to successfully either escape from or overcome Hobbes' account of political necessity, the challenges we face in doing so are increasingly being opened to engagement (Chapter 10). *Leviathan*'s angels persist, and persistently call on us to engage their challenges. Drawing from the strengths of the theorists I have engaged so far, I sketch an approach to Indigenous politics that seeks to problematize Hobbes' ground as our political starting point, and to reconceptualize the challenges posed by Indigenous political movements. The aspiration of this reconceptualization is to disrupt the "necessary" closures effected by the reproduction of the political space produced by sovereignty discourse, and thus to develop more productive political terrain for "marginal" forms of politics. Through this, I hope to suggest a broader political terrain than the struggles over the politics of identity currently occupy; in particular, to reinforce the necessity of opening up the political itself as a problem. Perhaps more importantly, though, I hope to give leverage to claims that the challenges these movements pose are not marginal but central to contemporary politics, and must be engaged as such by theorists of politics.

Note on terminology

Some specificity about the category of "Indigenous peoples," as well as the nuances of terminology in relation to Indigenous issues may be useful here. Definitions of Indigeneity are intensely politicized and contested, and it would not be useful to resolve them by fiat. However, a general indication of how I am conceptualizing Indigenous peoples, as well as of the complexity of definitional terrain, can be found in the United Nations Working Definition of Indigenous Peoples, the first part of which is:

> Indigenous populations are composed of the existing descendants of peoples who inhabited the present territory of a country wholly or partially at the time when persons of a different culture or ethnic origin arrived there from other parts of the world, overcame them, and by conquest, settlement or other means, reduced them to a non-dominant or colonial situation; who today live more in conformity with their particular social, economic and cultural customs and traditions than with the institutions of the country of which they now form a part, under a State structure which incorporates mainly the national, social and cultural characteristics of other segments of the population which are predominant.
>
> (Wilmer, 1993: 216)

The definition continues by extending consideration to other isolated and marginal populations. What I find useful about this definition is its emphasis on the social and political specificity embedded in their situations.

The peoples who inhabited North America when Europeans arrived have been referred to by many different names, the meanings of which are politically loaded and change across times and contexts. The most well-known reference is probably the colonial one of "Indians," which is still occasionally used—not infrequently as a self-reference—but has generally fallen from favor due to its colonial resonances. "Indigenous peoples" is perhaps the most general reference, and the one increasingly in favor in international forums. "Aboriginal peoples" is a similarly general reference, and is the formal term used by the Canadian government to refer to all Indigenous peoples in Canada.

In Canada there are also several long-standing terms, each connoting a specific political status: "Status" Aboriginal peoples include those groups and individuals covered under the Indian Acts, and thus having well-defined formal relationships with the federal government. However, some groups and individuals either declined, were overlooked, or lost "Status" over time and thus there are also "non-Status" Indigenous peoples who nonetheless claim Indigenous rights. "Status" groups are also sometimes referred to as "First Nations." "Inuit" refers to the Indigenous peoples of the Arctic. Canadian Inuit live primarily in four regions: Nunatsiavut (Labrador), Nunavik (northern Quebec), Nunavut, and the Inuvialuit region in the Northwest Territories. "Métis" are a specific group of descendents of Indigenous peoples and French trappers and settlers, who have now also gained official recognition as a distinct group by the Canadian government. Each of these four groups—Status, non-Status, Inuit, and Métis—is formally recognized by the Canadian government. As each group has a distinct history, status, and set of concerns, each is represented at the federal level by a distinct political organization.

The terms "Native," "Native American," "Amerindian," and "Native Canadian" are all used, but less frequently in contemporary political contexts. There are also, of course, names for each specific community, both self-identified and given by colonizers.

Each of these terms is politically loaded; their meanings change over time and across contexts. As the different resonances across these terms are politically relevant, rather than choosing one term and enforcing it throughout the text, I tend either to follow the usage of the texts I am drawing from or—when making analyses of more general relevance—to use "Indigenous." There is also no broad agreement on whether these terms should be capitalized; again, I will follow the usage of the texts or context.

Part I
Sovereignty and the political

2   Hobbes

Producing politics/effacing interrogation

As suggested in the last chapter, an analysis focused on the contemporary problem of the political must engage with sovereignty, as it is the discourses and practices of sovereignty that have, since early Modernity, framed the problem of the political, providing the logic and justification for the political spaces we have created and inhabited.[1] But why focus on Hobbes to explore the problem of sovereignty? There are certainly many other theorists with whom one might begin; the development of the modern state and the discourses of sovereignty that enabled it were complex processes and many theorists contributed to them in different ways. Hobbes famously wrote from within the chaos and violence of civil war in England; *Leviathan* was first published in 1651. This context defines what is at stake in his project: he wrote with an intense focus on how the horrific violence he saw around him might be contained. As such, the analysis was a response to the collapse of the forms of political authority that had previously contained violence, ordering it and enabling people to live their lives without the constant chaos and devastation of civil war. He wrote, in other words, to establish order, to argue for a basis for shared forms of political authority capable of stemming bloodshed. As such, his text contains an implicit analysis of the source of the conflicts around him, as well as a prescription for how authority might be constituted differently. His response to this was modern sovereignty, and his account of what it is—what assumptions and practices ground and enable it, and what exclusions are necessary to achieve it—remains paradigmatic. Starting with different theorists would provide different insights. I choose to begin with Hobbes not only because his account remains paradigmatic, but because it is so alert to and explicit in its engagement with the violences it effects. It also provides particularly sharp insights into not only the specific relationship between sovereignty and indigeneity, but contemporary politics more generally.

My engagement with Hobbes is thus concerned with how his formulation of sovereignty works, what enables it, what it enables, what its attendant violences and effects are.[2] I will focus especially on the implications of his practices of sovereignty for Indigenous peoples. The argument proceeds through three parts: I begin by looking carefully at how Hobbes lays the groundwork for sovereignty in the first few chapters of *Leviathan*, paying particular attention to how his establishment of an ontological foundation produces and locates identity and difference. I then move on to show how this foundation—expressed in the subjects he has produced—leads to a particular production of sovereignty and, again, how this series of maneuvers locates and defines difference. In the last part of the chapter, I begin to sketch some of the implications of this production of sovereignty.

Reading Hobbes

A reading of Hobbes that seeks to explore the relationship between sovereignty and indigeneity would most obviously begin with a passage in which he directly represents "savage peoples of America," such as the following:

> It may peradventure be thought, there was never such a time, nor condition of warre as this; and I believe it was never generally so, over all the world: but there are many places, where they live so now. For the savage people in many places of *America*, except the government of small Families, and concord whereof dependeth on natural lust, have no government at all; and live at this day in that brutish manner, as I said before. Howsoever, it may be perceived what manner of life there would be, where there were no common Power to feare; by the manner of life, which men that have formerly lived under a peacefull government, use to degenerate into, in a civill Warre.
>
> (Hobbes, 1968: 187)

This passage, and most others where he explicitly refers to "savages," is not difficult to unravel. "Savages" appears in his text at points where he needs to buttress his argument by drawing on an example—which may have seemed self-evident to his contemporaries—of "presocial" individuals, thus affirming his view of human nature. The "truth" of the representation aside, it functions in his text by drawing upon a series of associations about progress, development, time, history; about who his readers believe they are and how they are located in relation to "savages" and this place called America. A reading focused on this aspect of Hobbes' text might reveal a range of serious challenges to Hobbes, and for that matter to much of the history of modern political thought, by emphasizing the anthropological hierarchy he fixes, the limitations of his conception of time and history, and the pervasiveness of the imperialistic tendencies expressed in modern political thought: important lines of analysis, all. They reveal some of the most powerful assumptions, strategies, and legitimations of violence and inequality in modern political life, not least in situations confronted by Indigenous peoples in modern societies. Pursuing such analyses is thus crucial in relation to practices of contemporary Indigenous politics.[3]

For all their importance, however, and for all that the critique of contemporary structures of power still needs to come to terms with the contradictions in modern political life that they reveal, these analyses can only take us so far in understanding the relationship between the history of political thought and contemporary Indigenous politics. Even if, and it is a big if, one could expose all the traces of Hobbes' ethnocentrism, imperialism, orientalism, racism, or any other of the familiar expressions of the limits of modern political thought, we would be left wondering how it is that these limitations that now seem so obviously objectionable to us can have been so easily reproduced in the conventions and institutions of modern political life. Hobbes' references to the "savages" have a more crucial significance in this respect. Or rather, his explicit references to "savages" direct our attention away from aspects of his account of what sovereignty is and must be, aspects that have had much more significance for the way Indigenous politics is now framed than their overt othering as presocial beings.

Furthermore, the very attempt to call attention to Hobbes' distinction of Indigenous peoples as "others" takes place on ground already established by Hobbes. Even if the exposure of his "othering" is successful, if his thought in this matter is criticized and reformulated, Hobbes can still rest easy, for the grounding he established still largely orders and frames contemporary political life. It is this grounding that most directly frames and severely constrains contemporary Indigenous politics. So we have to start earlier in the text than the explicit appearance of Indigenous peoples; we have to start with the ground Hobbes produces. This ground is most clearly revealed in his production of sovereignty in the first thirteen chapters of *Leviathan*.

Producing man and/in difference

In the first part of *Leviathan*—"Of Man"—Hobbes is concerned with laying the groundwork for and producing individual subjects whose shared characteristics require that they come together into a common (sovereign) identity. To do this, he must truly begin at the beginning: with how and what men[4] can know. He thus begins by establishing three conditions: he bounds the world, by constructing and limiting space; he controls contingency, by disciplining time; and he establishes commonality, a shared basis for identity: language. These conditions comprise a series of ontological and epistemological distinctions necessary, for Hobbes, to ensure the potential for a shared social and political order.

The first crucial distinction happens immediately. He starts with the chapter "Of Sense," in which he begins to draw the distinction, completed in his next chapter, between sense—our apprehension of things—and imagination—decaying sense or memory. Sense, for Hobbes, is absolutely crucial, as it is through sense—our apprehension of motion—that we come to know the world. "The Originall of them all, is that which we call SENSE; (For there is no conception in a mans mind, which hath not at first, totally, or by parts, been begotten upon the organs of Sense.) The rest are derived from that originall" (Hobbes, 1968: 85). It is a simple enough assertion, as each assertion Hobbes makes seems to be: man comes to know the world through his senses. Contrasted with sense is imagination: "IMAGINATION therefore is nothing but *decaying sense*" (Hobbes, 1968: 88). There is, thus, no other basis for knowing than sense; our imaginations are not capable of understanding in relation to the world, they are only capable of holding and ordering sense information. Creativity of the imagination thus may be pleasant, beautiful, even insightful, but should not be mistaken for a basis of knowledge of or about the world, as these imaginings are not necessarily true to the world or to sense experiences. They are decaying, fading sense perceptions, likely to confuse or distort.

Some of the implications of this assertion of the primacy (exclusivity) of the senses become clear as Hobbes moves on to his next distinction, between different kinds of imaginings. Waking experiences, mediated through sense, constitute our imaginings while waking. But what of the imaginings we experience while asleep? These are dreams: inspired not by external senses so much as "What proceeds from the agitation of the inward parts of mans body; which inward parts, for the connexion they have with the Brayn, and other Organs, when they be distempered, do keep the same in motion; whereby the Imaginations there formerly made, appeare as if a man were waking" (Hobbes, 1968: 90). Thus these imaginings are also rooted in the body, though this time less in external sense perceptions than in internal activities of the body. However, since these imaginings are sometimes even more vivid than our waking imaginings, how are we to tell them apart?

> [I]t is a hard matter, and by many thought impossible to distinguish exactly between Sense and Dreaming. For my part, when I consider, that in Dreames, I do not often, nor constantly think of the same Persons, Places, Objects, and Actions that I do waking; nor remember so long a trayne of coherent thoughts, Dreaming, as at other times; And because waking I often observe the absurdity of Dreames, but never dream of the absurdities of my waking Thoughts; I am well satisfied, that being awake, I know I dreame not; though when I dreame, I think my selfe awake.
>
> (Hobbes, 1968: 90)

This passage begins the naturalization of particular epistemological criteria: waking thoughts, subject to external sense perceptions, are coherent, constant; dreams, sleeping imaginings, subject to internal agitation of the body, are incoherent, absurd. It is difficult, he acknowledges, to distinguish between the two, but because in one state he is "conscious" of the lack of constancy and coherency, and the absurdity of the other, and not vice versa, the distinction is enabled and waking imaginings validated as a proper basis for thought. Fair enough: one can easily see the necessity behind such a distinction, especially in relation to the context from which Hobbes was writing, where a range of groups, sects, and organizations were claiming moral and political authority on the basis of dreams, visions, apparitions, experiences neither shared nor necessarily subject to validation, and thus not particularly conducive to "rational" discussion and negotiation. Nonetheless, it is important to note the particularity of and fallout from such distinctions. These criteria satisfy him, but are hardly well defended—they are "obvious" rather than contentious. At issue is not only whether these ought to be the criteria, but what they mean as criteria. They are neither neutral nor universal. This valuing of the "conscious" (and assumption of what "consciousness" is) is a culturally and historically specific one, and it has a range of political effects. Very similar epistemological assertions have functioned to devalue a range of knowledge and authority claims on the part of Indigenous peoples.[5] By the time such examples emerge, these epistemological assertions are effectively naturalized and solidified, their particularity often forgotten. This was not the case when Hobbes wrote. The stability and stakes of this distinction thus differ between Hobbes' time and our own. I want to draw attention to it as a particular epistemological claim, and to how it functions to produce and authorize particular forms of knowledge and subjectivity. The location of these moves in Hobbes' argument is significant, indeed foundational. Once these assumptions are accepted and naturalized, their particularity becomes both more relevant and more difficult to resist.

In Chapter 3, he moves from considering thoughts and experiences singly to connecting them together into a train of thoughts, either unguided or regulated. By pursuing the idea of regulated thought—what links thoughts, and how they should progress logically from one to the other—he is able to introduce the notions of cause and effect, laying the groundwork for the introduction of time:

> The *Present* onely has a being in Nature; things *Past* have a being in the Memory onely, but things *to come* have no being at all; the *Future* being but a fiction of the mind, applying the sequels of actions Past, to the actions that are Present; which with most certainty is done by him that has most Experience; but not with certainty enough.
>
> (Hobbes, 1968: 97)

In this way, he effectively introduces and begins to *order* time: he gets it moving in a linear fashion, from past, to a bounded present (which only has a being in nature), to future. Lest the infinitude of the future overwhelm us, he then establishes the crucial boundary, the precondition for the bounding of identity: the boundary between the finite and infinite, between that which is and can be *known* and that which cannot:

> Whatsoever we imagine, is *Finite*. Therefore there is no Idea, or conception of anything we call *Infinite*. No man can have in his mind an Image of infinite magnitude ... When we say any thing is infinite, we

signifie onely, that we are not able to conceive the ends, and bounds of the thing named; having no Conception of the Things, but of our own inability ... A man can have no thought, representing any Thing, not subject to sense. No man therefore can conceive any Thing, but he must conceive it in some place; and imbued with some determinate magnitude.

(Hobbes, 1968: 99)

Hobbes thus establishes that in order even to think (to make sense), we must think *in a place*, a bounded and located space mediated by sense, moving through an ordered, linear time. This disciplining of time to space effectively orders it by containing and directing it from past to future, again establishing a particular set of constraints upon ways of conceiving and perceiving the world. By this point, then, Hobbes has managed to locate and solidify his epistemological stance. At the center is man, who can only perceive the world through sense perceptions: thus the importance of a bounded space for thought, for points of reference. In order to build these thoughts, to make sense of them, they must move in a linear temporal fashion. What and how one can know are thus ordered. However, it remains unclear how this particular subject might interact with other subjects.

In Chapter 4, then, we are ready for the introduction of language, the vital precondition for orderly social interaction:

But the most noble and profitable invention of all others, was that of SPEECH, consisting of *Names* or *Appellations*, and their connexion; whereby men register their thoughts; recall them when they are past; and also declare them one to another for mutuall utility and conversation; without which, there had been amongst men, neither Commonwealth, nor Society, nor Contract, nor Peace, no more than amongst Lyons, Bears, and Wolves.

(Hobbes, 1968: 100)

It is impossible to overemphasize the importance of language to Hobbes; this emerges throughout the rest of the text. Language is vital for several reasons. It is through language—the right (common, shared) naming of things—that time becomes further bound to space, as contingency (stemming from confusion of interpretation) is minimized. It is also through language—through the enforcement of right naming—that the sovereign can establish authority and order. Hobbes' discussion of language continues the process begun earlier of ordering space to produce the possibility of society. This depends upon a common and logical order of naming, a shared framework through which these different sensing beings can communicate. He thus stresses the *right* use of language, and guards against its abuses, as it is through this shared use of language that the possibility for order is established.[6] Again, each of these distinctions simultaneously enables a common identity and functions to inscribe difference. With each added set of distinctions, the identity which enables society becomes increasingly well defined and rigid. As he pursues the use of language he must begin to introduce potential for the universal: the precondition for a common, shared identity. If names can be agreed upon to the extent that a particular rule can become "true for all times and places" (Hobbes, 1968: 104), then we have a universal. Although such a universal would be true "in all times and all places," it would not extend beyond language, as time and place are dependent on shared space and communication: "For *True* and *False* are attributes of Speech, not of Things. And where Speech is not, there is neither *Truth* nor *Falshood*. *Errour* there may be, as when we expect that which shall not be; or suspect what has not been: but in neither case can a man be charged with Untruth" (Hobbes, 1968: 105). Truth thus becomes nothing more—or less—than "the right ordering of names in our affirmations." Thus the universal functions to homogenize the space within the bounds of language, but makes no claims beyond, as we cannot comprehend infinity.

It is here that we see the introduction of the epistemological assumptions and resolutions that will later enable a particular writing of difference to be grounds for exclusion. Hobbes has already established the political ground we—supposedly—share (in fact, that we *must* share in order to communicate), which consists of a very specific ordering of time and space, one that functions to enable and privilege a certain form of reason, providing the basis for an identity differentiated by these very specific forms of difference. Those who do not share this resolution of time and space (and that which follows from it) will come to inhabit—and mark—the "outside" of Hobbes' neatly delineated space, their "difference" enabling the recognition of something "we" share. Different resolutions of time and space are, of course, characteristic of many of those later excluded from political subjectivity not only in Hobbes' text, but in such political practices as colonialism.[7]

From Truth, Hobbes moves on to Reason. Here we see the same imperatives, the same process, the same awareness and fear of contingency as in his discussion of the right use of language. Again he details the definition and limits of Reason, "which is nothing but *Reckoning* (that is, Adding and Subtracting) of the Consequences of generall names agreed upon, for the *marking* and *signifying* of our thoughts" (Hobbes, 1968: 111). He emphasizes that the right use of reason lies in its process rather than its end, drawing attention again to the need for shared structures of communication. Again he details the dangers of absurdity, and its causes, and here again we see the kind of attention to the uses of language that is crucial to his project of producing a shared identity and also necessarily crucial to the production and writing of difference. The tension that guides the discussion of reason, as well as much of Hobbes negotiation of identity and difference, can be characterized by one sentence: "For all men by nature reason alike, and well, when they have good principles" (Hobbes, 1968: 115). The first part of the sentence functions to further homogenize reason and provide grounds for the exclusion of difference ("These people reason differently and are thus not 'us,' or indeed men"), but the last part reveals the contingency of such a claim.[8] Thus the discussion of reason continues the same tension as above, but each move increases the stakes. The barriers that were originally arbitrary markers of difference dig more deeply as the potential structures of identity become more focused.

With reason guaranteed, Hobbes moves on to introduce its benefit: Science. In his introduction, he stresses the "industry" required in the pursuit of reason and the nature of its achievements:

> By this it appears that Reason is not as Sense, and Memory, borne with us; nor gotten by Experience onely; as Prudence is; but attayned by Industry; first in apt imposing of Names; and secondly by getting a good and orderly Method in proceeding from the Elements, which are Names, to Assertions made by Connexion of one of them to another; and so to Syllogismes, which are the Connexions of one Assertion to another, till we have come to a knowledge of all the Consequences of names appertaining to the subject in hand; and that is it, men call SCIENCE.
>
> (Hobbes, 1968: 115)

Here we see the first hints of what is possible through right (shared, common, logical) reasoning, and what it enables: a common identity, collaboration, "progress." Interestingly, even as he begins to emphasize the potential successes of science, he also marks the contingency of his project:

> No Discourse whatsoever, can End in absolute knowledge of Fact, past, or to come. For, as for the knowledge of Fact, it is originally, Sense; and ever after, Memory. And for the knowledge of Consequence, which I have said before is called Science, it is not Absolute, but Conditionall. No man can know by Discourse, that this, or that, is, has been, or will be; which is to know absolutely: but onely, that if This be, That is; if This has been, That has been; if This shall be, That shall be: which is to know conditionally; and that not the consequence of one thing to another; but of one name of a thing, to another name of the same thing.
>
> (Hobbes, 1968: 131)

All knowledge—and all science—then, is conditional. In these two passages, Hobbes suggests both the possibilities and limitations of his own project. Done well, a project such as his would enable science, and all of the possibilities that flow from science. No matter how well done, however, such an achievement is necessarily limited and conditional, bounded by what and how we can know, and especially by our capacity for shared knowledge, for order. His project thus maintains a crucial awareness of the limits of the possible, a deep caution or skepticism about any claim to universality. We cannot, as emphasized above, even apprehend infinity. This reinscription of limits enables a potential acknowledgment of different makings, different negotiations of political and social organization, in different times and spaces. However, he clearly wants to claim a primacy for his own making—which he does through giving it the appearance of necessity—in relation to his own time and space.[9]

In these first few chapters, Hobbes has produced the basic framework for his new subjects. He has established an ontological foundation, a common basis for communication, for the production and evaluation of knowledge, and for the authority of an appropriate science. He has struggled with the limits of what we can know, the dangers of believing in what we cannot. We have a good sense of the basic parameters and limitations of his project, of the limits and bases of shared knowledge, of where we can and indeed must begin to construct the possibility of the political and social order. Here I would mark a shift: with the ontological and epistemological groundwork for his project laid and ensured through important limits on language and reason, Hobbes' discussion from here consists of a layering and naturalizing of these bases, of giving form and specificity to the general geography he has constructed.

Ordering difference

As he shifts from establishing the ontological and epistemological ground of his project, Hobbes becomes much more focused on giving form and substance to his subjects, to their natures, to the language in which we can speak of, with and about them. At this point, differences become more explicitly marked. Here we begin to have the first explicit writing of "others":[10] "Children therefore are not endued with Reason at all, till they have attained the use of Speech: but are called Reasonable Creatures, for the possibility apparent of having the use of Reason in time to come" (Hobbes, 1968: 116). The "otherness" of children is marked temporally: they have not *yet* developed, but they contain the potential. In the same paragraph, he also notes that most men have little need of or use for reason. They fumble along, using what they need, but have no knowledge of the right use of it, or of science. Yet, because of their potential, of what they share in capacity, they are not marked as different, they are just "most men." At worst, they are "like children": *potential* users of reason.

He turns to the substance of his subjects, to their social psychology: to the passions. The passions are important to Hobbes' argument. While these passions are potential sources of conflict and violence, they are also what drive all people's behavior. They cannot be erased, ignored, suppressed. They must, rather, be channeled, disciplined, enabled. He begins by defining and naming them, firmly locating them within his epistemological framework, explaining them as appetites and aversions. This functions at the same time to discipline them and to indicate their excess of this disciplining (Hobbes, 1968: 129). Perhaps the most important function they serve is as explanations for differences amongst men: "It [difference of wits] proceeds therefore from the Passions; which are different, not onely from the difference of mens

complexions; but also from their difference of customes, and education"
(Hobbes, 1968: 138–39). The stakes of difference are raised once again when
the description of passions and the importance, effects, and dangers of belief
enter in. Suddenly, we not only begin to see the explicit markings of "otherness" (the "difference of men's complexions"), we begin to hear almost direct
arguments used against "others":

> The Passions that most of all cause the differences of Wit, are principally,
> the more or less Desire of Power, of Riches, of Knowledge, and of
> Honor. All of which may be reduced to the first, that is Desire of
> Power. For Riches, Knowledge, and Honour are but several sorts of
> Power.
>
> And therefore, a man who has no great Passion for any of these things;
> but is as men terme it indifferent; though he may be so farre a goode
> man, as to be free from giving offence; yet he cannot possibly have either
> a great Fancy, or much Judgement.[11]
>
> (Hobbes, 1968: 139)

These two passages suggest the necessity of the passions: without passion,
men cannot excel; indeed, cannot even be very bright. However, the passions
are also dangerous:

> For as to have no Desire, is to be Dead: so to have weak Passions, is
> Dulness; and to have Passions indifferently for every thing, GID-
> DINESSE, and *Distraction*; and to have stronger and more vehement
> Passions for any thing, than is ordinarily seen in others, is that which men
> call MADNESSE.
>
> (Hobbes, 1968: 139)

Further, the excess passion that leads to madness in an individual is also a
danger to society as a whole:

> And if this be Madness in the multitude, it is the same in every particular
> man. For as in the middest of the sea, though a man perceive no sound of
> that part of the water next him; yet he is well assured, that part contrib-
> utes as much, to the Roaring of the Sea, as any other part, of the same
> quantity: so also, though wee perceive no great unquietnesse, in one, or
> two men; yet we may be well assured, that their singular Passions, are
> parts of the Seditious roaring of a troubled Nation.
>
> (Hobbes, 1968: 141)

Thus, although passions may vary amongst men—even to the point of
"dullness" and "madness"—the manifestation of these passions is intimately
linked to the state of the social body as a whole. This indicates a tension

between expressions of "different" passions—itself not a bad thing—and the danger to society of the too extreme expression of any passion. This tension is an expression of the problem of authority in the "horizontal" space Hobbes has created—the space defined on the one hand by the fundamental identity of all subjects, and on the other by their different passions and desires. This sets up the crucial maneuvers that follow, maneuvers that enable the sovereign state to become the condition of possibility for the negotiation of this tension.

Hobbes begins chapter 11 by characterizing men in terms that affirm the (contradictory) demand of modern liberalism: liberty and equality among individuals. It is precisely their basic similarity and equality of condition that throws men into conflict: creating the "security dilemma." This proto-typical structuralist analysis of the "security dilemma" depends upon his prior analysis of the passions. In a world of similarities, it is the passions that are made to account for differences. Men—all men—are motivated by desires that are unceasing, are, indeed, the condition of life: "No more can a man any more live, whose Desires are at an end, than he, whose Senses and Imaginations are at a stand" (Hobbes, 1968: 160). Because men want not just to fulfill a desire but to assure that they will be able to fulfill it in the future, they can never cease to strive for the power to fulfill their desires.

> And therefore the voluntary actions, and inclinations of all men, tend, not only to the procuring, but also to the assuring of a contented life; and differ onely in the way: which ariseth partly from the diversity of passions; in divers men, and partly from the difference of the know-ledge, or opinion each one has of the causes, which produce the effect desired.
>
> (Hobbes, 1968: 161)

The basic difference amongst men, then, is a diversity of passions and of knowledge of causes and effects; what they share is a constant pursuit of desires:

> So that in the first place, I put for a generall inclination of all mankind, a perpetuall and restlesse desire of Power after power, that ceaseth onely in Death. And the cause of this, is not alwayes that a man hopes for a more intensive delight, than he has already attained to; or that he cannot be content with a moderate power: but because he cannot assure the power and means to live well, which he hath at present, without the acquisition of more.
>
> (Hobbes, 1968: 161)

Whereas some of these desires throw men into conflict, others encourage men to submit to a common power. Hobbes goes on to detail each of these, emphasizing especially those desires that might facilitate agreement to a common power. As he details these, some consistencies begin to emerge: in particular, both the dangers and the possibilities of men's "ignorance of causes":

> Want of science, that is Ignorance of causes, disposeth, or rather constraineth a man to rely on the advise, and authority of others. . . . Ignorance of the signification of words; which is, want of understanding, disposeth men to take on trust, not onely the truth they know not; but also the errors; and which is more, the non-sense of them they trust: For neither Error, nor nonsense, can without a perfect understanding of words, be detected.
>
> (Hobbes, 1968: 165)

These passages, especially combined with his earlier argument that most men have little knowledge of or need for Reason or Science, set up an interesting line of argument about why men believe in God. Such an argument is crucial for Hobbes' argument as it is belief in divine authority that Hobbes must subvert or obscure from civil matters in order for his production of sovereignty to work. Until people believe that government/civil authority is a construction of men, but one founded on principles that exceed them (necessity), Hobbes argued there would be no shared agreement amongst men to command authority. However, Hobbes had to wrestle carefully with ecclesiastical authority: divine authority may have been highly contested, but the power of the Church remained nothing to sneeze at. Hobbes' negotiation of this tightrope is expressed, for example, in the double reading one can make of his account of political obligation as a matter of prudence on the one hand, and duty to preserve what one's Maker has made on the other.

The remainder of Chapter 11 and all of Chapter 12 are devoted to negotiating this fine line between science and religion. He repeats that it is a lack of knowledge of natural causes that leads men to false belief, and he details the dangers of "false belief," especially when combined with an excess of passion. Belief in God, however, arises from a (much more positive) impulse to learn natural causes:

> Curiosity, or love of the knowledge of causes, draws a man from consideration of the effect, to seek the cause; and again, the cause of that cause; till of necessity he must come to this thought at last, that there is some cause, whereof there is no former cause, but is eternall; which is it men call God. So that it is impossible to make any profound enquiry into naturall causes, without being enclined thereby to believe there is one God Eternall; though they cannot have any Idea of him in their mind, answerable to his nature.
>
> (Hobbes, 1968: 167)

This passage contains an important distinction: though it is a curiosity of natural causes that leads to a belief in God, through such inquiry one cannot come to know God, or anything of his nature. This is important because a common belief about God could be (and had been) enough of a glue to hold society together. However, once that set of beliefs comes into question, there is no way—no method, process, standard, set of laws—by which one can resolve the disputes. There is no court of appeal—except the sword—where competing knowledge claims about God or his will can be reconciled. This, again, is the crucial background for Hobbes' effort to establish an alternate ground of shared belief in how we must perceive the world around us.[12]

Chapter 12 thus walks a fine line: Hobbes must critique religious belief as being insufficient to achieve peace in a commonwealth in order to make an argument for another basis for civil authority. However, given his context, he had to do so without discrediting a belief in God. The distinctions he makes in order to negotiate this tension are continuous with his argument: between what is and can be known and that which cannot, and between a belief in a higher authority and a belief in a particular religion. He repeats a brief and universalized history of the causes of religion and the relationship of religion to commonwealths:

> And therefore the first Founders, and Legislators of Common-wealths amongst the Gentiles, whose ends were only to keep the people in obedience, and peace, have in all places taken care; First, to imprint in their minds a beliefe, that those precepts which they gave concerning Religion, might not be thought to proceed from their own device, but from the dictates of some God, or other Spirit; or else that they themselves were of a higher nature than mere mortalls, that their Lawes might the more easily be received.
>
> (Hobbes, 1968: 177)

While this had been successful for a long while, it was becoming increasingly clear to Hobbes and others that it was no longer successful. Another ground of civil authority was necessary. However, he is careful to note that this does not mean that there is no necessary relationship between "God himselfe" and a particular commonwealth. Rather, that, considering the limits of what we can know, this is not a particularly viable basis for civil authority (Hobbes, 1968: 178–79). Religious and civil authority are thus not irreconcilable, as he goes to great pains to justify elsewhere. However, because of the impossibility of knowledge of God, and thus of a shared verifiable basis of authority, religious authority should not any longer be the basis of civil authority. Hobbes is very careful, though, to point the blame not at belief in God or at religion per se, but at unscrupulous clergy: "So that I may attribute all the changes of Religion in the world, to one and the same cause; and that is, unpleasing Priests; and those not onely amongst Catholiques, but even in that Church that hath presumed most of Reformation" (Hobbes, 1968: 183).

Having—however provisionally—dealt with Religion as an effective ordering force for civil society, Hobbes proceeds in chapter 13 to establish the architecture for his proposed form of authority: the sovereign Leviathan.

Producing sovereignty

Chapter 13 is where Hobbes begins to give form to this identity he has constructed, creating a geography through which some of the pressing questions of the time can be engaged. In particular, it is here that he bounds the identity he has produced, locating it in preparation for the sovereign state to take on the task of providing not only security but meaning for its citizens. By the end of this chapter, the reader must be convinced that to be part of a sovereign unit is not only to be secure from harm, but to be a part of a larger identity, spatially bounded, progressing through time, achieving feats of science, technology, advancing knowledge, and so on. In other words, there is a sense of community one is a part of that potentially not only provides a space for the satisfaction of one's desires but gives a collective range of possibilities for them, provides a backdrop of meaning for them. This challenge is resolved through a maneuver enabled by his earlier ordering of time and space: sovereignty is produced by ordering difference spatially to enable identity. By this point, he has produced a "natural"(ized), ahistorical man-subject, which has in fact emerged from a very particular set of historical and epistemological specificities. He has produced a homogenized man-citizen running about in "natural" chaos, which he can now move on to discipline into the formation of one common overarching sovereign identity. This is the trick—he must now make this distinction explicit: produce an "outside" that is so awful, and so close, as to coerce those "inside" to bind together, to produce a common "sovereign" identity. Fortunately, as we've seen, he has also produced these subjects such that this maneuver is not only necessary, but desirable.

The chapter begins with the reassertion of the fundamental equality of men—both mental and physical. Because all men are more or less equal, they have an equal hope of attaining their goals. However, as we have already seen, this also means there is no security that men can achieve, or maintain, these goals:

> And from this diffidence of one another, there is no way for any man to secure himselfe, so reasonable, as Anticipation; that is, by force, or wiles, to master the persons of all men he can, so long, till he see no other power great enough to endanger him: And this is no more than his own conservation requireth, and is generally allowed.
>
> (Hobbes, 1968: 184)

The restlessness of desires and inability to secure them throws men into constant conflict: "Againe, men have no pleasure, (but on the contrary a great deal of griefe) in keeping company, where there is no power able to over-awe them all" (Hobbes, 1968: 185). Men have a great deal of difficulty keeping company "naturally," yet there is a potential solution for this difficulty: an overarching form of authority. This is an interesting move on Hobbes' part as, in the past, this has been the form of power that has, more or less, maintained peace: a monarch, a power to overawe. However, the first part of his book has been devoted to producing an argument for a basis and system of authority that is far more subtle and deeply rooted than the power of a monarchy. If we think of this chapter as establishing the geography or form of sovereignty, this statement gives a sense of where we are headed. So far we know men require a power to overawe them all in order not to be in constant conflict. We can suspect from what has preceded that the matter or content of such power might be different from a monarchy, but the form seems perhaps familiar. Without a power to overawe them, thus, men are in conflict because of their constant pursuit of desires and lack of security for their achievement.

This state of affairs would seem to encourage men towards the formation of a common authority. However, Hobbes doesn't stop there; he goes on to produce a much stronger and more specific border at the edges of his commonwealth. He produces an "outside" that is truly horrific in order to cause those "inside" to recognize themselves, to realize their good fortune, what they owe to the state, what the state enables. Without a common power, men are in conflict, but more:

> Hereby it is manifest, that during the time men live without a common Power to keep them all in awe, they are in that condition which is called Warre; and such a warre, as is of every man, against every man. . . . So the nature of War, consisteth not in actuall fighting; but in the known disposition thereto, during all the time there is no assurance to the contrary. All other time is PEACE.
>
> Whatsoever therefore is consequent to a time of Warre, where every man is Enemy to every man; the same is consequent to the time, wherein men live without other security, than what their own strength, and their own invention shall furnish them withall. In such condition, there is no place for Industry; because the fruit thereof is uncertain; and consequently no Culture of the Earth; no Navigation, nor use of the commodities that may be imported by Sea; no commodious Building; no Instruments of moving, and removing such things as require much force; no Knowledge of the face of the Earth; to account of Time; no Arts; no Letters; no Society; and which is worst of all, continuall feare, and danger of violent death; And the life of man, solitary, poore, nasty, brutish, and short.
>
> (Hobbes, 1968: 186)

These passages accomplish a series of key moves, establishing the boundary of a commonwealth, of sovereignty, by producing a series of distinctions marking the separations between what is enabled by sovereignty and what exists "outside" it. First he broadened the definition of state of war from a condition of explicit aggression to any condition where there is a lack of security. This broadening of the definition of war is crucial because it enables sovereignty to offer much more than just peace, and it homogenizes a whole range of forms of social organization into the non-sovereign. Then he goes on to layer a series of other effects—ostensibly characteristics of those "outside" resolutions of sovereignty, in fact also serving to produce a positive identity for those "inside." Sovereignty offers more than just order and peace, though that is most important. It offers promises of all these other things, enabled by Hobbes' shared epistemological system: shared knowledge, technology, etc. The "outside" is awful. Life "there" is not pleasant. But it is also more than that: it is brutish. There is no account of time, no way to give one's life meaning, no way to change one's condition, no way to create or relate to a collective, a community. There is no progress. Thus sovereignty is marked not only by peace, but by an entire—quite specific—attitude towards time, history, meaning. In this passage, then, without establishing a specific spatial border, Hobbes has created an inside and an outside. "Inside" is characterized by a set of sovereign resolutions, by a shared belief system which grants authority to the sovereignty to mediate conflicts amongst men, because, given who "we" are, without that we could have no science, letters, arts, knowledge, industry, etc. Thus "we," because of our natures as humans, must come together to create an overarching authority, to enable us to move through time, attain our desires, progress. All of these, of course, require a bounded space, the precondition for thought, the production of knowledge, the account of time, identity. Thus Hobbes provides an explicit set of markers for sovereignty, all of which are enabled by a preaccomplished resolution of space, time, identity, by an assertion of who we are and what we are capable of.

Perhaps most importantly, this tricky set of resolutions is naturalized, written as a description based on necessity. If one accepts Hobbes' epistemological system and the portrayal of human behavior that emerges from it, there is no other way it can be. The world is neatly divided into sovereign and non, with those living under sovereignty having a place in the world, a structure of meaning, a location from which to make sense of the world and act within it. All else, on the "outside," is a state of war, suffering through various degrees of violence or not, but lacking the security to develop, pursue knowledge, live well. In order to illustrate and ensure this boundary, Hobbes then marks it with an explicit writing of difference as—who else?—the Savages of America: "For the savage people in many places of *America*, except the government of small Families, and concord whereof dependeth on natural lust, have no government at all; and live at this day in that brutish manner, as I said before" (Hobbes, 1968: 187). The appearance of "the Savages" at this point is hardly surprising; their usefulness as a disciplining tool apparent. The passage functions to say: "We may be in a civil war and this is terrible, but look at the possibilities we have available to us. We are not, after all, the Savages, though if we don't get it together, we shall be soon." Read in this context, then, Chapter 13 is vital in that it *produces* the "outside," the state of nature, the "other" which we can (only) avoid by binding together to establish an identity, an identity precisely grounded in a particular ontology of sovereignty and established in difference from the outside, which lurks in the realm of possibility (if we give up those things which mark the difference: language, reason, science, order). We need the overarching sovereignty because we cannot live together in peace without it, our sameness (our subjectivities as produced by Hobbes) precisely prevents it: "Againe, men have no pleasure, (but on the contrary a great deale of griefe) in keeping company, where there is no power able to over-awe them all" (Hobbes, 1968: 185). Thus both inside—order, culture, art, science, time—and outside—nasty, poor, brutish, short life—are possible results of our nature; the only key difference is the authority of the sovereign. For this if for no other reason, we owe our allegiance to the sovereign. Who we are—in our positive aspects—is only enabled by our identity, in language, as produced through and by sovereignty.

As part of this, then, the "other" can be explicitly rewritten as well; the difference can be more directly and easily marked now. The "other" becomes those who lack the nation-state identity, as marked by (what else?) order, shared language, reason, science, resolutions of time and space—all as measured against Hobbes' writing of them. The difference is not necessarily "outside" spatially, but outside or under the resolutions of state sovereignty. It is the Savages of North America. What marks "the savages" is thus not a difference at the level of ontology or even epistemology. "They" are in essence the same as "we." *All* men, if we are to believe Hobbes, must apprehend the world the way Hobbes has described; it is just that some men haven't yet managed to achieve a sovereignty (commonwealth) that will enable them to enter into history, to pursue commerce, and so on. Thus, "savages" are no different from "other people." Their "society" is merely marked by a lack. They are marked by a failure to understand themselves and their world appropriately and so lift themselves from their nasty and brutish condition by establishing a shared system to allow them security in the pursuit of their desires. This portrayal of "savages" is hardly unique; it is more or less standard for the day (1650s). Crucial to his specific use of the "savage" is that despite the fact that the structures of authority Hobbes has produced are a response to the conditions around him (i.e. the necessity of countering claims to divine authority), when selecting a specific form for the collective "difference" to encourage people to bind together, to recognize their "identity," he reaches for something very far away: the "savage peoples of America." In choosing the "savage," he chooses an identity which only exists for most of his readers in the abstract and has no material expression in the lives of his countrymen. In this sense, his use of the "savage" is designed to minimize violence—the violence of neighbor against neighbor—rather than to legitimate it against the savage. He thus calls upon a "different/ce" that is clearly distant, far "outside" the nation, in order to discipline a plethora of "differences" within the nation, differences that were effecting great violences. In this sense, Hobbes' quest is to marginalize violence. That he fails to take account of the violence of this particular act of representation makes some sense, given the circumstances, especially as he is so careful to mark the limits of his own claims, for example, by resisting the expansionary state. This is in part why I argue that his representation of the "savage" in and of itself does not pose the most serious problem for Indigenous peoples today. In this sense, Hobbes' text is symptomatic of the presence/absence of "others" in modern political thought: savage peoples are explicitly present in Hobbes' text as the "savages of America," but they are implicitly present as his neighbors, those "mad" enough to kill their fellow citizens. Thus, the representation of "savages" tells us much more about 17th century England than about 17th century America.

However, in part due to how these assumptions are embedded in the practices of an expansionist and imperialistic state, they ultimately resonate far beyond the borders of England. The implications of the larger architecture in which this representation makes sense are and were played out on a much larger canvas than Hobbes perhaps envisioned. What is far more significant to contemporary Indigenous politics than this explicit production of a universalized and ontologically homogeneous "man" and the location of "savages" as less developed versions of "man," however, is the way in which this is embedded in the ontology that grounds Hobbes' production of sovereignty and thus of politics. This is the element of Hobbes work that has received far too little attention.

Put differently, what is more important than the fact that Hobbes has badly misrepresented Indigenous peoples at this point is that this misrepresentation is a necessary consequence of his production of the conditions under which we can think about or imagine politics at all. If, as I am arguing, Hobbes, in articulating the ground of modern politics, has not only misrepresented Indigenous peoples, he has ensured that they *must* be misrepresented, as the framework through which representation occurs already tells us what they must be. To address the political implications of Hobbes' misrepresentation thus requires challenging the conditions of possibility that ground our contemporary thinking about politics: sovereignty. By the same token, because of the crucial role the production of identity and difference, and the representation of the "savages," plays in determining those conditions, Indigenous politics also contains the possibility of posing this challenge. Developing these assertions is the work of the chapters that follow.

Sovereignty of/and knowledge

In the brief but important chapter 9 of *Leviathan*, one that I have so far neglected, Hobbes produces a typology of knowledge. He categorizes knowledge into two general kinds: "Knowledge of Fact" and "Knowledge of the Consequence of one Affirmation to another" (Hobbes, 1968: 147).

Knowledge of fact is knowledge involving sense and memory; it is "Absolute knowledge; as when we see a Fact doing, or remember it done" (Hobbes, 1968: 147). This knowledge he calls history, either natural or civil.

The other form of knowledge (knowledge of the consequence of one affirmation to another) is science, also known as philosophy. This knowledge is conditional; it is the knowledge of the relation of one affirmation to another. This field of knowledge is much larger and more complex than the former; Hobbes produces a diagram to illustrate this complexity (Hobbes, 1968: 149). The interesting aspect of the diagram is that "Science" immediately divides two ways: "Consequences from the Accidents of Bodies Naturall; which is called NATURAL PHILOSOPHY" and "Consequences from the Accidents of *Politique* Bodies; which is called POLITIQUES, and CIVILL PHILOSOPHY" (Hobbes, 1968: 149). While the first category divides further into a myriad of different "disciplines" of study (from Geometry, Arithmetique and Astronomy, to Geography, Astrology, Musique, Ethiques, Poetry, Logic and "the science of Just and Unjust"), the latter category divides only once, into: "1. Of consequences from the *Institution* of COMMON-WEALTHS, to the *Rights*, and *Duties* of the *Body Politique*, or *Soveraign*, and 2. Of Consequences from the same, to the *Duty*, and *Right* of the Subjects."

This diagram illustrates (at least) two crucial things about the structure and effects of Hobbes' argument. First, the definition of politics comprises the study of the relative rights and duties of the sovereign and the subjects. "Politics" is thus what happens within already constituted political communities. "Politics" is confined to and defined as the negotiation of rights and duties between already-constituted "subjects" and their "sovereign." "Politics" begins after Hobbes' Chapter 13. In order for sovereignty to "work"—to provide the necessary guarantee on the security of life, the fruits of the pursuits of men (including knowledge)—its conditions of possibility must be excluded from the realm of the political. Thus, although all that has happened in the first twelve chapters—including the production of an ontological ground that renders the difference expressed by Indigenous peoples as uncivilized and barbaric—is political in that it determines the possibility for and nature of politics, according to Hobbes it must be forgotten, naturalized, excluded from the study (and practices) of "politics." Again, given the tight-rope between ecclesiastical faith and "scientific" authority that Hobbes was walking, this is hardly surprising. In order for a commonwealth to work, Hobbes argued, people would have to accept its authority. Given that faith was no longer broadly capable of inspiring such acceptance, this faith must be transferred to "science," but, more precisely, to the necessity of this form of authority. If that question were to remain open, Hobbes felt we would remain without any basis upon which to agree enough to trust a power higher than our own.

But this diagram and chapter also imply more than this. They also indicate the centrality of the relationship between how and what we think—knowledge—and the question or problem of social order, authority, of sovereignty.

According to Hobbes, all of Science, or Philosophy, is conditional knowledge. It is the knowledge of the relation of one affirmation to another, conditional upon the terms of the affirmations having shared meanings. In other words, this science is dependent upon the shared system of meaning that Hobbes has produced thus far in the *Leviathan*. It is dependent upon the epistemological and ontological resolutions that are embedded in the languages and subject-ivities of the knowledge producers, of "men" and citizens. It is dependent upon precisely that which enables it: sovereignty.

The production of knowledge thus emerges from and within the system that requires sovereignty—resolutions of space, time, meaning, location, and so on in an inside/outside move—as its necessary result and condition. This would suggest a certain limitation on the search for "truth" or "fact," a limit on what kinds of questions can be asked. This limitation is clearly indicated by Hobbes' insistence that "science" is conditional knowledge, and is motiv-ated not by a search for fact so much as by the search for consistent relations amongst affirmations, for the knowledge of the consequences of our produc-tions of meaning. The status of "fact" is reserved for history, natural or civil, for the telling of eyewitness accounts of natural or civil bodies.

In other words, Hobbes here indicates that knowledge is produced in reference to sovereignty. It is the establishment and success of sovereignty, the determination of the limits of identity and meaning, that determines the effectiveness or "truth" or consistency of knowledge. Rather than existing "outside" of the state, knowledge is an expression of how sovereignty "works" to produce a common identity, the possibility for order, communica-tion. This suggests the importance of knowledge and knowledge production in the reproduction of sovereignty. All knowledge exists in reference to and reproduces the resolutions that enable sovereignty. Sovereignty exists in as much as things "make sense," as there is a way in which, a basis upon which, disputes can be arbitrated (science, objectivity). In the absence of this guaran-tee of meaning, of security, knowledge loses its capacity to make sense, and thus there is no basis for an assertion of legitimate authority.

Sovereignty thus requires the naturalization of the resolutions that Hobbes accomplishes prior to Chapter 13. It requires the erasure of the specificity of its own conditions of possibility, the protection of them from political engagement. It requires that there be an authority higher than the will of another. Since "God" or religion can no longer provide this authority, know-ledge itself must produce and guarantee this authority through and in relation to sovereignty. Sovereignty in this way becomes the principle that structures the intellectual, as well as physical, world, as it reinforces the ontological and epistemological principles that guide our own activities and practices as knowledge producers, as "subjects" who apprehend the world as Hobbes describes. His production of "man" as a "knowing subject" thus provides the basis for a reorientation of authority along two parallel axes: the subject (who knows with authority) and the sovereign state (who embodies/ guarantees this authority). Knowledge, subjectivity, and sovereignty are intimately interwoven, yet "politics" is confined to the realm in which they are already constituted. It is no coincidence that Hobbes is often referred to as a father of political science.

Here we have, then, the constitutive paradox of both modern knowledge broadly speaking and modern politics more precisely: knowledge requires sovereignty (not to mention a knowing subject), yet sovereignty is enabled by the production of a shared ontological (and epistemological) system. Sovereignty is necessary because the men who it is sovereign over are constituted so that they need sovereignty, yet this constitution, for Hobbes, is not political. It is the precondition for politics yet, for Hobbes, it must not be part of the political realm. It is both what we—subjects—must be and must forget we are. It is the insistence that we cannot be otherwise (without sovereignty) and maintain who we are, because we already are a particular way (that requires sovereignty). The principle of sovereignty, as established by Hobbes in Chapter 13, is thus the limit that tells us who we are, what we can know, and what happens if we refuse who we are. It tells us what can be political and what cannot. It establishes much more than a commonwealth, though it reassures us that what matters is the establishment of the commonwealth, as that is the precondition for all else. It is a beginning point for the science of politics.

Conclusion

The first ten chapters of *Leviathan* thus produce the groundwork for sovereignty: an ontological ground that produces an epistemological system that enables authoritative claims. This system rests on a series of exclusions, a rigorous—and universalized—production of identity. This identity is neither neutral nor universal, yet the moves Hobbes makes both naturalize his ontology and make this ontology into the ground for modern politics. As his argument progresses and his system is increasingly naturalized, differences get marked more explicitly, located much more firmly into a temporal developmental scale. The chapters leading up to and including Chapter 11 then take this ontology and epistemology and produce a naturalized, essentialized "human nature" which creates particular kinds of conflicts requiring sovereign mediation. After bracketing religious authority, Hobbes can then in Chapter 13 come in and provide the explicit framework for his proposed response: sovereignty. And, considering the options—the dangers lurking all around—it looks pretty appealing. Chapter 13 is crucial because it executes the bounding of identity, the melding of ontology, epistemology, identity, sovereignty. It constructs the space of the state as the space of identity and meaning. It sets up sovereignty as the answer to all that ails, an answer meant to minimize violence and enable men to pursue their desires. It sets the terrain for the rest of his thought. What concerns him, and any other political scientist, can from now on be bounded by the wall of the state. Modern politics is enabled.

At the same time, "savages" and other "others" without sovereignty are produced as "different,"[13] as marking the outside, the margins, of "our" new political imaginary. It tells those of us "inside" how to think about the world (and those "outside"); it provides for us the limit that enables us to evade the problem of "infinity" or "difference." Most remarkably, it does so openly, explicitly, self-consciously. It tells us what we must be and what we must forget in the name of order, progress, security. The strongest testament to the power of the story Hobbes tells is how remarkably compliant most modern theorists and practitioners of politics have been in accepting his starting point for politics and averting their eyes from the violences that enable it.

Hobbes spends much of the rest of his volume working out the characteristics, operations, functions, limits, and so on of the sovereign state and subjects he has established. Many others have spent many more volumes. Even more have simply begun with the distinctions and discriminations embedded in Hobbes' account of sovereignty and embarked on other projects from there. Thus begins the substitution of the study of government for the study of politics. Still others have contested the philosophical method he used, or his epistemological system. The ontological grounding of politics—the spatial and temporal resolutions of the sovereign state—however, has remained largely uncontested by political theorists. In what follows, I am particularly interested in the strength of his production and practices of sovereignty, in not only how sovereignty functions in Hobbes to resolve the tensions of his time, but more crucially how it still does and how this forces a continuation of the effects of Hobbes' representation of the "savages" even as his representation is increasingly seen as flawed. In one way or another, all of the thinkers and situations I engage in what follows begin with or are structured by the geography Hobbes sets up. I want to show how this is the case, see how far they get within or against it, and suggest the range of effects it continues to have on our thinking and our politics, especially through and in relation to Hobbes' border guards: the original inhabitants of North America.

3 Violences of sovereignty

The "regrettable necessity" of civilization

This chapter explores the resonances between Hobbes' relatively abstract account of sovereignty and some of the actual practices of sovereignty in the early histories of state building in North America. Tracing the workings of sovereignty in practice, and their resonances with Hobbes' account, reveals both the complexity of sovereignty and how it has shaped possibilities for Indigenous peoples. The chapter thus extends the analysis of sovereignty developed in Chapter 2, emphasizing sovereignty not just as an abstract concept cleverly adapted to modern contexts by theorists such as Hobbes, but also as a wider range of practices through which authority is constituted and legitimated, whether in a text like *Leviathan* or in the building of states.

For texts or stories such as Hobbes' to be authorized, they must convince: they must create their authority. Hobbes enacts this in his text through a combination of careful, logical argumentation and telling a story that is intended to be so frightening that we will be convinced that sovereignty is the obvious and necessary precondition for political community. But Hobbes' production of sovereignty in his text does not necessarily translate into the world: states, or other forms of authority, must produce and legitimate their own authority. They must produce, and reproduce, their sovereignty, in part through convincing others—their citizens, other states, global institutions—of its existence and legitimacy. Although sovereignty is frequently assumed to be natural and given, as we saw in Hobbes' text this itself is an effect of how sovereignty works, how the practices of sovereignty encourage us to see the world in a particular way and to believe in the inevitability and necessity of this way of seeing the world. We do not have sovereign states because they are inevitable or necessary, but because their inevitability and necessity have been produced; we have been and must continue to be convinced of them. In order to understand this process, as well as its implications, we need to examine sovereignty not only as a discourse, as in Hobbes' text, but as a practice, as the discourse is enacted, reproduced, rearticulated, and acted upon.

This chapter will examine practices of sovereignty at two different sites: first, in the analysis of emerging forms of democracy in America by Alexis de Tocqueville and, second, in the legal and political practices through which the Canadian state historically engaged Indigenous peoples. Alexis de Tocqueville was a French aristocrat who came to the United States in the early 1800s to develop an understanding of this new country, and of its new practice of governance: democracy. His account of democracy in America is extraordinary for the grasp of political culture and institutions it expresses, so much so that he has come down to students of contemporary politics as one of the fathers of American pluralism. His text is also revealing in that, unlike Hobbes, for whom the "Savages of North America" were a distant abstraction, in Tocqueville's case the mythical "savage" inhabited the same land as the emerging forms of political authority, and thus understanding their situation and treatment posed an immediate challenge. As a consequence, Tocqueville's text engages Indigenous peoples very directly and this engagement, importantly interwoven with his influential analysis, provides key insights into how practices of (democratic) sovereignty have determined political possibilities for Indigenous peoples. In particular, it reveals the way that practices of sovereignty produced the exclusion and subsequent ill-treatment of Indigenous peoples as a "regrettable necessity" for the emergence of democracy in America.[1]

The practices of sovereignty expressed in law and policy towards Indigenous peoples in Canada are revealing for similar reasons. Tocqueville witnessed, and sought to understand and justify, the treatment of Indigenous peoples in the United States. Lawmakers in Canada had to shape their own policies about how to respond to the presence of Indigenous peoples, under their own specific constraints. An analysis of their responses—their apprehension of Indigenous peoples, their communities, worldviews and aspirations, and the possibilities for responding to them—reveals crucial resonances with the discourses and practices of sovereignty already discussed. This is not to say that policy towards Indigenous peoples was the same in Canada and the United States. On the contrary, it is to show how despite the important differences between the two countries in how they produced their sovereignties, the outcome for Indigenous peoples was strikingly similar. This reveals how the underlying logic and structure of sovereignty articulated by Hobbes has consistently worked to frame the possibilities not only for Indigenous peoples, but also for the production of modern political space much more widely.

The violence of democracy in America

Alexis de Tocqueville's project in *Democracy in America*, first published in 1835, is to usher in a new age: the Age of Democracy. He argues that a democratic revolution is sweeping the Christian world and that unless "those who direct our affairs" adapt to it, they will be swept away. Democracy is inevitable, he argues, but nonetheless malleable, and he is concerned with how it might be shaped and molded. His book is an attempt to provide a foundation for "a new science of politics" to effect this taming of democracy:

The first of the duties that are at this time imposed upon those who direct our affairs is to educate democracy, to reawaken, if possible, its religious beliefs; to purify its morals; to mold its actions; to substitute a knowledge of statecraft for its inexperience, and an awareness of its true interest for its blind instincts, to adapt its government to time and place, and to modify it according to men and to conditions. A new science of politics is needed for a new world.

(Tocqueville, 1990: 7)

This "new science of politics" involves both an analysis and a production of this new form of authority, this new relationship between "people" and "state." In this way Tocqueville, like Hobbes, is struggling to respond to the collapse of hierarchical (ecclesiastical and aristocratic) forms of authority. Unlike Hobbes, however, he has access to and is intrigued by the possibilities of democracy as way of responding to the problem of authority in the context of the horizontal forms of authority expressed by modern sovereignty. The problem of sovereignty is thus quite centrally Tocqueville's problem, and although Hobbes makes no explicit appearance in the text, his framing of the problem echoes throughout it.[2]

For Tocqueville, as for Hobbes, sovereignty rests upon a shared body of beliefs, a core of discursive resonance. It is this shared set of beliefs, the identity and self-consciousness of a people as a people that provides the most fundamental basis for government:

A government retains its sway over a great number of citizens far less by the voluntary and rational consent of the multitude than by that instinctive, and to a certain extent involuntary, agreement which results from similarity of feelings and resemblances of opinion . . . Society can exist only when a great number of men consider a great number of things under that same aspect, when they hold the same opinions upon many subjects, and when the same occurrences suggest the same thoughts and impressions to their minds.

(Tocqueville, 1990: 392)

The taming of democracy is thus intimately bound up with the production, maintenance, and shaping of this commonalty, this resonance. This is the self-conscious significance of Tocqueville's text: he works not only to produce a study of America for translation to other sites, but to *produce* the sovereignty of America in the text. He seeks to tell a story about democracy in America that will function to produce and effect the resonance necessary for a particular form of authority, to produce democratic sovereignty as it should be. As such, the story he tells is doubly important, and deeply embedded in ongoing struggles over legitimate political authority in both America and Europe.

In this context, the "Indians"[3] pose a particular challenge to Tocqueville.

The mythology of the "Indian" was by his time well developed in Europe, as an expression of both the highest ideals and greatest fears about human nature: the "noble savage" and "barbarian" respectively.[4] Tocqueville comes to the New World informed by these myths, but once he arrives he must deal with the reality of the presence of Indigenous Americans, as well as of their treatment at the hands of democracy. Like Hobbes, he can and does use them as an imagined outside that defines the social core of resonance. But unlike Hobbes, for whom they remain essentially an abstraction, he has to material-ize this in some way in relation to the particular narrative of a nation with a violent past (and present). He negotiates this difficulty in ways consistent with the treatment of non-Europeans in most European texts. He produces them as different in specific, predictable ways, and then makes their differ-ence the justification for the violence of their treatment. Once this treatment has been justified, made to appear as natural and necessary, its violence must be concealed or forgotten lest its injustice haunt the nation. The "Indi-ans" must be banished from the core of democracy because they do not resonate with its identity (although they constitute it). Crucial to Toc-queville's argument, however, is that although he sees the treatment of the "Indians" as a necessary effect of the production of democratic sovereignty, he argues that Americans—in order to believe in their sovereignty—must understand it as a failure of the "Indians" rather than as an effect of democratic sovereignty.

Tocqueville begins the process of marking and establishing their difference in the first chapter of the book, which focuses on the form and territory of the future nation. He marks this difference by reproducing the well-known argument made by Locke that the "Indians" did not have the proper relation-ship to the land for them to be considered civilized, and thus as possessing the land:[5]

> Although the vast country that I have been describing was inhabited by many indigenous tribes, it may justly be said, at the time of its discovery by Europeans, to have formed one great desert. The Indians occupied without possessing it. It is by agricultural labor that man appropriates the soil, and the early inhabitants of North America lived by the produce of the chase.[6]

> (Tocqueville, 1990: 25)

Because they do not properly possess the land, they cannot claim sovereignty over it, and thus need not be treated as "real" societies or states.[7] This enables Tocqueville to write the "Indians" as caretakers: their purpose was to inhabit the land, to hold it ready for the real owners to arrive and take possession of it:

> They seem to have been placed by Providence amid the riches of the New World only to enjoy them for a season; they were there merely to wait till

others came . . . the whole continent, in short, seemed prepared to be the abode of a great nation yet unborn.

(Tocqueville, 1990: 25)

In this way, "Indians" become a part of the territory, another aspect of the landscape the settlers had to confront and subdue as part of the building of their nation. While the "Indians" have lived on the land "timelessly," not marking their space and histories in ways recognized by European settlers, the settlers are destined to bring the land into history by cultivating and "improving" it. Within the first chapter, the "Indians" are thus produced as different on the basis of their level of civilization, as indicated by social organization (tribal) and relationship to land (wandering). Simultaneously, democratic sovereignty is connected to civilization and a specific relationship to territory.[8]

After the first chapter, the "Indians" largely disappear from the text, except for occasional references, only to reappear in the final chapter of volume 1; in the text, as on the ground, they inhabit the margins. Between lies the substance of Tocqueville's work, in which he produces the core of resonance that enables democratic sovereignty in America. He identifies three crucial points of resonance which provide the basis for American democracy: "the peculiar and accidental situation in which providence has placed the Americans," the laws, and the manners and customs of the people. Interwoven within these three categories are the rich subtexts of belief which he argues characterize American national identity or character: equality of condition, independence and the cult of the individual, freedom of—but not freedom from—religion, freedom of opinion (though more in theory than in practice), and so on. Together, these three conditions for democracy and their subtexts frame a narrative of America that locates and justifies the state in time, history, and destiny and provide the social resonance that authorizes its sovereignty. They also, insofar as they rest upon the prior exclusion of the "differences" expressed by "Indians," reinforce their exclusion from democracy in America.

The first enabling condition for democracy in America is the peculiar situation the Americans inherited, a situation already hinted at in the first chapter of his book. Unlike peoples elsewhere in the world, Tocqueville explains, Americans find themselves on a "boundless continent" that is essentially "uninhabited," such that "Nature herself favors the cause of the people" (Tocqueville, 1990: 290–91). For Tocqueville, this land was made for this (European) people, for this form of government. It was given by the Creator for this purpose:

Everything is extraordinary in America, the social condition of the inhabitants as well as the laws; but the soil upon which these institutions are founded is more extraordinary than all the rest. When the earth was given to men by the Creator, the earth was inexhaustible; but men were weak and ignorant, and when they had learned to take advantage of the treasures which it contained, they already covered its surface and were soon obliged to earn by the sword an asylum for repose and freedom. Just then North America was discovered, as if it had been kept in reserve by the Deity and had just risen from beneath the waters of the Deluge.

That continent still presents, as it did in the primeval time, rivers that rise from never failing sources, green and moist solitudes, and limitless fields which the plowshare of the husbandman has never turned. In this state it is offered to man, not barbarous, ignorant, and isolated, as he was in the early ages, but already in possession of the most important secrets of nature, united to his fellow men, and instructed by the experience of fifty centuries.

(Tocqueville, 1990: 291–92)

This passage locates the arrival of Europeans within a grand narrative of human history and divine (Christian) destiny. America becomes the promised land: promised and waiting for the civilized Europeans, who have learned how to properly organize themselves and their use of land and resources. It is Eden, but an Eden whose passage is guarded by specific narratives of economy, civilization, history. In this way, the territory of America is brought into the temporal resolutions of European civilization.

The specificity of this relationship between land and peoples emerges more clearly in his discussion of one nagging problem: the land does appear vast and uninhabited, but there are these "Indians" running about. How do they fit into this Edenic narrative?

In what part of human history can be found anything similar to what is passing before our eyes in North America? The celebrated communities of antiquity were all founded in the midst of hostile nations, which they were obliged to subjugate before they could flourish in their place. Even the moderns have found, in some parts of South America, vast regions inhabited by a people of inferior civilization, who nevertheless had already occupied and cultivated the soil. To found their new states it was necessary to extirpate or subdue a numerous population, and they made civilization blush for its own success. But North America was inhabited only by wandering tribes, who had no thought of profiting by the natural riches of the soil; that vast country was still, properly speaking, an empty continent, a desert land awaiting its inhabitants.[9]

(Tocqueville, 1990: 291)

Here we see the emergence of the narrative that justifies violence in the name of civilization. Celebrated communities were founded in violence, because they were founded in the midst of "hostile" peoples. Communities in South America were founded through violence because they were founded amidst an "inferior civilization," despite the fact that they were civilizations that cultivated the land, which in Lockean terms should mean they had a legitimate claim to it. Nonetheless, their extirpation was "necessary" for the founding of new states, and "civilization" blushed for its successes. The North American situation is even easier for Tocqueville: these "wandering tribes" have not even achieved that level of social organization or relationship to land that their treatment even registers as violent. They simply need to be chased away, to wander elsewhere: "Three or four thousand soldiers drive before them the wandering races of the Aborigines; these are followed by the pioneers, who pierce the woods, scare off the beasts of prey, explore the courses of the inland streams, and make ready the triumphal march of civilization across the desert" (Tocqueville, 1990: 292).

The first characteristic that enables democracy in America thus establishes the basic narrative of the nation: a promised land, full of riches, the birthplace of a new nation, one emerging as and from the pinnacle of civilization. It is a return to nature, but a return enabled and over-determined by an historically specific relationship to land, economy, and social organization. The land is given to them, by the Creator and history, for the projects of man, for the development of a state, for human artifice. The previous inhabitants of the land are but remnants of the past, those that live outside of time. Simultaneous with the founding narrative, one of the key sites of resonance that enables sovereignty, is the inscription of the "Indians" as uncivilized, or at least (as in the case of the South American Indigenous peoples) as of an inferior civilization. Not only is their claim to the land denied, but any violence committed against them is either erased or justified as the necessary violence of civilization.

While Tocqueville considers the physical situation of America to be crucial to the development of democracy, there are two other key conditions. The second is the laws of the new state, an analysis of which is the primary target of Tocqueville's book. Perhaps more important for Tocqueville than the specific character of the laws, however, is the source of the power of the laws. This power does not necessarily emerge from their quality (in fact he argues they are not usually as good as laws produced by an aristocracy), but from the belief that they are created by the people who are ruled by them. They belong to and represent the people of the nation, and thus the people uphold them:

> [I]n the United States everyone is personally interested in enforcing the obedience of the whole community to the law; for as the minority may shortly rally the majority to its principles, it is interested in professing that respect for the decrees of the legislator which it may soon have occasion to claim for its own. However irksome an enactment may be, the citizen of the United States complies with it, not only because it is the work of the majority, but because it is his own, and he regards it as a contract to which he himself is a party.
>
> (Tocqueville, 1990: 248)

This, combined with the flexibility of the laws (the feeling that they can be changed if proven harmful) compels the population to support and believe in law, and in turn in democratic sovereignty. That the laws would provide a point of resonance is not surprising in relation to Hobbes' analysis, in that processes of law are processes by which the meaning of words—so vital to foundation of sovereignty—is negotiated and determined, making laws the expression of the core of agreement that constitutes sovereignty. For Hobbes, laws made by the sovereign would thus be the expression of the core of agreement that constitutes sovereignty. What is distinct in Tocqueville is the emphasis on process: the crucial point of resonance is not that all citizens agree with or believe in each law, but that each citizen can see the value of upholding the laws because they can be made and remade to express citizens' wills, and because they feel the laws thus express their will. In the case of both Hobbes and Tocqueville, however, the crucial thing is that the laws—in process or in substance—express the shared core of resonance of the nation, they express the agreement that constitutes sovereignty.

While the laws are important to the maintenance of democracy in America, however, Tocqueville does not believe them to be as important as the influence of customs and beliefs, the third aspect of the core of resonance that enables sovereignty. The first and most central "custom" he discusses in this section is religion, which he believes is crucial to the operation of democracy.[10] While he argues that the direct influence of religion on democratic politics is relatively small, the indirect influence is not: "In the United States religion exercises but little influence upon the laws and upon the details of public opinion; but it directs the customs of the community, and, by regulating domestic life, it regulates the state" (Tocqueville, 1990: 304). This is not to say, however, that religion is not a political institution: "Religion in America takes no direct part in the government of society, but it must be regarded as the first of their political institutions" (Tocqueville, 1990: 305). As with the laws, the importance of religion to the state is not direct, but rather felt in its regulation of mores, customs, manners. Not accessible through politics, it nonetheless fulfills a crucial function in the institution and maintenance of political stability. Crucial also is that the shared religious assumptions are those of Christianity, which themselves reproduce the notions of time and space into which Hobbes neatly slotted the state, and—as we saw in the Edenic narrative above—Tocqueville neatly slotted America. As with Hobbes, then, the elements most crucial to sovereignty, to the authorization and legitimation of the authority in the state, are naturalized so deeply as to be inaccessible to the political as he has defined it, even as they are the most important of political institutions. They are crucial preconditions of the political; they shape its character and direction, and express the core of resonance that enables it, but themselves remain shielded from political engagement.

These, then, are the three crucial points of resonance which, Tocqueville argues, function to maintain democracy in America: the physical circumstances of the founding of the nation, its laws, and the customs and habits that regulate it. All three implicitly and explicitly reinforce the location of America in time and space, and reinscribe the location of the "savage" outside of, marking the edges of, these resolutions. They are explicitly excluded from the founding narrative. As non-Christian, not to mention non-European, they cannot resonate with the most important customs and habits that regulate the nation. As non-citizens, with no capacity to participate in the making of the laws, they do not resonate with these. At times, the mental gymnastics required to maintain this separation boggle the mind. For example, although the "Indians" are condemned because their government is grounded in opinion and custom, Tocqueville argues that it is precisely opinion and custom that provide the most crucial glue for American democracy (Tocqueville, 1990: 333).

It is in the last chapter of the book that Tocqueville completes the narrative of civilization that locates and justifies the treatment of the "Indians." This chapter focuses on those things which are "American without being democratic": the future of the three races (Anglo-Americans, "Negroes," and "Indians") within the United States and the dangers which threaten the Union. That this chapter, focused on the dangers to the Union, should be the context in which Tocqueville effects and justifies the violence inherent in the treatment of the "Indians" is telling: it is a violence inherent in the constitution of the Union itself. Having established the core of resonance that enables democracy, Tocqueville turns to examine those things that might threaten it. Prominent among these is the threat posed by those races excluded from democracy in America: the "Indians" and the "Negroes." Each group, Tocqueville argues, has responded differently to this exclusion: the "Negroes" have fought for inclusion, whereas the "Indians" have chosen to reject civilization: "Far from desiring to conform his habits to ours, he loves his savage life as the distinguishing mark of his race and repels every advance to civilization, less, perhaps, from hatred of it than from a dread of resembling the European" (Tocqueville, 1990: 334). Tocqueville sees this as perhaps a wise decision, though tragic: if they were to desire acceptance in the social core, they would be in the same position as "the Negroes," forever consigned to the lower margins of society, not real citizens because to admit them as citizens would require an unwriting of their absolute difference and thus a recognition of the violence of their treatment, the violence inherent in the social core of democracy. Tocqueville fears that this is something the core of resonance that enables democracy could not live with:

> As long as the Negro remains a slave, he may be kept in a condition not far removed from that of the brutes; but with his liberty he cannot but acquire a degree of instruction that will enable him to appreciate his misfortunes and to discern a remedy for them. Moreover, there exists a singular principle of relative justice which is firmly implanted in the human heart. Men are much more forcibly struck by those inequalities

which exist within the same class than by those which may be noted between different classes. One can understand slavery, but how allow several millions of citizens to exist under a load of eternal infamy and hereditary wretchedness?

(Tocqueville, 1990: 373)

Although regrettable, then, for Tocqueville the exclusion of "Indians" and "Negroes" from democracy is necessary. It is a self-conscious violence on his part, necessary because the "social core" or sovereign imaginary would be unable to maintain its resonance in light of an acknowledgment of its own violences. The assertion of the "identity" of those marked as "different" will thus always be politically volatile, so much so that it poses the greatest challenge to American democracy in Tocqueville's eyes. Although he marginalizes "Indians" in the text, he does not marginalize their potential political significance to the future of democracy in America.

Unlike the "Negroes," "Indians" choose to reject civilization. However, it is not really a choice, as the "choice" of civilization does not result in any advantage for the "Indians": either choice effectively results in their extermination. Tocqueville claims that they choose not to assimilate (be civilized), suggesting that the fault ultimately rests with them, effectively drawing attention away from his point above about the dangers to society of assimilating them, given that its identity rests precisely upon their absolute difference. Because of their danger, the potential they carry for revealing the myth of the social core, they must be written out, erased, their treatment justified. Again, in Tocqueville's text the critical tool for effecting this "necessary choice" is civilization. In the face of such an "advanced" civilization the "Indians" simply cannot survive, according to Tocqueville (1990: 349), and the inevitable Westward march will force them further and further on to their own death, in as legal and bloodless manner as possible:

From whichever side we consider the destinies of the aborigines of North America, their calamities appear irremediable: if they continue barbarous, they are forced to retire; if they attempt to civilize themselves, the contact of a more civilized community subjects them to oppression and destitution. They perish if they continue to wander from waste to waste, and if they attempt to settle they still must perish. The assistance of Europeans is necessary to instruct them, but the approach of Europeans corrupts and repels them into savage life. They refuse to change their habits as long as their solitudes are their own, and it is too late to change them when at last they are forced to submit.

(Tocqueville, 1990: 354)

The violence of their treatment is thus concealed; the blame for their disappearance rests in the necessity of progress, the triumph of civilization, the triumph of the particular resolutions of sovereignty. Their treatment is necessary, regrettable, inevitable: the difference they express cannot be accommodated within the core of resonance that enables democratic sovereignty in America. In this way, by the end of the text the erasure is so complete that Tocqueville can call the Anglo-Americans "natives" (Tocqueville, 1990: 430–31) and present a picture of American democracy that is completely dependent on this particular writing of sameness, of identity:

> At a period that may be said to be near, for we are speaking of the life of a nation, the Anglo-Americans alone will cover the immense space contained between the polar regions and the tropics. . . . Whatever differences may arise, from peace or war, freedom or oppression, prosperity or want, between the descendants of the great Anglo-American family, they will all preserve at least a similar social condition and will hold in common the customs and opinions to which that social condition has given birth.
>
> (Tocqueville, 1990: 432–33)

Tocqueville's text enacts an impressive gymnastic. Within his description of democracy in America he produces a new myth of democracy and sovereignty, one grounded in the American experience: settlers landed on this continent, eager to create a new world, a new government, a new kind of state. They encountered a continent perfectly suited to their project, ripe and waiting for cultivation, civilization. They also encountered some wandering tribes of "Indians," proud, beautiful, but unfortunately uncivilized peoples who, because of their lack of civilization, held no real claim to the land. The interaction between the two peoples was predetermined from the start: the settlers needed land to expand and build their new state; when the two "civilizations" came in to conflict, the superior one, obviously, triumphed. Further, this triumph comes through only the most "civilized" means:

> The Americans of the United States have accomplished this twofold purpose with singular felicity, tranquilly, legally, philanthropically, without shedding blood, and without violating a single great principle of morality in the eyes of the world. It is impossible to destroy men with more respect for the laws of humanity.
>
> (Tocqueville, 1990: 355)

The erasure of violence effected by this statement is truly breathtaking, even though it will not be unfamiliar to historians of American mythmaking. Sovereignty is thus established, both in his text and on the land.

However, in order to produce this myth he enacts a double violence. He not only legitimates and erases violence against the "Indians," removing responsibility for it onto "regrettable necessity," he also reproduces an identity for them that leaves them trapped in an impossible choice between assimilation and extermination. He writes them as fundamentally different, utilizes this writing to produce the core of resonance upon which sovereignty depends, and then erases them, banishes them to the borders, the outside of democracy. In this process, democracy and sovereignty become linked in a complicated way. Democratic sovereignty requires a core, an identity. This is produced in part by a writing of otherness defined by civilization. The violence of state building is thus a violence of identity (and difference) building and must be concealed in the language of regrettable necessity. However, there is a weakness in this resolution because the very treatment which enables sovereignty also threatens it, should those marked as "different" ever come to be seen as part of the collective identity, in that the violences committed against them would discredit this core of resonance. Sovereignty thus rests on a continued violence: it must maintain its differences as its own boundaries, as non-subjects, because to acknowledge them as subjects would force democracy to face its own violent necessities.

Producing Canada/producing "Indians"

Tocqueville, of course, wrote about the United States, and marveled at its uniqueness. But discourses and practices of sovereignty repeat certain necessities across contexts, indeed produce contexts in particular ways. The remainder of the chapter illustrates this in relation to the treatment of Indigenous peoples in Canada. Although practices of sovereignty have helped to produce stability and order in both places, and their successes should not be forgotten, the analysis here, as above, emphasizes some of the darker sides of these practices, the ways in which their successes depended on certain kinds of violence. Understanding this violence—its logic, character, and justification—is crucial to understanding not only sovereignty as a practice, but also the nature and significance of contemporary Indigenous politics.[11]

Initial contacts between Indigenous peoples and European explorers and settlers in the future territory of Canada tended to be more cooperative than in the United States. Because this area was exploited at first mostly for trading purposes—fur and fish—rather than for agricultural settlement, and because of the harsh, unforgiving environment, Indigenous cooperation was vital to European interests. Indigenous groups were not only valuable trading partners; the explorers were absolutely dependent upon their knowledge of the area in order to survive. In addition, they were crucial military allies, first for the French against the British and later against the growing American menace. This cooperation does not mean, of course, that the Indigenous peoples suffered no ill effects from these encounters, as the effects of disease, for example, were significant.[12] Towards the end of the 18th century, the dynamics of this relationship began to change as the fur trade ceased to be the dominant economic interest in the area and the number of colonists coming from Europe with an eye to agricultural settlement began to dramatically increase. The War of 1812 and the Rush–Bagot Convention were the crucial turning points in this respect. With the American menace more or less controlled and peace assured, the Indigenous peoples' last area of importance to settlers—their importance as military allies—faded. In 1830, Great Britain transferred jurisdiction for Indian affairs in Canada from military to civilian officers, marking a significant shift in the relationship between Indigenous peoples and Europeans.[13]

Once Indigenous peoples were no longer useful to the colonists, they were also in the way: colonists wanted access to their land. Facing this situation, those responsible for "Indian Affairs" had to figure out how to remove the "Indian" (and his claims to land) as easily as possible so that the land could be settled. However, because they were still under British jurisdiction, they had to be attentive to the *Royal Proclamation of 1763*, which stipulated that "Indian" land could only be sold to the government, not to individual citizens.[14] Working within these limitations, those responsible for policy making had to come up with some way to cause the "Indians" to renounce their claim to the land. The two most apparent ones were assimilation—turn them into good productive citizen-farmers, each with his own small plot of land and without special claims on large tracts of land—or elimination—a more aggressive campaign to force them off the land, such as had been pursued in the United States. There was little to motivate the latter, a policy that was likely to be costly both economically and politically, especially because the relatively cooperative relationship of the past meant there was little public fear or hostility towards "Indians." Thus, Canadian policy focused on the peaceful transfer of "Indian" land through a program of assimilation. The shift to a policy of land appropriation through "protection" and assimilation from one of partnership and cooperation was enabled through a fortuitous (for Britain) concurrence:

> The policy of assimilation was the result of a concurrence of sentiment and interest: the sentiment that a superior race (the British) had definite responsibilities towards an inferior (the Indians) coincided with the self-interest of the British government in cutting the costs of colonial administration.
>
> (Upton, 1973: 51)

Here, as in Tocqueville, the narrative of civilization provided crucial authorization for a policy of assimilation: in this case a "benevolent" rather than explicitly violent one, but the logic—as well as its apparently coincidental benefits for the settlers—remained the same.

What was to follow for almost two centuries were systematic policies of assimilation, pursued first by the British, then the Canadian colonial governments, and later—after confederation—by the Canadian government. The first systematic articulation of this policy was that of the Bagot Commission (1844), whose recommendations established the key components of the policy that was to guide the Canadian government for the foreseeable future. While the Commission reaffirmed government and Crown obligations to the "Indians," especially regarding land tenure, it also recommended both eliminating Indians' distinctive relationship to the land by enforcing settlement and individual land ownership, and reducing the government's obligations to them by turning them into productive farmers and artisans (Miller, 1991: 104). The government's acceptance of the Commission's recommendations resulted in a reorganization of the Indian Department and a concerted effort to settle and assimilate the "Indians." It also led to significant resistance from the "Indians," especially regarding the question of land and land use (Miller, 1991: 104–05). Thus began a dynamic of the Canadian government forcibly instituting policies to which Indigenous groups explicitly objected, to no avail. It was a dynamic that was to become very familiar.

The policy that followed, though periodically revised, was consistent in its focus: the "Indian problem" must disappear through their assimilation, which would be accomplished through their "civilization." This required three things: education, Christianity, and a settled way of life, preferably agricultural. As Upton describes the policy:

> First of all it would be necessary to overcome his preference for his own way of life which was doomed to vanish in the face of white settlement. To do this it would be necessary to Christianise him, and the missionaries would be the executive arm of assimilationist policy. Unless sanctioned by religion 'civilized life is too tame, to [sic] insipid, to charm the roving barbarian,' explained one witness before the Parliamentary enquiries. . . . Christianity [would give] them the material desires of white men, and for that reason the Indian [would] now [have] to work like a white man. He could no longer be drunken, indolent, improvident. He [would be] inducted into civilization, on his way to assimilation—the end which . . . was 'the only possible euthanasia of savage communities.'[15]
>
> (Upton, 1973: 54)

The assumptions that were embedded in Tocqueville's analysis clearly ring through here. Most obvious is the conviction that "civilization" is the only possible future for the "Indians"; their only alternative is to be "doomed to vanish." The necessary mechanisms of this civilization are settlement, Christianity, and education. The positive effect of this is that the "Indian" would become a Hobbesian man: a desiring, productive contributor to society. The tone is benevolent, but there is no less conviction that assimilation through "civilization" is the only option for the "Indians" than was present in Tocqueville's justification for their more explicitly violent treatment at the hands of democracy in America.

This emphasis on assimilation and its development into an increasingly coercive policy is evident in even the briefest examination of the major legislation regarding "Indian" affairs. In 1850 Canada passed *An Act for the better protection of the Lands and Property of Indians in Lower Canada* and *An Act for the protection of the Indians in Upper Canada from imposition, and the property occupied or enjoyed by them from trespassing and injury*. As can be guessed from their titles, these Acts were intended to protect "Indians" and their land. However, they also purported to define "Indians." While the definition used was very broad—anyone with "Indian blood" or living with "Indians" was included—the significance of this maneuver lay in the fact that "civil government, an agency beyond the control of Indians, a body in which Indians were not even eligible to have representation, arrogated to itself the authority to define who was or was not Indian" (Miller, 1991: 109). This move opened the door for increasingly coercive attempts to control "Indians" in the next bit of legislation: the 1857 *Act for the Gradual Civilization of the Indian Tribes of Canada*, which made into law the goals of Canada's Indian policy. Drawing again from the recommendations of the Bagot Commission to justify the policy, this Act spelled out how "Indians" could become full citizens and leave behind their "Indian" status. In order to become enfranchised, an "Indian" would have to prove to a board that he was literate, free of debt, and of good moral character. Upon enfranchisement, the "Indian" would gain freehold tenure of 20 hectares of reserve land. In this way the legislation functioned to break up "Indian" landholdings in order to enable settlers to gain access to them. Again, this desired outcome was concealed in a rhetoric of the necessity of civilization.

As Miller and others have pointed out, this Act created a crucial legal paradox. Even though the Act was designed to offer citizenship to "Indians," it did so by first defining them as non-citizens: "In other words, legislation whose purpose was 'to remove all legal distinctions between Indians and Euro-Canadians' actually established them in law" (Miller, 1991: 111). This legal paradox is an expression of the practice of sovereignty: the "Indians" must be defined as different in order to establish the identity and sovereignty of Canada; however, this sovereignty is simultaneously grounded in the assumption that "we" all ultimately must be the same, just as Hobbes argued in *Leviathan*. Some differences, such as a difference in material desires, are acceptable and even necessary. Others, such as that expressed by the "Indians"—differences in ontology, in land use, "civilization"—must be overcome (or eliminated) in order to establish the resonance necessary for sovereignty. Thus the differences expressed by "Indians" must be understood as temporal ones: they must be markers of an inferior civilization, of having "not yet grown up" to be as we all must be: modern, rational, desiring individuals. This paradox is thus a necessary and constitutive one: the production of sovereignty requires this particular disciplining of difference. The paradox, of course, cuts most deeply for those marked as "different," who are left with the options familiar from Tocqueville's analysis: remain "different" and thus excluded, or reject their difference in order to access political subjectivity. This option was rejected by the "Indians" almost universally; their reaction to this new policy was unequivocal:

The reaction of the Indians to at least these provisions of the Act was swift and blunt. It was, said a tribal leader, an attempt 'to break them to pieces.' It did not, he continued, 'meet their views' because it ran counter to their wish to maintain tribal integrity and communal land ownership. Equally revealing was the response of the Indian Department: 'the Civilization Act is no grievance to you,' it replied brusquely.

(Miller, 1991: 111–12)

The most clear example of their response, however, is that they simply refused to comply. Between the *Gradual Civilization Act of 1857* and the next significant piece of legislation in 1869, only one "Indian" chose to become enfranchised (Miller, 1991: 114).

The government response was to become more coercive. In 1869, another *Gradual Enfranchisement Act* repeated all of the provisions of the 1857 Act and added two more critical ones. The first was the "location ticket": the government would have reserves surveyed into individual lots, which the government-recognized leadership of each group could then assign to individual band members. As title, they would be given a "location ticket." If he then used the land during the subsequent three years "as a European might," and if he was fully qualified for membership into Canadian society, he would be enfranchised and given title to the land. "[This] was a means by which the Indian could demonstrate that he had adopted the European concept of private property, which was an additional test of whether he had become 'civilized' " (Tobias, 1976: 17). In this way, again, attitudes towards land and property become layered onto civilization as necessary components of resonance.

The second change in the 1869 Act was an explicit attack on self-government:

Recognizing that the obstacle to enfranchisement was Indian resistance that expressed itself through political organizations, the new act empowered Indian Affairs officials to remove elected leaders 'for dishonesty, intemperance or immorality.' The interpretation and application of these vague terms was conveniently left to bureaucrats in Ottawa. The 1869 act also restricted the jurisdiction of band councils to matters of municipal government. And, finally, the same measure established a governmental veto of Indian legislation by making all band measures 'subject to confirmation by the Governor in Council.'

(Miller, 1991: 152–53)

This trend towards increased coercion in attempts to prevent resistance to assimilation expressed through political organization and mobilization became yet more pronounced in further legislation. Although the 1876 *Indian Act* consolidated previous legislation with relatively few changes, subsequent revisions increased the Department of Indian Affairs' ability to intervene in tribal self-government, further attempted to control movement, and banned traditional cultural celebrations such as the Sun Dance and the Thirst Dance on the prairies, and the Potlatch on the West Coast.[16] In 1920, legislation even went so far as to make enfranchisement and loss of Indian status compulsory for those who could meet the standards (Miller, 1991: 206).

Despite its consistent failure, the goal of this long sequence of legislation remained clear. In the words of Canada's first prime minister: "[T]he 'great aim of our legislation ... has been to do away with the tribal system and assimilate the Indian people in all respects with the inhabitants of the Dominion, as speedily as they are fit for the change'" (Miller, 1991: 189). Or as Department of Indian Affairs deputy minister Duncan Campbell Scott put it in 1920: "Our object is to continue until there is not a single Indian in Canada that has not been absorbed into the body politic, and there is no Indian question, and no Indian Department" (Miller, 1991: 207). Precisely what this assimilation looks like is also consistent and clear. Prime Minister Macdonald again:

> So I say that the Indians living in the older Provinces who have gone to school—and they all go to school—who are educated, who associate with white men, who are acquainted with all the principles of civilization, who carry out all the practices of civilization, who have accumulated round themselves property, who have good houses, and well furnished houses, who educate their children, who contribute to the public treasury in the same way as the whites do, should possess the franchise.
>
> (Miller, 1991: 195)

Citizenship, in other words, is the reward of modern subjectivity, which is expressed in a range of familiar ways: education, association with "white men," civilization, and property (including well-furnished houses).

Macdonald's statement raises one of the darkest chapters of Canada's "Indian" policies: residential schools. Education was seen as so crucial to "civilizing" Indigenous peoples that there was a systematic policy across Canada throughout this time, and in some cases well into the 1970s, of enforcing school attendance for "Indian" children. What this meant in practice was forcibly removing children from their families and communities at an early age, sometimes as young as four or five, and putting them into residential schools, usually run by religious groups.[17] Given the remoteness of many Indigenous communities, these schools were frequently a significant distance from their families, so this would mean an almost complete severing of contact between the children and their families and cultures for months, or years, at a time. Given the "corrupting" temptation of the "savage" lifestyle, however, this was seen as desirable by policy makers and school administrators, who focused their efforts on systematically "civilizing" the children, not least by denying them access to their culture. They were punished for speaking their own languages or for expressing preferences for their traditional foods or dress; they were taught nothing about their own cultures or histories, and, in a pattern that has unfortunately become familiar in such contexts, physical, emotional, and sexual abuse were not uncommon. The effects of these practices, especially as they were reproduced across generations, were absolutely devastating. A horrific number of children either died while at residential schools from inadequate nutrition, health, and medical care or indeed from abuse. An even larger number were permanently damaged by their experiences, emotionally, physically, psychologically. Intergenerational bonds, crucial to the maintenance of any society, were fractured in a number of different ways. Children would return home as strangers, often unable to communicate effectively with their parents or grandparents. They would never have had the opportunity to learn the skills necessary to survive on their lands and contribute to their communities; they would have little understanding of their cultural contexts, histories, and values; and, perhaps worst, they would have been taught to disdain and reject these inheritances. Having never been parented, they would have inadequate parenting skills to deal with their own children, and—struggling against the long-term effects of their experience, which often meant alcohol or other drug abuse—would at times reproduce the kinds of behavior shown to them in the context of the schools. The residential school policy was an absolute plague for Indigenous communities, one that is at the root of many of the social problems they face and remains the focus of much of their activism. It was also no more successful in its stated ambitions than were other assimilationist policies: the generations of children who left these schools were much more likely to be destroyed by the experience, ending up on the streets or in their communities struggling with the after-effects, than they were to go on to become "productive" members of society. It was a violent, brutal policy, pursued—again—in the name of "civilization," legitimated by the necessities of sovereignty.[18]

Resonances

There are several striking things about "Indian" law and policy in Canada, as even this brief glance might suggest. One is its overall consistency: despite little indication of success, and plenty of failure, the insistence that the ideal of assimilation must guide "Indian" policy was maintained, even as the policies to achieve it varied some over time, usually by becoming more coercive. This ideal continued to guide policy well into the 1990s, and some would argue that it still does, although as we will see below the forms it takes are more subtle now. Perhaps more to the point, the particular form of assimilation should be familiar: strategies and structures for the production of political resonance hearken back clearly to Hobbes. The assumptions contained within the laws and the insistence of the practices they reproduce thus underline the conviction that identity—a shared sense of space, time, history, language—is the necessary precondition for shared inhabitation of territory.

They also illustrate the ways in which these assumptions are deeply embedded in and are reinforced by the laws and institutions of a country. Further, these are assumptions that, as we have seen, not only depend upon the exclusion of any other ontological ground, but are also explicitly constructed in opposition to the differences expressed by Indigenous peoples.

Perhaps more striking is the consistency of resistance to this policy on the part of Indigenous peoples, even when this resistance must have truly seemed futile. It was clear to them throughout, however, that these legal trends and policies would lead to the destruction of their communities. As levels of coercion increased, even though devastated by the effects of this legislation, by disease and social problems that were the effects of these policies, Indigenous communities continued to resist, insisting that they would not assimilate, would not give up their identities or political claims. The price was too high. This in itself suggests an important critical commentary on Canadian society, one that is taken up in Part III.

For the purposes of the argument here, though, the most striking thing that emerges from the analysis above rests precisely in the resonances between the policies towards Indigenous peoples in Canada, and the productions of sovereignty in both Tocqueville's analysis of democracy in America, and Hobbes' *Leviathan*. Despite significant differences in the history of Canada and the United States, and in each country's policies towards Indigenous peoples, the general terrain of possibility for them was produced and constrained in very similar ways. In all three contexts, the necessity for sovereignty was the establishment of a core of agreement, a resonance, an identity. In all three cases, the figure of the Indigenous in some way marked the edges of that agreement, the boundary of what was acceptable, or what a modern individual, and a modern society, should be. That such a figure was needed is revealing about the workings of sovereignty. But what is also important are the practices through which the marginalization was effected, how sovereignty worked in this context: in a text, through laws, policies, and most importantly through the underlying assumptions that guided them all and legitimated the violences they effected. This is revealing about sovereignty as a problem, about its character, and the difficulty and complexity of analyzing it, insofar as it is a dynamic discourse and practice, but one that works through a surprisingly consistent underlying architecture.

So, for example, one response to the analysis above would be that the policies and practices simply indicate misguided, prejudiced views about "savages" prevalent at the time. However, if this treatment of Indigenous peoples were primarily a consequence of ignorance, false information, or prejudice, it would be much easier to respond to, and would have been much less persistent. What emerges from the analysis here, and particularly from the resonances amongst the different sites of analysis, is that there is much more at stake than that. The treatment of Indigenous peoples is a consequence of more than assumptions about who they are; it emerges from tensions that are deeply embedded not only in the explicitly political structures and institutions of modern governance, but in the underlying assumptions and practices that ground and enable them. As Tocqueville argues in relation to the laws of America, the laws of Canada express something of the core of resonance of the majority, as such working simultaneously to construct the identity of non-Indigenous peoples, the necessity and superiority of that identity, as well as legitimating the treatment of Indigenous peoples. As Hobbes reveals, words, or laws, express agreement about who we think we *must* be, to be sovereign. The treatment of Indigenous peoples thus emerges from the discourses and practices through which modern sovereignties have been created. It emerges from the same practices that have enabled democratic sovereignty to function. It emerges from how we moderns have resolved the problem of authority in the collapse of hierarchical forms of authority. As such it expresses a very real problem: the conditions which have allowed sovereignty to "work" in Canada and the United States (and other "successful" states) are deeply implicated in the treatment of Indigenous peoples; their treatment is not incidental, but constitutive of the success of these democracies.

4 Sovereignty and disciplinarity

The previous chapters have introduced modern sovereignty as a particular response to the problem of constituting legitimate forms of authority after the collapse of hierarchical forms, first as articulated in Hobbes' *Leviathan* and then in practice in the treatment of Indigenous peoples in Canada and the United States. This chapter extends the analysis of sovereignty in another direction: into an examination of the disciplining of knowledge, the production of the categories through which we understand and explain the world. As we saw in Hobbes' analysis of the relationship between the constitution of political authority and the production of knowledge in Chapter 2, practices of sovereignty are intimately interwoven with the production and disciplining of knowledge. To illustrate this, I focus here on how the disciplines of international relations and anthropology are constituted through and reproduce the necessities of modern sovereignty, and how this shapes their apprehension of and response to the challenges posed by Indigenous politics. My goal is not especially to critique international relations or anthropology, or indeed disciplinarity in general, but to use these specific sites to illustrate a broader problem.

All thought is, of course, "disciplined," not necessarily by formalized academic disciplines, but by the assumptions and conventions embedded in language, subjectivity, culture, context. The expression and effects of this disciplining vary significantly across contexts, as indeed do disciplines of the formal academic type. My concern here is to draw attention to how claims to authority rely upon and reproduce practices and assumptions of sovereignty, and how these function to constrain expressions of political possibility for Indigenous (and other forms of "marginal") politics.

The formal disciplining of knowledge is one particularly important site at which this occurs. More importantly for my purposes, it is a site at which these processes and their effects can be seen, in part because of the work by a range of thinkers such as those I draw on in this chapter. My purpose here is thus to illustrate how discourses and practices of sovereignty "work" to establish limits of conceptual and political possibility, and—more specifically—how they work broadly across sites of knowledge production, not just within political science.[1] This analysis suggests that an effective response to the violences of sovereignty discourses and practices to Indigenous politics requires an interrogation of the conditions under which we think about politics and authorize political discourse more broadly.[2]

International relations, sovereignty and Indigenous marginality

Few scholars of international relations have turned their attention to issues raised by Indigenous politics, for reasons that both are obvious and require unpacking. Most obviously, scholars of international relations have shown little interest because Indigenous political movements are not a significant presence in international politics: apparently an understanding of their intricacies is not necessary to an understanding of international relations or world politics. On this reading, Indigenous political movements lie outside the sphere of interest of international relations; they inhabit the realm of domestic politics, perhaps, or anthropology. This position is enabled by the discipline's self-definition, in turn grounded in the acceptance and naturalization of sovereignty as establishing the preconditions for thinking about international relations. By effectively reproducing the assumptions and practices of sovereignty, the discipline also reproduces the marginalization of Indigenous peoples, repeatedly identifying them as relics of another time, as out of time. We can see the effective marginalization of Indigenous peoples manifest in the work of even those international relations scholars who are the most concerned about making the international arena as fair and just as possible, scholars who, if asked whether Indigenous peoples' concerns should be included as part of the focus of international politics, would certainly reply in the affirmative. However, in the struggle to represent the international arena as open to normative analysis, these scholars rely upon the self-definition of the discipline in ways that shape the apprehension of Indigenous peoples such that their concerns can never be more than marginal to the study of international relations. In this way, the reliance on assumptions and practices of sovereignty simultaneously authorizes and constrains the discipline of international relations, rendering it both a problematic site for Indigenous peoples and a revealing example of how the assumption and practices of sovereignty work to shape not only political but conceptual possibilities.

A classic example of this is Hedley Bull's text *The Anarchical Society*. Bull's text is particularly revealing because it is a focused attack upon the Hobbesian tradition within international relations, at least in part because of the way in which this tradition has functioned to exclude a range of questions from discussion. Bull is thus critiquing particular practices of exclusion, and is trying to assert a reading of international relations that will enable a broader range of questions to be taken up by the discipline. However, his critique is itself enabled by a reliance upon the assumptions and practices of sovereignty in ways that necessarily curtail the questions that can be taken up.

He begins his argument by setting out the crucial preconditions for his analysis:

The starting point of international relations is the existence of states, or independent political communities, each of which possesses a government and asserts sovereignty in relation to a particular portion of the earth's surface and a particular segment of the human population. On the one hand, states assert, in relation to this territory and population, what may be called internal sovereignty, which means supremacy over all other authorities within that territory and population. On the other hand, they assert what may be called external sovereignty, by which is meant not supremacy but independence of outside authorities. The sovereignty of states, both internal and external, may be said to exist both at a normative level and at a factual level.

(Bull 1977: 8)

In this short passage Bull asserts states, and the sovereignty of states, as the starting point for the study of international relations. What makes a state? Government, sovereignty, territory, population. The basic subject matter for the discipline is thus framed, its primacy established. Any unit which does not display these characteristics—which, for example, perhaps claims sovereignty but does not or cannot appropriately exercise it over a particular territory or population—does not qualify as a constitutive element of the discipline. Consequently, Bull quietly excludes all those who have not achieved the Western state form from the constitution of international relations. He acknowledges that other units exist and may be in some way significant or worthy of study, just not by the discipline of international relations (Bull 1977: 9).

This first exclusionary move in Bull's text is then compounded by a second. At the same time as he insists on the state as the enabling assumption for the study of international relations, he also seeks to establish the analytical primacy of relations between states: "The first function of international law has been to identify, as the supreme normative principle of the political organization of mankind, the idea of a society of sovereign states" (Bull 1977: 140). This statement goes beyond an assertion that states are the primary actors in international politics; it asserts the primacy of the society that these states form as the universal form of the international. In so doing, it also reinscribes a particular modern, European form of social-political organization as the universal norm. While it introduces the debate of whether the state or the states system should be most central to the study of international relations, it clearly enforces and justifies the disciplinary focus of international relations on states and their relations, thus doubly excluding all other forms of social or political organization from the purview of international relations. Why should international relations be concerned with these other modes of organization? They are all simply steps towards statehood, the supreme normative principle of the political organization of mankind.

In this double move, the move that enables his argument and upon which the meaning of the rest of the text is based, Bull thus reinscribes the assumption of sovereignty as the crucial precondition of international relations. This move enables international relations and relegates Indigenous (or other forms of social organization) elsewhere, into an earlier time, into pre-history. In anticipation of the question of how order exists in areas other than the international realm where there is no overarching authority, Bull must reinscribe the difference between the timelessness of the international realm and the way that primitive societies are not only out of time, but behind the times. As one example:

> [P]rimitive stateless societies rest not simply on a culture that is homogeneous but also on one that includes the element of magical or religious belief. . . . International society, by contrast, is part of the modern world, the secular world that emerged from the collapse of ecclesiastical and religious authority.
>
> (Bull 1977: 64)

In this way, despite the fact that Bull wishes to contest a particular Hobbesian or Realist prescription for the space of the international, he accepts the framework of sovereignty—with its attendant spatial and temporal assumptions and exclusions—as the precondition for international relations. For all that Bull tries to escape from the stereotypes of political Realism, to emphasize the importance of history, culture, ethics and law, he is forced to return precisely to a form of political Realism in which anything other than the necessities of states remains marginal.[3] Without explicitly wishing to exclude Indigenous peoples from international relations, his argument clearly establishes the international arena as a particular—modern, secular—space in which their ontologies are inappropriate.

This logic for the exclusion of Indigenous peoples from the study of international relations illustrated by Bull's text—the preconditions established by the assumption of sovereignty as the ground of analysis—provides the basic tension that any attempt to include Indigenous peoples in disciplinary conversations must negotiate. Insofar as one wants to argue that international relations should take Indigenous political movements (or Indigenous peoples, for that matter) seriously, there are two apparent arguments that can be pursued. One can argue that these movements are a crucial part of international politics, and therefore their exclusion from the study of international relations is not justifiable, i.e. they are important to and contained within the realm of international relations and one cannot understand this realm properly without engaging them. Alternatively, one can argue that they have not been a part of international relations and their exclusion from this realm contains precisely their significance to it. From their location outside, they are positioned to provide a critique of and challenge to existing understandings of international relations; they express the possibility of being otherwise than international relations assumes. Each of these lines of argument potentially opens space for Indigenous peoples to enter the discipline. However, in each case the space opened remains tightly constrained by the terms of its creation. A brief survey of two texts from recent international relations literature on Indigenous politics will serve to illustrate this, as well as the dangers it creates for Indigenous political movements.

Other than the occasional text about the rise of Indigenous politics through international cooperation,[4] or the increasing presence of conversations about the status of Indigenous peoples in international law,[5] the literature of Indigenous politics within international relations comprises a rather slim file. One of the only exceptions is Franke Wilmer's study of Indigenous activism in the context of international relations, *The Indigenous Voice in World Politics*. Wilmer's book is an argument both for the legitimacy of Indigenous political claims and for their relevance to the study of international relations. She writes with the intent of strengthening and validating Indigenous presences in the study and practices of world politics, and makes a persuasive case for this. However, her argument relies upon the assumptions of sovereignty in ways that create a risk that the terms for the inclusion of Indigenous political concerns will simultaneously increase the legitimacy of international relations and the strength of the resolutions that enable it, thus reproducing the marginal status of Indigenous peoples.

Her book begins with an examination of the historical treatment of Indigenous peoples. Victims of early (16th- to 18th-century) colonization, largely by European powers, Indigenous groups have been subject to successive waves of "modernizing" policies by their colonizers. Their histories are thus characterized by sustained resistance to the—supposedly universal—concepts of modernization, progress and development imposed by their colonizers. Unlike the victims of later waves of colonization (19th- to early 20th-century) Indigenous peoples have not been decolonized. Rather, they remain in a colonial situation within larger states. Thus their struggles are characterized by their efforts to achieve autonomy within their respective states. For this they have often turned to the international political and legal systems, seeking to bring extra-sovereign force to bear on their colonizers. Although this kind of activism dates back as far as the history of colonization, according to Wilmer it has been ineffectual until quite recently. Much of Wilmer's book carefully traces the specificities of their colonization, resistance and contemporary forms of activism, emphasizing in particular the range and depth of the challenges posed to and by contemporary Indigenous activism.

This history is paralleled in Wilmer's book by a history of the international realm. The overall narrative of this story is characterized as follows:

> [T]he overall progression of world order, as reflected in international legal norms developed among European nations but extended to the world system, has been in the direction of greater inclusiveness and a reduction in the arbitrariness with which force may be used by the state.
>
> (Wilmer, 1993: 162)

In particular, Wilmer reads this history as a shift from the development of the norms of conquest and colonization to an emphasis on self-determination (Wilmer, 1993: 189). This shift in the normative basis of international political community suggests the need for a shift in the way the international arena is studied. In particular, Realism, she argues: "speaks to us as an historical paradigm, accurately describing the basis and configuration of world politics from the sixteenth to the early twentieth centuries" (Wilmer, 1993: 196). However, Realism's limitations have become apparent because this shift in the normative ground of international politics is accompanied by a shift towards the increasing importance of norms in international political activity (Wilmer, 1993: 40).

Wilmer's history of the international realm thus contains two related arguments: first, the international realm has moved away from norms of conquest and towards those of self-determination, in the process becoming more sensitive to normative issues in general; and, second, our study of international politics needs to parallel this shift and move towards an understanding of the essentially normative character of international relations (Wilmer, 1993: 24).

These two histories—of Indigenous politics and the international realm—are logically intertwined through a double move in Wilmer's argument. First, her argument about the rise of Indigenous politics functions to support her argument for a normative approach to international relations. She argues that if one reads the international system through Realism, there is no way to explain the rise of Indigenous politics, as these movements lack the "currencies of power" that are recognized by Realism (Wilmer, 1993: 20). All that they have available to them is a particular ethical/normative claim in relation to the international system. She argues that the fact that this claim is now finally receiving attention provides evidence for the increasing significance of the normative element of world politics (Wilmer, 1993: 25). In the second part of the double move, this case for a normative approach to world politics in turn provides the basis for Wilmer's argument for why international relations scholars should be attentive to Indigenous political movements. The power of these movements rests, according to Wilmer, in their normative claims. If normative issues are becoming increasingly important, as she asserts, these movements will become more important to the practices and theories of international politics (Wilmer, 1993: 27).

Wilmer's book thus makes a strong argument that Indigenous political issues should be taken seriously in international politics and grounds this argument in a reading of the international system that makes it seem likely that they will. This argument, however, hinges on the assumption that the discipline and practice of international relations have changed from the bad old (Realist) days and that it is this change that explains the rise to prominence of Indigenous peoples. This assumption is vulnerable to a number of critiques arising from other accounts of international history and norms, such as those that suggest that state-centric Realism is far from passé, and those that argue that emerging norms have as much to do with new forms of domination in a modern globalizing economy that are not obviously conducive to Indigenous struggles against colonialism and neo-colonialism.

For my purposes, however, what is most crucial is that her analysis relies upon and fails to problematize the role of sovereignty in structuring the study and practice of international relations.[6] Because the terms available to her within the story of sovereignty are limited, her argument necessarily reinforces the "central" status of international relations as both practice and discipline and the location of Indigenous peoples on/as margins. This happens despite her best intentions and efforts to do precisely the opposite. It happens through a series of moves in her text, moves that are inescapable if one begins from the assumptions of international relations, and thus of sovereignty, rather than taking these to be a problem.

First, her argument rests upon an assertion that Indigenous peoples were outside of international politics and now are moving towards inclusion. This story of the past of international relations and Indigenous peoples erases the ways in which Indigenous peoples have always been present in international relations, and not only as activists for their own rights.[7] The extent to which Indigenous peoples have not been incidental frills at the edges of but have always been central to international relations—both as a discipline and as practices of politics among nations—should not be erased. In particular, at the very least we need to understand how the active marginalization of Indigenous peoples has been necessary for international relations to appear and function.[8]

On this telling, then, international relations does not require the presence of Indigenous peoples, *or their exclusion*. Thus their inclusion is a (generous) expansion of boundaries and their status is reproduced as marginal; in Wilmer's language, the "core" might adapt to "noncore" views and assumptions (Wilmer, 1993: 27). This telling erases the ways in which the discipline is and always has been about the determination of limits, and historically it has relied in part upon Indigenous peoples to enable this. This telling also erases the role of discourses and practices that remain crucial aspects of international relations (such as international law) in the dispossession of Indigenous peoples and the necessity of this dispossession in order for international relations to develop as it has, i.e., the material contributions of Indigenous peoples' resources to the establishment and maintenance of Euro-American global hegemony in the form of international relations.

Second, as a result of this, Indigenous peoples remain essentially objects of rather than subjects in international relations. Their inclusion at this point is not primarily due to their own assertion of agency (as Wilmer shows, they have been active opponents of their colonization throughout), but rather is explained by the development, advancement, progress, dynamism, generosity of the international arena. Indigenous peoples are becoming empowered by the international arena, an arena previously indifferent to them, rather than one that actively required their exclusion. Despite their incredible survival in the face of all odds, it is essentially their good fortune to be located at the time when the international realm is becoming "more normative" such that their voices might be heard.

Third, again following from the above, the representation of Indigenous peoples thus serves not necessarily to empower them, but to empower and legitimize the international realm, to legitimize it as the discourse which is and must be central, universalizable. International relations is what has changed, progressed, become more tolerant. It is thus flexible, dynamic, capable of change. Its violences are safely located in the past (their sources un-interrogated, assumed to be historically necessary), and it remains the crucial ground upon which conflicts must be mediated. International relations (as relations between states or state-like powers) remains the central, dominant element of the analysis of world politics. The disciplinary margins have been expanded to include normative concerns and thus a broader range of actors, but the geography of center/margin has not.

This in turn poses a dilemma for Indigenous peoples: the narrative that should cause them to have faith in the international realm—it has progressed beyond its past violences—is precisely the one that, as Wilmer acknowledges, has enabled five centuries of violence against them: the narrative of progress and modernization. The sovereigntist story prevails: the state/international realm moves from violence to peace, from a focus on unity and identity to an appreciation of diversity and plurality. This is a story Indigenous peoples have heard before, and one that should hardly inspire confidence. They will be included because those with power have decided to be nicer.

All this is also not to say that Wilmer's book is not an important text or that it will not have a range of political effects. It is (and may) for at least two reasons. First, it engages with and thus reveals and expresses the limits of international relations theory. It illustrates in its struggles what can and cannot be spoken about, and on what terms. It draws attention to the problem of Indigenous peoples in relation to the study of international relations. In doing so, it opens a space for Indigenous peoples to see themselves as legitimate actors in the international arena, however tenuously they are located there. It also acknowledges and names the violences of their past exclusions from this arena. Second, and perhaps more importantly, in drawing attention to the problem, it also opens space for further conversation, potentially producing a disruption in conversations of international relations, insisting that there are questions that need to be addressed that may ultimately prove to be rather awkward for the discipline. In this sense, it is a crucial precondition for my own analysis, and I am indebted to it.

Wilmer's book thus illustrates one of the approaches to Indigenous politics enabled by the discipline, and its limitations. It expresses the limits of arguing for inclusion within the terms of sovereignty. What about the other side of the binary mentioned earlier? Is there more space to be gained by respecting and drawing attention to the ways in which Indigenous peoples articulate political options other than those expressed by the international realm? Is there something to be gained, in other words, from taking them on their own terms rather than trying to make space for them within an existing understanding of international relations?

This question was taken up by David Bedford and Thom Workman in an article examining *The Great Law of Peace*, a document from the Iroquoian Confederation, as the articulation of a vision and practice of international relations that provides the basis for a critique of Realism (Bedford and Workman, 1997). Their analysis is in part a response to a reading of the same document by another scholar of international relations, Neta Crawford (1994). While Crawford's effort is "praiseworthy in its effort to introduce Aboriginal experience to contemporary international relations scholarship," according to Bedford and Workman it is fundamentally flawed by "the forceful application of Realist-derived terms upon the Iroquoian document" (Bedford and Workman, 1997: 90).

Crawford analyzed *The Great Law of Peace* as a premodern version of a security regime, arguing that its success as a security regime was rooted in the democratic character of its members. The problem with this kind of analysis, according to Bedford and Workman, is that "the interest that the author finds in *The Great Law of Peace* does not lie in the uniqueness of the Iroquoian confederacy but rather in its supposedly (Western) democratic character" (Bedford and Workman, 1997: 91). They contrast this with their own approach:

> In sharp contrast, our interest in *The Great Law of Peace* is animated by the nonmodern character of the text. It registers a thoroughly non-Realist practice between peoples or nations, and as such it embodies understandings and practices that are incommensurate with Realist orthodoxy . . . It is the contention of this article that *The Great Law of Peace* must be appreciated on its own ethical and philosophical terms. To disregard this injunction will result in the violent imposition of modern modes of thought upon fundamentally unmodern expressions of human being, and the tragic loss of the opportunity to explore an alternative form of life.
>
> (Bedford and Workman, 1997: 91)

Their project contributes to a broader critique of Realism in international relations thought by "unearthing the presence of non-Realist practices in the relations of nations in the past" (Bedford and Workman, 1997: 91). In particular, then, their goal is to challenge the transhistorical claims of Realism by revealing that there have been times and places in which the assumptions and practices of Realism have not been dominant or even present.

The article examines three themes contained within *The Great Law of Peace*: understandings of the nature of human being, and a sensitivity to the relationship between politics and the order of being; the generic properties of social being, especially inter-nation(al) relations; and the embeddedness of inter-nation(al) relations within intra-nation(al) life (Bedford and Workman, 1997: 92). The description and analysis in the article are rich, illustrating and insisting upon the unique conceptions of selves, societies, politics and international relations that run through the document. However, what I want to draw attention to is that, although Crawford's article was criticized for using an Aboriginal document to reflect upon a fundamentally modern question, Bedford and Workman's article is caught on the obverse side of the same position. The end result is apparently different—a reification rather than erasure of the difference between the ideas expressed in *The Great Law of Peace* and Realism—but the effects of this apparent difference on the critical force of the argument and the representation of Indigenous peoples are similar. Bedford and Workman, as I will argue below, end up in more or less the same position as Wilmer and Crawford: despite their best intentions and the richness and sensitivity of their representation of *The Great Law of Peace*, their argument potentially reproduces the agency and centrality of international relations and freezes Indigenous peoples as at best marginal contributors to its questions and endeavors.

Bedford and Workman locate *The Great Law of Peace* as an expression of Indigenous social and political organization fundamentally outside of and different from the discourses of international relations, either past or present. Like Wilmer, then, they draw attention to the exclusion of Indigenous paradigms from consideration in international relations. Unlike Wilmer, however, they don't argue for their inclusion so much as for the acknowledgment of the critical perspective provided by their excluded status. Although different from Wilmer, their argument encounters the same dangers of reproducing the centrality of international relations, as well as the apparent accidental location of Indigenous peoples outside the boundaries of international relations discourse. In other words, *The Great Law of Peace* might function as a critique of universalizing claims of Realism, and illustrate the possibility of being otherwise (at least under premodern conditions) than Realism says the world must be. Realism might even be responsible for some of the violences committed against the Indigenous peoples who ascribed to *The Great Law of Peace* (although the authors don't go so far as to say this). But the assumption that international relations as discourse and practice has operated essentially independently from the histories and paradigms of Indigenous peoples remains unquestioned.

Further, in Bedford and Workman's article the location of *The Great Law of Peace* as an idealized "outside" is not necessarily connected to the disciplinary practices of Realism or international relations more broadly. Although the ideas of Realism are different from and antagonistic to Indigenous peoples' paradigms, this is an historical accident rather than a closely related problematic. So, for example, *The Great Law of Peace* is examined in the abstract as a philosophical paradigm rather than, for example, drawing attention to the fact that the peoples of this law have been in international relations with expressions of Realism for five centuries. In other words, the relationship between Indigenous peoples and colonizing nations is not treated as international relations. The confrontation between these two paradigms is erased in order for *The Great Law of Peace*—the apparent loser of this conflict—to be presented as an alternative to the dominant paradigm of international relations. While these paradigms may indeed be incommensurate, they have been constantly in conflict, and this conflict has had an effect on the theory and practices of Realism, not to mention on the development of *The Great Law of Peace*.

To present *The Great Law of Peace* as an alternative is to reinforce the status of Realism specifically, and international relations more broadly, as independent of the historical treatment of Indigenous peoples. Thus, while perhaps international relations—as both practice and discipline—should consider the possibility of being otherwise, such as suggested by the non-modern document of *The Great Law of Peace*, why it would remains unclear. Bedford and Workman thus must in the end rely on the same rather weak normative argument as Wilmer to encourage people to take *The Great Law* seriously:

> Part of what has been destroyed are inter-nation(al) practices permeated with balance and moderation—practices diametrically opposed to the extremely aggressive conduct of capitalist states in the late twentieth century. This can be expressed as a paradox. Western subjugation of North America reflects the capacity for unbounded and limitless behaviour, a capacity formalised in the Realist vision of international relations. In the process, it has all but destroyed an example of moderate inter-nation(al) relations. It has all but destroyed that which it most needs to save itself, particularly by deadening the imagination.
>
> (Bedford and Workman, 1997: 108)

Thus international relations should be attentive to this different way of approaching international politics. It may even need to be. However, an argument for taking up a document that emerges from an idealized premodern world in order to guide our practices in the "real" world of contemporary international relations seems hardly persuasive. It is precisely Realism as an expression of contemporary international relations that ensures that *The Great Law of Peace* can never appear as anything other than a dreamy (im)possibility, not least because its existence as part of international relations for the past five centuries is erased in the move to assert its critical status.

Like Wilmer, then, Bedford and Workman accept the self-definition of international relations to provide a basis for their critique, and thus accept resolutions expressed by sovereignty. And like Wilmer, this assumption functions to ensure that their critique will not be taken seriously by many scholars of international relations, but instead functions, as an invocation of the margins always does, to reinforce the centrality of the center. This failure to interrogate the grounds of international relations also leads the authors to necessarily represent Indigenous peoples in problematic ways, as dictated by the ontology of sovereignty. Indigenous peoples as peoples are barely present in Bedford and Workman's article; they appear as historical and essentialized expressions of *The Great Law of Peace*, itself represented as an essentially historical document. The agency and dynamism of contemporary international relations remain unquestioned, and the agency expressed in Indigenous peoples' past and present struggles against their colonizers remains invisible. Their offering to international relations, the vision in *The Great Law of Peace*, exists only in their memories. It is an historical document, not a living practice, and it is a document that can be understood without reference to the experience of the peoples who have lived with it for centuries. What it *is* is less relevant than what it was:

> *The Great Law of Peace* reveals above all else that it is a text about living well, especially regarding the establishment of inter-nation(al) practices conducive to the attainment of the good life. It survives as a spiritual text rather than a document guiding the conduct of nations. And while the great binding law survives to this day in the memory of the Iroquois people, the sociocultural milieu that engendered it has been undermined by the European subjugation of Turtle Island.
>
> (Bedford and Workman, 1997: 108)

This document thus emerges from the past of a damaged people (objects of the brutality of "our" vision) rather than from the present of a dynamic people, of subjects struggling against ongoing practices of international relations. Thus once again the cost of representing Indigenous peoples in the dominant discourse is the reinforcing of their essentially frozen marginal status as objects of international relations. And the long practice of Indigenous peoples providing the idealized or despised "outside" reference point to explain and/or produce what is "really" going on is continued.[9]

However, as with Wilmer, this critique of what happens when Indigenous people are "brought in" to international relations is not intended to suggest that Bedford and Workman's article is not important. It is to point out the limits within which such critiques will necessarily operate when the resolutions of sovereignty are reproduced by assuming the disciplinary parameters of knowledge production. Articles like Bedford and Workman's perform the important task of drawing attention to and challenging closures and resolutions within international relations, and potentially provoke further conversations and disruptions in various official stories of the discipline.

As these texts illustrate, grappling with the issues raised by Indigenous politics within international relations is no simple matter. The way in which international relations as a discipline has developed not only directs scholarly attention away from issues such as these (makes them, in fact, incomprehensible), but actively requires their exclusion for its own endeavors and conversations to make sense. Thus, any effort to focus attention on these issues requires a justification of their significance to a discipline whose self-definition requires their insignificance. Indigenous peoples (among others) thus function as border guards to remind us of the limits of political possibility. Whether premodern brutes or noble savages, they remain out of modern time and space, despite their continuing presence in both discourses and practices of international relations. If one begins from the assumptions of international relations, then, there is actually very little of interest that can be said about Indigenous politics (all descriptions are actually more telling of international relations). If one accepts the underlying resolutions of sovereignty as a way of bounding an examination of the world, one has already determined how and where Indigenous peoples can appear in the discourse and practice.[10]

This is certainly not to say that international relations as a discipline is irrelevant to Indigenous peoples; quite the opposite. Both the discipline and practice of international relations play a crucial role in maintaining structures that both enable Indigenous politics and reinforce the marginalization of Indigenous peoples' concerns, ensuring that their issues (issues which emerge in part because of their implication in the international realm) can only have relevance to the extent that they appear in particular forms. International relations, as both discipline and practices, contributes to a framing of options for the shape and expression of Indigenous politics, not least by providing the conditions of entrance to the discourse. The position that international relations is only about relations between states (which would require sovereignty as a precondition for entrance) has given way (not coincidentally, just as sovereignty is being broadly asserted by Indigenous peoples) to a more complex set of conversations about what international politics is and might be. However, as we see from the analyses of Wilmer, Bedford, and Workman, it is by no means clear that the practices of sovereignty that reproduce the marginalization of Indigenous peoples will also change.

There are important histories to be written: histories of how international relations as a discipline has produced its identity and object of study in and through the exclusion of all expressions of politics and subjectivity other than its own story/subjectivity. There are other important stories to be written about how the development of the modern states system specifically, and practices of international relations more broadly, are also dependent upon and reproduce a series of violences towards and exclusions of a range of peoples, something that finds some expression in analyses such as Wilmer's. Both of these, of course, would be to take international relations as object rather than subject of inquiry, which in turn requires an interrogation of its conditions of possibility to provide the critical leverage point for the analysis. It requires the sustained engagement with sovereignty as both practice and ontology.[11] In the absence of this kind of interrogation of these histories, international relations will continue to function as a border guard, constraining influence of all marginal forms of politics even in attempts to legitimate and respond to them.

I return to these questions in the last section of the chapter (see pp. 83–85). First, however, I turn to examine the "twin" discipline of international relations. If international relations as a discipline is responsible for one "outside" of sovereignty, the space of the inter-sovereign, anthropology is the discipline supposedly responsible for another "outside": for those who live outside the temporal boundary of sovereignty, for the "pre-state." This poses the question of whether anthropology provides a space in which the concerns of Indigenous peoples can be engaged more effectively than does international relations. Does it provide a basis for a challenge to Hobbes' ground (sovereignty) as the necessary precondition for political analysis, or does it, too, fall victim to the simultaneously enabling and constraining practices of sovereignty?

Anthropology: life out of time

Perhaps to a greater extent than any other discipline, anthropology has struggled with the politics of knowledge production, with its roots in and reproductions of the power relations of colonialism. Anthropology has also, of course, engaged with the contemporary situations facing Indigenous peoples in far more depth than any other discipline. Often, this anthropological work is today providing crucial leverage in Indigenous legal and political battles. Anthropologists are called upon to document consistent use and habitation of land or resources, social and political organization, "civility," and so on. These studies often prove crucial to the success of particular legal or political claims. Although many criticisms can be made of anthropology's past, to condemn anthropological work for its colonial past is to miss the point. Such a condemnation only conceals the extent to which anthropology is only one expression of a much larger problem. "It" is not the problem. On the contrary, as I argue below, the struggles of anthropologists with anthropology as a discipline and practice provide crucial insight into the limitations and violences of modern practices of knowledge production. Paralleling my engagement with international relations above, my analysis here begins with an older text from the discipline, one that seeks to open the discipline to engagement with Indigenous politics, then moves on to examine a more recent struggle with the same challenge.

I begin with Pierre Clastres' text *Society Against the State* (1977), a text—like Bull's—that stands in a critical, and somewhat "marginal," relation to its discipline.[12] Clastres' analysis proceeds through a critique of the ethnocentrism that has characterized the analysis of power and politics in anthropology. In essence, he argues that anthropology has assumed a particular definition of power as coercion—a particularly Western understanding of power—and used it as a universal norm by which all other societies should be measured. This, he argues, is a notion of power that presupposes and requires a state form, as well as a very specific relation between state and society. With this (particular) notion of power as a (universal) starting point, then, anthropology turned its attention to "other" societies. How did it determine which societies were "other"? It marked those without the corresponding notion of power, without a state with coercive authority over a society. Thus, when anthropology looked at societies without this kind of state form, without corresponding power relations, it saw not difference, but lack (Clastres, 1977: 189). In this way, ethnologists translated difference into lack, read difference as a deficiency to be measured against the norm: Western social arrangements, the state. This lack was then located on a temporal scale: the state became the necessary teleology for all societies. "Primitive" societies—those lacking the state—were thus pre-state, earlier in time than state societies, but moving towards them. In this way, difference is explained and disciplined: written as lack, it is located temporally in an earlier form of "ourselves," as "our society" used to be. Because the West has "arrived" at the end, it is authorized to explain and understand, to produce and speak knowledge of its own past: primitive society. The project of anthropology is enabled and authorized. Difference is reduced to identity and thus contained. This ethnocentrism, which rapidly extends to evolutionism, is where Clastres focuses his attack, arguing that this logic of evolutionism forces anthropologists into a series of conundrums when they try to think about the political (or power) in relation to primitive societies (Clastres, 1977: 19–20).

In response to this problem, Clastres argues for a "Copernican revolution" in how political anthropologists frame their subject matter, for a complete reconceptualization of the political in order to enable political anthropology to more appropriately study "primitive" or non-state societies on their own terms. To this end, Clastres suggests three shifts necessary for a new political anthropology: First, it must reject the notion that there is only one form of power, and thus that there are societies with power (state societies) and those without (primitive), and instead acknowledge that power manifests in two primary modes: coercive and non-coercive. Second, coercive power is only one possible form of power and thus there is no scientific reason that it should be privileged. Third, even where there is no political apparatus resembling a state form, still there is power and thus the political: the political can and must be understood separately from violence. If we follow these three shifts, Clastres argues, we can remedy this form of ethnocentrism, open the discipline of anthropology by enabling it to see and represent difference: to see power and the political in forms other than the Western—coercive—form.

He proceeds to enact this new vision in his analyses of power, the state and society in several South American societies, emphasizing the ways in which power can be seen to operate non-coercively through the structure of social relations. He concludes that indeed there is a fundamental difference between societies with a state and those without, but not one that can be explained by putting them on a developmental scale (Clastres, 1977: 199). He marks the difference, rather, in the relation between the state, time and history:

A massive reduction, seeing that history affords us in fact only two types of society utterly irreducible to one another. . . . On the one hand, there are primitive societies, or societies without a State; on the other hand, there are societies with a State. It is the presence or absence of the State apparatus (capable of assuming many forms) that assigns every society its logical place, and lays down an irreversible line of discontinuity between the two types of society. The emergence of the State brought about the great typological division between Savage and Civilized man; it created the unbridgeable gulf whereby everything was changed, for, on the other side, Time became History.

(Clastres, 1977: 200)

For Clastres, the critical difference is still marked by the presence of the state. However, instead of privileging the presence of the state form as marking a level of development, he seeks to maintain this difference as an absolute difference, one that cannot be reduced by locating the societies on a temporal scale. Rather, he argues, it is actually a difference in time—in what time is for each—that divides the two. Whereas states live in historical (linear) time, primitive societies live in non-historical (non-progressive) time:

The essential feature (that is, relating to the essence) of primitive society is its exercise of absolute and complete power over all the elements of which it is composed; the fact that it prevents any one of the sub-groups that constitute it from becoming autonomous; that it holds all the internal movements—conscious and unconscious—that maintain social life to the limits and direction prescribed by the society . . . Primitive society, then, is a society from which nothing escapes, which lets nothing get outside itself, for all the exits are blocked. It is a society, therefore, that ought to reproduce itself perpetually without anything affecting it throughout time.

(Clastres, 1977: 212)

What characterizes the primitive, he argues, is not a backwardness, a slowness on the scale of progress, but rather a rejection of the state and, more specifically, the relations of time and space, power and history that it carries with it:

[W]hat the Savages exhibit is the continual effort to prevent chiefs from being chiefs, the refusal of unification, the endeavor to exorcise the One, the State. It is said that the history of peoples who have a history is the history of class struggle. It might be said, with at least as much truthfulness, that the history of peoples without history is the history of their struggle against the State.

(Clastres, 1977: 218)

Rather than seeing the state as an achievement, Clastres casts it as a failure, as the point at which primitive societies, because of failure to control demographic growth, cannot any longer sustain their eternal, timeless existence, cannot stave off the centralization and flattening of power consistent with the state, and must enter history.

Clastres' critique reveals within political anthropology the same logic Hobbes reproduces in his production of sovereignty. Indigenous "savage" societies are pre- or non-state societies, to be distinguished from our own by their lack of sovereignty. Against Hobbes' representation of "savages" as having no society, peace, or order Clastres would assert that these societies do have social organization, order, society, and peace. This, of course, has been one of the crucial contributions of anthropology to our contemporary understanding of Indigenous peoples—it turns out the "savages" weren't as "savage" as we thought. His analysis thus does provide a logic one could use to challenge Hobbes' representations of Indigenous peoples, not to mention most other modern thought. It might also provide a basis for a more "accurate" political anthropology. However, even as Clastres' attack on evolutionism functions to challenge the ethnocentrism within anthropology, ultimately he reinscribes the difference between "savage" and civilized, this time by making a historical/non-historical distinction. By reinscribing the difference in this way—as absolute and marked by a temporal/spatial distinction consistent with the resolutions of state sovereignty—Clastres closes down much of the terrain that his analysis could have opened up. He accomplishes his primary goal of challenging the ethnocentrism which arbitrarily privileges the state as the necessary teleology of all societies, but he maintains the state/non-state temporal distinction. Further, he still places state/non-state in a relation of succession: the state does emerge from societies without a state, just not through a gradual process of evolution. Rather, the shift happens through a failure of primitive society caused by demographic pressures. He thus rejects one form of ethnocentrism—that which privileges our own state/society relation—but ultimately cannot escape reproducing another version of it. In this way, while politics may slide over into the study of "primitive" societies, the boundaries of anthropology remain firm: anthropology is concerned with "primitive" or "savage" or—still—non-state peoples, peoples who exist out of (historical) time. With no container (state), no sovereignty through which their space and time can become properly ordered, they remain "other"—out of time and, consistently, denied their space, identities, autonomy. The message is clear: until they achieve sovereignty, they exist outside the regime of the political as we know it, and they therefore have no voice in it.

The reinscription of the distinction between historical and non-historical societies has (at least) two significant effects in Clastres' writing. The first is the homogenization of the "savage" or "non-historical" society, which also leads to the continued homogenization of Indigenous peoples. Even though he bows to the tyranny of detail in places, he nonetheless goes on to generalize his conclusions to the whole of South America, indeed to all "primitive" societies, producing statements like: "The whole political philosophy of primitive society can be glimpsed in the obligation of the chief to be a man of speech" (Clastres, 1977: 153); or "It is in the nature of primitive societies to know that violence is the essence of power" (Clastres, 1977: 154); or "It [primitive society] is a society, therefore, that ought to reproduce itself perpetually without anything affecting it throughout time" (Clastres, 1977: 212). These kinds of statements serve to reproduce the very homogeneity he explicitly disavows, effecting the erasure of difference amongst "primitive" or "non-state" societies. It also reproduces the history of the West writing the "savage other" in order to reinforce its identities. Their "difference" is measured and conceived in relation to our "identity": we remain in historical time; they live in another, timeless, world. Yet the assumption remains that we can somehow neutralize these assumptions, "see" their politics as "authentic" without acknowledging that we are determining their authenticity by reference to conceptual categories that are enabled by their exclusion.

The second effect of this reinscription of difference is that it freezes these societies, giving them only one option for change: into states. Again, Clastres' distinction is between those societies which live in time as history, where a story can be written about past, present, and future, and changes are usually marked as progress, and "non-historical" societies, which live in timelessness, stasis, the eternally repetitious and self-contained. With time and change thus disciplined, the researcher can focus on structure alone, weaving together the threads of meaning through "reading" social ritual and interaction. The problem with this, of course, is that these societies do change and adapt. The meanings of social interactions are never stable, uncontested. Yet the eye of the researcher focused on structure has no way to mark this.[13]

This freezing of primitive societies in time functions to trap Indigenous societies: their identity becomes dependent upon the maintenance of these timeless rituals, and they cannot change and adapt without endangering their identity, their place. Again and again, when Indigenous groups seek to make claims against states, they are forced to "prove" their "authenticity," usually judged by how closely their activities resemble those of their ancestors.[14] This would be an absurd demand of any "modern" group, yet this is the demand— enabled by the kind of temporal distinction made by Clastres—that is repeated again and again to Indigenous groups, often resulting in the denial of their claims because they fail to be "Indian" enough in a world where being "Indian" in that way would doom them to starvation or self-destruction. In resisting the idea that "primitive societies" are less developed versions of our own—and the ways this erases their differences—Clastres thus creates them as absolutely different in ways that reify their differences, denying them the capacity for change.

Clastres thus presents an interesting puzzle: he seeks to challenge anthropological ethnocentrism, to open some space for a more authentic representation of Indigenous societies. More precisely, he recognizes that in part the past limitation is due to the concept of the political usually assumed and reproduced in anthropological discourse. However, in order to challenge this concept of the political in the context of anthropology, he is forced to reproduce the exclusion of Indigenous peoples from the politics of state societies. He must locate them "out of time," just as Hobbes did. While this opens space for a different kind of analysis of Indigenous societies, this study reinforces their difference from and exclusion from the "properly political": politics as framed and enabled by sovereignty.[15]

Anthropology as border guard: losing the good fight

The central problem that drove Clastres thus continues to haunt anthropology. Unlike, say, scholars of international relations who must fight for legitimacy to address Indigenous politics, anthropologists speak from within the discipline that has historically been authorized to speak about them. Thus, they can and do engage with Indigenous peoples' situations in a rich variety of ways. However, since Clastres' time the situations of Indigenous peoples have become increasingly politicized and at times desperate. This has meant that anthropologists have continually been forced into the realm of politics, not only "on the ground" in their efforts to support Indigenous peoples, but also (and not coincidentally) in relation the political stakes of their own disciplinary work. This has led to an explicit engagement with at least three different expressions of politics within anthropology. First, the subfield of political anthropology has expanded and developed, resulting in a blossoming of research into cross-cultural forms and conceptions of political activity.[16] Second, there has been an extensive conversation about the political effects of anthropological work, ranging from critiques of the historical connection between anthropology and colonialism to explorations of the ways in which power relations are reproduced in the disciplinary practices of anthropology, such as writing ethnographies.[17] Finally, in part emerging from the previous two conversations, the field of applied anthropology has emerged as a crucial conversation and practice concerned with putting anthropology to work for the communities it studies (and the tensions and problems that emerge from this practice), thus directly implicating anthropological work in political struggles within these communities. These developments make anthropology one of the more rich and interesting sites for thinking about the political within contemporary academic work.

However, as I argue below, these conversations and practices also—not surprisingly—remain crucially constrained, producing difficulties for both theories and practices of anthropological work.[18] In part these constraints emerge from how anthropology is located by sovereignty, both in relation to the disciplinary production of knowledge (i.e. anthropology's location and identity within the social sciences)[19] and, more crucially, by the philosophical resolutions that provide the logic and authorization for these disciplinary divides (i.e. the larger ontological resolutions of modernity that enable contemporary knowledge claims).

To illustrate this, I turn below to a recent text by John Gledhill, *Power and Its Disguises: Anthropological Perspectives of Politics* (1994). Gledhill's text is exemplary in that it explores and expresses these constraints with impressive clarity, illustrating the complexity of the ground that contemporary anthropologists must negotiate. However, his assumption of anthropology as determining the starting point and scope of his analysis also necessarily constrains his analysis, limiting it to illustrating the disciplinary situation of anthropology, rather than providing an explanation of how this situation—and the constraints experienced by anthropologists—is itself produced and reproduced. My reading of Gledhill's text below emphasizes how the assumptions and practices of sovereignty remain crucially constraining forces for anthropological attempts to engage with Indigenous politics, and thus of how the challenges posed by Indigenous politics require an interrogation of the disciplining of thought more broadly.

As indicated by the title of his book, Gledhill's main goal is to illustrate and argue for the contributions that anthropology can make to the understanding of contemporary politics. For him, these contributions emerge from anthropology's commitment to cross-cultural research, rather than—as he acknowledges is more common—its methodological commitments (Gledhill, 1994: 7–8). Drawing on the work of Clastres, he argues that the major barrier to past anthropological efforts to study politics lay in anthropology's historical acceptance of Western forms and practices of politics as its starting point when looking for politics elsewhere: "One major problem here is that the subfield of political anthropology has failed to reflect adequately on what is peculiar to the political life and systems of Western societies in world-historical terms" (Gledhill, 1994: 8). Thus in part what political anthropology needs to do is understand what is peculiar and specific about Western forms of politics, to resist the tendency to universalize the Western political experience but rather to make it "one amongst many," to subject it to the assumption of cultural relativism that drives anthropological research rather than holding it as the baseline against which this relativism should be measured. This shift in the approach and project of political anthropology reveals crucial insights about both Western forms of politics and the ways in which these are not universal. This in turn illustrates the need for anthropology to "fill in the gaps," to document the variations in political forms and practices in all their specificity, rather than relying upon the West's (universalized) explanations and practices of politics.

This description of anthropology's distinctive contribution to the social sciences runs into trouble, however, at particular points. This trouble emerges from the fact that although Western forms and practices of politics might not be universal, Western domination in various forms is characteristic of political life in most places, either directly or through how Western forms have transformed the ways in which political struggles are articulated and pursued

(Gledhill, 1994: 23). This situation throws the assumption of cultural relativism into some question, as thinking about politics across cultures will always in some way bear the mark of and need to be understood in relation to these forms of Western domination. This in turn leads Gledhill to refine and expand his initial characterization of anthropology's contribution towards one concerned with revealing and potentially rearticulating the relationship between global and local: "In my view, a political anthropology adequate to the world of the late twentieth century must seek to relate the local to the global, but in a more radical way than has been attempted in the past" (Gledhill, 1994: 8). Or, more precisely put:

> Though particular situations always reflect the interaction of the local and the global, local social and cultural histories now find expression in action in ways that are part of a common experience of modernity . . . which focuses on the contemporary articulation of the local and global. Only concrete, contextualized analysis of particular situations will enable us to understand what is happening and why it is happening. . . . But little that is happening anywhere can be understood without reference to the historical discontinuities produced by the rise of the modern state and modern forms of power.
>
> (Gledhill, 1994: 23)

This is an intellectual problem that is far more complex than a mandate to investigate the "cultural element of politics" would initially seem to imply, not least as it is a characterization that situates anthropology within a social and political context that both constrain and enable it.

This (re)definition of the project of anthropology leads him back, if reluctantly, to an endorsement of anthropology's research method as central to the contribution anthropology can make to the social sciences. It also leads him to introduce "politics" into his analysis as more than an object of inquiry: "Such studies enable anthropologists to challenge analyses and explanations offered by other disciplines in ways which are politically as well as intellectually significant" (Gledhill, 1994: 9). Thus "politics" enters the conversation in a second manner, in relation to the political impact or significance of disciplinary work. The relationship between these two senses of the political—as an activity to be studied and as a field such studies enter into—however, begins to get Gledhill's analysis into some conceptual murkiness. It is here that we begin to see the ways in which resolutions of sovereignty, and his reluctance to consider that the problems of anthropology might emerge in part from anthropology's implication as well as role in the social sciences, begin to constrain his analysis.

While the anthropological study of the cultural dimensions of politics leads to the necessity of thinking about the political role and impact of the discipline, the "politics of anthropology," or the political force and effects of anthropological work, poses a problem. While there is greater discussion of political and ethical issues in the discipline than perhaps ever before, the discipline itself, in Gledhill's view, remains unchanged in any profound way (Gledhill, 1994: 210). He attributes the discipline's failure to change largely to the constraints emerging from the structures of academic knowledge production (Gledhill, 1994: 224–25). In particular, anthropology is constrained by its history and location within the social sciences:

> There are certainly causes where a particular anthropological expertise is recognized as having salience, but much of this perceived salience is based on a construction of anthropology as the 'science of the exotic other.' Anthropologists are likely to be drawn to issues which concern minority groups neglected by other advocates. It would be ridiculous to deny the importance of such advocacy, but there is no logical reason why anthropological engagement in the political arena should be restricted in this way.[20]
>
> (Gledhill, 1994: 220)

However, as he documents with reference to the fate of anthropologists' careers when they speak out against political events (such as the Vietnam War) or advocate on behalf of their subjects' political claims, it is precisely when anthropologists turn their efforts to apparently "political" effect that they are "disciplined" most severely, especially from within their own discipline.[21]

The effect of these constraints is that in this moment when an understanding of anthropological perspectives on politics is perhaps most crucial—the argument that occupies most of Gledhill's book—these perspectives are least likely to be heard. This is because anthropology's position and authority in the social sciences are too often guaranteed by its historical identity. Gledhill's response to this is a passionate plea for anthropologists to retain their political ideals and remain on the side of the angels (Gledhill, 1994: 225) and a simultaneous reluctant argument that these political ideals are perhaps best pursued not in their role as anthropologists, but in their roles as citizens: "To a great extent, no doubt, the action in which anthropologists should participate as individuals should be pursued outside the academy in concert with other citizens" (Gledhill, 1994: 220). The politics of anthropologists as anthropologists, in other words, seem to run aground on the shoals of (inter)-disciplinary conflict. Anthropologists must be political, but they cannot be political as anthropologists, or bring their disciplinary authority to bear on political questions.

The story of contemporary anthropology is thus tinged with tragedy and heroism. It is heroic not only because anthropologists remain the crucial defenders of the angels in a fight they seem doomed to lose, but because anthropology itself continues to provide the best hope for a resolution to the dilemma we all find ourselves in (Gledhill 1994: 10). Alas, however, in practice anthropology is constrained and misunderstood, both inside and outside of the discipline, thus reinforcing its marginalization:

This maximalist account of the anthropological project remains one which can be advocated in principle, but more modest claims for the discipline's role have tended to prevail in practice. Funding agencies, non-governmental organizations and governments are told that the world needs anthropologists to add 'cultural' dimensions to research projects designed by specialists in other fields. Thus anthropologists help reinforce the conviction of others that they are exclusively specialists on non-European peoples . . . these selling points of the discipline are valid, but they also invite continuing marginalization.

(Gledhill, 1994: 10)

Gledhill's story about the politics of anthropology thus remains a rather sad tale, even as his accounts of what anthropology can contribute to an understanding of politics are rich and glowing.

However, there is a missing piece in this puzzle. It is a piece that Gledhill gestures to but doesn't follow through, both in the quotations above and at other moments:

Anthropology is a Western mode of knowledge, and it continues to revolve around the definition of cultural 'otherness' as non-Westernness because that was the problem Western power historically constituted anthropology to investigate. This makes the centrepiece of anthropology's claims to enlightenment and radicalism, its commitment to cultural relativism, somewhat problematic.

(Gledhill, 1994: 225)

Although Gledhill carefully documents and fervently supports the struggle to "decolonize" anthropology, he stops short of exploring the ways in which anthropology itself is an expression of the very context he takes to be crucial: "little that is happening anywhere can be understood without reference to the historical discontinuities produced by the rise of the modern state and modern forms of power" (Gledhill, 1994: 23). He criticizes anthropology's colonial past, but stops short of situating anthropology within the broader disciplining of knowledge so as to enable a more general critique of the sources of the binds that "progressive" anthropologists find themselves in. In holding on to a desire to rescue or support the value of anthropology and its project, he leaves himself trapped within the very colonial past from which he wishes to extract the discipline. He urges anthropologists to redefine anthropology in a progressive frame, rather than querying the broader structures of knowledge production that force anthropology into such a bind. Thus, despite all of his rich analysis of the history of the discipline and the insights it can offer to the study of politics, ultimately the politics of anthropology are unfortunately—from Gledhill's perspective as much as my own—reduced to a plea to act outside of the discipline in concert with other citizens. The discipline must remain what the discipline was constituted to be:

marginal; and anthropologists should confine their political actions to those of citizens in the realm of the "properly political."

The limitations of this position are expressed in Gledhill's own text and analysis, in his expression of frustration at the limits within which anthropology operates. What Gledhill can't consider without fitting anthropology into a broader analysis of disciplinarity is the politics of these limits and the way in which his reproduction of "anthropology" might contribute to the reproduction of these limits. If one approaches anthropology from the perspective of its location within the resolutions of sovereignty, Gledhill's sad story makes perfect sense. Anthropologists are caught in a losing battle: they are constituted to produce, examine, defend, and reproduce the "margins" of sovereignty, those who are "out of time" in a world structured by the logic of sovereignty. Sovereign states move through time, create history, monopolize space, producing the marginal as those who cannot live in the present, even as they make it impossible for them to do so. Anthropologists are thus constituted as the defenders of those who are doomed to disappear. They, perhaps more than those in any other discipline, have witnessed the workings and effects of Western political, cultural, and intellectual expansion, the violent reconstitution of the margins. They have thus become the defenders of the very margins that the logic of sovereignty maintains a constant assault on. Even as it defends these margins, the very authority of anthropology depends upon and reproduces the logic of sovereignty: its necessity and inevitability. This leaves anthropologists to write stories of necessity, and regret.

None of this, however, is to dismiss anthropology or anthropologists as fighting the wrong battle. There is no other battle to be fought. There is no "outside"; or rather, they are the "outside." On the contrary, because of their location within the structures of sovereignty, anthropology potentially provides some of the most acute critiques of the effects and operations of sovereignty. Gledhill expresses very clearly the problems that anthropology faces. He fails, however, to see how the constitution of the discipline of anthropology itself is a problem, and not one to be dismissed. Rather, it is one that needs to be taken very seriously. Further, the problem is not that it is a child of "colonialism"—although this is one expression of it—but the location of anthropology within and by the ontology and practices of sovereignty discourse; more specifically, the exclusion of anthropology from the realm of the "properly political" and the ways in which anthropology—in concert with many other disciplines, particularly political science—too often reinscribes the conditions of this exclusion.

Put differently, part of the problem anthropology is facing has to do with modern definitions of what politics is, where it happens, and who does it. Although anthropologists have challenged the universalization of this definition in important ways, they also often unintentionally participate in reaffirming it in practice (as do many of us), in part because so much appears to hinge on the maintenance of it. Further, anthropologists are in a sticky situation—being border guards is not a pleasant business—but if their interrogation of the past violences of their own discipline fails to disrupt the ways in which the disciplining of knowledge itself (re)produces the position/problem of anthropology, they run the risk of getting stuck there. Thus, the disciplinary conversations going on within anthropology, just as those going on within international relations and political theory, must engage with the problem of sovereignty, with the modern disciplining of thought as an expression of sovereignty, and thus of the violences and closures sovereignty requires. What this engagement involves varies from site to site, discipline to discipline, just as the constraints and their effects do. Anthropologists have already pushed this engagement further than most, as Gledhill's analysis illustrates. However, they, as the rest of us, remain face to face with the limits and constraints effected by sovereignty.

Conclusions

So where does this all leave us? The previous analysis is an effort to illustrate and reframe a problem—the problem posed by Indigenous politics but also by a range of other political dilemmas—rather than to suggest a solution. The problem arises precisely from the complex relationship between the production of knowledge and of authority, as described by Hobbes so many years ago. Discourses of international relations and anthropology depend on the spatial and temporal resolutions expressed by state sovereignty to resolve the fundamental questions that ground their analyses. History begins and ends with modern sovereign states: states as spatial containers discipline Time into History, and within the bounds of state sovereignty History continues its one-way path of Progress. Outside these neat boundaries, anarchy and timelessness reign: either in the realm of the pre-state/primitive, "known" (and produced) by anthropology, or in the modern inter-state world, "known" (and produced) by international relations. With the spatial domination of the state/international relations boundary, anthropology is thrown out of space and into time, into either the premodern or the static and unlocatable realm of "difference." State sovereignty thus enables and marks the boundaries of both disciplines. Between lies the proper place for modern political life: the state, "known" by disciplines such as politics and sociology. In this way, the disciplining of thought expresses and reinscribes sovereignty, rendering it both obvious and necessary.

Variations on this general claim, however, have been developed by a range of other thinkers in all three disciplines, and the basic structures of my argument are already clearly present in Hobbes. Indeed, the fact that what I am arguing is not drastically new poses another layer of challenge: knowing this about sovereignty and how it works, about the questions that are closed off when one invokes it as unproblematic ground, does not necessarily change anything. It is not as if, having realized these exclusions effected by sovereignty, one can adjust one's efforts, perhaps pick up a different paradigm and carry on having resolved the problem, as the analysis of recent disciplinary work above suggests. Since we can now see that even the "outsides" of sovereignty (international relations and anthropology) are constructed on the ground of sovereignty, since even language as our medium of communication cannot be separated from its imbrication in these relations, we remain right where we began. To arrive at this point, in other words, is just to repose a problem that is already familiar to many, not to provide an answer.

The problem for those of us who are interested in politics, of course, is that all kinds of things hinge on these resolutions. It is not only a ground that legitimizes violences, exclusions, and endless circular debates. It is also the ground that—as Hobbes promised—enables order, peace, security, knowledge. It legitimizes Indigenous politics, even as it constrains it. Thus once we begin to take seriously this ontology as political and as always necessarily effecting erasures and closures in order to enable shared understanding, the problem only becomes more acute. This is what partially drives the above analyses: all of these authors are attempting to respond to and engage with the violences and exclusions of their disciplines, yet they remain constrained by the ontology of sovereignty in ways that effect a reinscription of some of the necessities they seek to avoid. While constraints are an inevitable effect of knowledge production, what this analysis reveals is how the *particular* constraints they reproduce are neither arbitrary nor neutral. Rather, they effect closures that systematically reproduce the marginalization of Indigenous peoples, particularly in relation to their attempts to achieve political subjectivity.

This leaves us with the problem of the political with which we continue to struggle today. We have no choice but to work both politically and intellectually from and against the disciplining of knowledge we have inherited, but doing this requires engagement with both the conceptual and political problem of limits. In this context, anthropology and international relations are crucial expressions and sites of renegotiations of these limits. As these resolutions that have structured much of modern thought and politics come under increasing strain, however, these disciplines are beginning to reflect this strain, as each increasingly struggles with its own limits and violences. Parallel to this is the rise to prominence of a range of different movements that in some incarnations cast serious doubts on the capacity of modern institutions and structures of knowledge to accommodate them. One of these is Indigenous politics. In this context, the problem of how to think about the political becomes increasingly acute. It is increasingly clear that accepting Hobbes' answer to the political problems of our age will not suffice; however, taking his problem seriously provides one entry point. Doing this requires an engagement with the disciplining of knowledge as a problem expressed not only in academic disputes but in our struggles to understand and act in the world. In this context, our inability to understand some movements might correspond with their apparent effectiveness (or intractability), their "irrationality" an expression of their struggles against the constitution of the limits of sovereignty. Thus, not unlike Gledhill's assertion about the potential of anthropology, though with a different twist, I would argue not only that we must pay careful attention to these movements, but that the study of these movements must necessarily become a study of the limits of our own assumptions and practices of understanding the world, and the articulation and reformulation of these limits must become a crucial political practice.

That said, this is not an obvious task, and the impossibility of seeing a clear answer to the problem can invoke despair, in turn leading us to re-inscribe the "least bad" solution, which often reinscribes familiar limits, as we saw in Gledhill's analysis. Part II seeks to chart ways forward in relation to this challenge, through an engagement with three different sites at which it appears and is being negotiated. While none of these provides an entirely satisfactory solution, each I think reveals important insights about the potentials contained within, and importance of, contemporary struggles against the violences of sovereignty.

Part II

Negotiating the limits of the political

5   Resistance
Negotiating the interstices of sovereignty

The previous chapters have sought to provide contexts for interpreting and understanding both what is being negotiated and what is at stake in contemporary forms of Indigenous politics, specifically in relation to broader political and philosophical challenges of our day. The next three chapters seek to illustrate this, and—more importantly—to draw attention to the ways Indigenous movements are negotiating these contexts. In these negotiations reside critical perspectives on and resources for ongoing efforts to engage contemporary challenges. The focus of the analysis is especially on the dynamics of sovereignty in the following cases because it is in their engagements with and rearticulations of sovereignty that Indigenous peoples' movements present both the greatest challenges to and opportunities for contemporary political theorists and others.

Each of the next three chapters focuses on a specific site during the 1990s where these struggles and their stakes emerged with particular force and clarity: during the Constitutional Referendum of 1992, the Delgamuukw legal cases, and James Tully's book *Strange Multiplicity*. Other sites could have been chosen, and would have enabled complementary lines of analysis: sites of violence between the state and Indigenous peoples, such as the conflicts at Oka, Ipperwash, Gustafson Lake, or Burnt Church; sites of negotiation such as the Meech Lake Accord, the Nishga Treaty, the creation of Nunavut, or the Royal Commission on Aboriginal Peoples; or sites of much less prominence—locally based or less well-known efforts to address the concerns of Indigenous peoples. I focus on these three sites because they seem to me each to illustrate the dynamics of sovereignty, and thus to implicate the activities of political theorists most powerfully. However, as I will argue below, sites of violence illustrate the stakes and failures of political theory with greater clarity. To be clear, though, these are what I take to be illustrative moments, rather than an overview of recent Indigenous politics in Canada; for that there are more comprehensive sources.[1]

I begin, in this chapter, with a reading of the 1992 Constitutional Referendum, and more precisely with a reading of the broader implications of the Native Women's Association of Canada's opposition to it. Contained within their opposition is an analysis of the legacies of colonialism that is crucial to understanding how sovereignty has provided perhaps the greatest resource for and danger to Indigenous peoples' movements, just as for other forms of "marginal" politics. Situated within a broader analysis of the political terrain faced by Indigenous groups at the time, it reveals the complex and high stakes contexts produced by and negotiated through practices of sovereignty.

The Constitutional Referendum: precipice or turning point?

In 1992, after long and often torturous negotiations, including the most extensive and intense debate over Indigenous rights the country had even seen, a new proposal for Constitutional reform in Canada—the Charlottetown Accord—was announced.[2] To many people's surprise, it included a Constitutional guarantee of Aboriginal[3] peoples' right to self-government.[4] This appeared to be a crucial victory for Indigenous peoples of Canada, and was touted as such extensively by the negotiators. With great fanfare, the Charlottetown Accord was presented to the public for approval in the form of a non-binding referendum. The guarantee of a right to self-government was only one of many proposed reforms, and Aboriginal leaders were concerned that if the referendum was defeated this would be taken as a defeat for self-government when the majority of voters might be rejecting the Accord for other reasons. However, with their reservations expressed they agreed to the referendum and launched into an intensive campaign to promote the Accord.

The referendum thus looked promising as a crucial victory for Aboriginal politics. Though the exact meaning and effects of the self-government guarantee were far from clear, it indicated a formal foothold on which future relationships could be based, a potentially very different basis for interaction between the Canadian government and Aboriginal peoples. However, as the referendum campaign progressed the inclusion of the self-government guarantee began to look increasingly problematic. Not only was there significant opposition to the Accord for a variety of reasons unrelated to the guarantee, but—more importantly—one after another Aboriginal organizations and groups began to speak out in opposition to the proposal. While this opposition was not unexpected by negotiators, it sent shock waves through many observers of Aboriginal politics. It appeared that just at the moment of unprecedented success the identity of interests that facilitated the rise of Aboriginal politics to the national agenda was fracturing deeply, throwing into question the future of federal-level Aboriginal politics.

Things took a turn for the worse when the Referendum failed to pass. Initially, Ovide Mercredi, chief of the major pan-Indian organization that negotiated the Accord, accused Canadians of once again turning their backs on the plight of and their responsibilities to Aboriginal peoples. He called for a separate tally of the Aboriginal votes. However, when this tally came in he was forced to confront a very different picture:

Of the Indians who did bother to cast a ballot, 62.1 percent were against the Charlottetown deal—an even higher percentage than among other Canadians. The Northwest Territories was the only place west of the Maritimes where a majority of Indian voters supported it. Saskatchewan Indians rejected their leaders' pleas and voted 55 percent against. Mercredi's home province of Manitoba led all comers with an 81.6 percent rejection. It was a different story amongst the Inuit, in whose isolated villages individual votes could be identified. They voted 75 percent in favour.

(Smith, 1993: 231)

The reasons for this opposition varied widely. Some didn't trust the federal-level Indian negotiators; some were content with the status quo; some disliked particular elements of the Accord, and so on. However, all of these specific complaints had combined into a significant oppositional force.

This apparent fracture was a turning point for Aboriginal politics. By splintering what had come to appear as a solid and widely accepted identity of political interests, it made visible the complexity of and potential conflicts within Aboriginal politics. Some commentators have mourned this as a setback (Smith, 1993: 231). However, I believe that the complexity it revealed, and the explicit engagement with the nature, potential, and dangers of the dominant productions of sovereignty that have ensued, have considerably enriched contemporary Aboriginal politics. In particular, the resistance of some groups revealed the ways in which the struggle for sovereignty and self-determination was in danger of perpetuating past violences that can be traced to the embeddedness of discourses and practices of sovereignty in colonial relations. This danger was revealed perhaps most effectively in the campaign of the Native Women's Association of Canada (NWAC), which brought to the surface a history of Aboriginal–settler interaction and an analysis of the current state of Aboriginal politics which had previously received relatively little attention from either the mainstream press or the large pan-Indian organizations.

NWAC's challenge

NWAC's opposition to the Charlottetown Accord centered around two related concerns.[5] First, they protested the lack of representation of Aboriginal women's concerns at the negotiating table. Although the federal government had funded four organizations representing Aboriginal peoples to participate in negotiations, they refused to fund an organization specifically focused on representing Aboriginal women.[6] In response to this, NWAC argued that one effect of colonization on Aboriginal communities was the disruption of traditional gender roles through the imposition of patriarchal structures and forms of government. As stated in a NWAC position paper on the referendum:

The legal and political struggle by Aboriginal women was not only against an insensitive federal government. It was also against the Aboriginal male establishment created under the *Indian Act*. The *Indian Act* has imposed upon us a patriarchal system and patriarchal laws which favour men. Only men could give Indian status and band membership. At one time, only men could vote in band elections. By 1971, this patriarchal system was so ingrained [through]out our communities, that 'patriarchy' was seen as a 'traditional trait.'

(Moore, 1992: 4)

Because of this, they argued, Aboriginal women were not—and could not be—adequately represented at the Constitutional negotiating table by male Aboriginal leaders:

Some of our women say that our governments—White and Aboriginal— don't give a damn about us! We are telling you this situation will not change without our involvement in self-government and in Constitutional discussions. Aboriginal men could take the initiative and give us a place at the table. Have they done that? No they have not. Aboriginal women want to take their rightful place at the Constitutional table. We are a 'distinct and insular' minority belonging to another culture from which we have been separated.

(Moore, 1992: 6–7)

This argument in turn leads to their second concern: they argued that the political disempowerment of Aboriginal women, combined with the other effects of colonialism that continued to plague their communities, meant that institutionalizing self-government at this time and without the participation of Aboriginal women was premature and dangerous:

Some Aboriginal women have said no to self-government. Some of our women do not want more power, money and control in the hands of men in our communities . . . We do not want you to create Aboriginal governments with white powers and white philosophies in our communities. We do not want the western hierarchical power structure which you have given us.

(Moore, 1992: 9)

Why are we so worried as women? We have never discussed self-government in our communities. There is much to be learned. We are living in chaos in our communities. We have a disproportionately high rate of child sexual abuse and incest. We have wife battering, gang rapes, drug and alcohol abuse and every kind of perversion imaginable has been imported into our daily lives. The development of programs, services, and policies for handling domestic violence has been placed in the hands of men. Has it resulted in a reduction in this kind of violence? Is a woman or a child safe in their own home in an Aboriginal community? The statistics show this is not the case. As one woman said, people are killing each other in our communities. Do they want to govern that? Men rarely speak of family violence. Men rarely speak of incest. Men rarely speak of gang rape and what they are doing about it.

(Moore, 1992: 16)

Although they strongly supported the argument that self-government is an Aboriginal right and should be recognized (Moore, 1992: 8), they argued that the definition and implementation of this right must include Aboriginal women in a way that so far had not been the case:

What we want to get across to Canadians is our right as women to have a voice in deciding upon the definition of Aboriginal government powers. It is not simply a case of recognizing that we have a right to self determination and self-government. Aboriginal women also have sexual equality rights. We want those rights respected. Governments cannot simply choose to recognize the patriarchal forms of government which now exist in our communities. The band councils and the Chiefs who preside over our lives are not our traditional form of government. The Chiefs have taken it upon themselves to decide that they will be the final rectifiers of the Aboriginal package of rights. We are telling you, we have a right, as women, to be part of that decision. Recognizing the inherent right to self-government does not mean recognizing and blessing the patriarchy created in our communities by a foreign government. Aboriginal women are not asking for chaos in our communities. We want the equality to which we are entitled as women.

(Moore, 1992: 8–9)

Addressing these questions thus would require broader participation than is currently in effect in the Constitutional negotiations. Indeed, it would perhaps require a different locus for those negotiations:

We want community decision making. We want consent powers. We want the people in the communities to decide upon their form of government. We want those Aboriginal women who are still banished from their communities to have a vote, some land, and a house in their homeland, in the community in which they were born. There are those among the Chiefs who would deny us a voice, who would deny us a place and those who wish we would simply go away until they have settled this political business. We are not going to go away.

(Moore, 1992: 9–10)

At the very least, they argued, the Canadian Charter of Rights and Freedoms should apply to Aboriginal governments in order to ensure that Aboriginal citizens have recourse to a higher legal authority than their local tribal governments, in this way ensuring that they are able to exercise their political rights. This was a position that was strongly opposed by the representatives of most of the organizations at the negotiating table.[7] These organizations claimed that the Charter's basis of individual rights was in conflict with Aboriginal philosophy and culture, where rights are held by the group rather than the individual. Further, many Aboriginal leaders argued, the application of the Charter to Aboriginal governments would limit Aboriginal sovereignty (Moore, 1992: 9–10).

In response to this argument, NWAC's position paper invokes the *Charter of the United Nations* and the *Universal Declaration on Human Rights* to support the position that individual rights are fundamental and cannot be compromised for the benefit of the collective:

> The Native Women's Association of Canada supports individual rights. These rights are so fundamental that, once removed, you no longer have a human being. Aboriginal Women are human beings and we have rights which cannot be denied or removed at the whim of any government. That is how fundamental these individual Charter rights are. These views are in conflict with many Aboriginal leaders and legal theoreticians who advocate for recognition by Canada of sovereignty, self-government and collective rights. It is their unwavering view of the male Aboriginal leadership [sic] that the 'collective' comes first, and that it will decide the rights of individuals.
>
> As Aboriginal women, we can look at nations around the world which have placed collective and cultural rights ahead of women's sexual equality rights. Some nations have found sexual equality interferes with tradition, custom and history. Sexual equality rights have been guaranteed to women around the world. But, like Canada's Charter, the United Nations has allowed nations to 'opt out' of these international instruments.[8]
>
> (Moore, 1992: 11–12)

The history of the Aboriginal leadership's treatment of Aboriginal women's concerns shows a frightening tendency to repeat the decision to rank women's rights second to collective rights. Thus, they argue, the application of the Charter should not be left to Aboriginal governments:

> The Native Women's Association of Canada recognizes that there is a clash between collective rights of sovereign Aboriginal governments and individual rights of women. Stripped of equality by patriarchal laws which created 'male privilege' as the norm on reserve lands, Aboriginal women have a tremendous struggle to regain their social position. We

want the *Canadian Charter of Rights and Freedoms* to apply to Aboriginal governments.

(Moore, 1992: 13)

Further, they argue, they want the federal government to take responsibility for other effects of colonization in their communities as well:

Yes, we want rights—individual and collective rights. But we want our governments to have responsibilities, too. The Federal government does not get off so easy, either. We are not asking the Federal government to dump us out the door. Self-government is not going to solve our social, economic, cultural and political problems. After 400 years of colonization, Aboriginal communities, Aboriginal families, and Aboriginal structures are devastated. Self-government will be meaningless without the land, money and resources to ensure our self-determination.

(Moore, 1992: 17)

NWAC's position paper is a fascinating document. It draws on some of the most powerful concepts in contemporary political thought—human rights, representation, autonomy, the individual, community—in order to negotiate a treacherous political terrain. It also seeks to disrupt not only the existing context of Aboriginal politics, but also the political space constituted by sovereignty, appealing as it does to international discourses and institutions in an attempt to counter the dual sovereignties of the Canadian state and Aboriginal organizations. It expresses a hairline judgment and willingness to pursue a potentially risky strategy. The achievement of a potential constitutional guarantee of the right to self-government in the context of hundreds of years of colonization seemed incredible. And to many—not least Aboriginal leaders—for NWAC to stymie this was irresponsible to say the least. Although they combined their position with a commitment to self-government in the longer term, it was not an easy position to take. That they were motivated to do so is in part an expression of their perception of the stakes of the struggle: the stakes of sovereignty. Before exploring this in more depth, I want to trace some of the context revealed by NWAC's intervention. This context, in turn, reveals the depth of challenge their intervention posed.

The context, and the politics of context

Perhaps the most important aspect of NWAC's paper is the way it contextualized the problematic of self-government within the complex history of colonialism. This history—both distant and recent—that grounds NWAC's argument provides a crucial background to understanding the effects of their strategy and, importantly, the ways in which the terrain of politics has been deeply shaped and framed by discourses and practices of sovereignty. For Indigenous peoples in North America, as we have seen, discourses and practices of modern sovereignty are simultaneous with those of colonialism. In addition, as has been argued in relation to colonial processes elsewhere in the world,[9] the history of colonization of Indigenous nations in Canada is characterized by a systematic attack upon and reorganization of gender roles and hierarchies within Indigenous communities. As M. Annette Jaimes argues, because Indigenous women often traditionally held significant political and social power in their communities, "[t]he reduction of the status held by women within indigenous nations was a first priority for European colonizers eager to weaken and destabilize target societies" (Jaimes, 1992: 318–19). This resulted in the fact that: "[t]he disempowerment of native women corresponded precisely with the extension of colonial domination of each indigenous nation" (Jaimes, 1992: 391).[10]

As we saw already in Chapter 3, there is significant evidence to support this claim in the history of "Indian policy" in Canada. Along with a sustained attack on Aboriginal sovereignty and self-government, Canadian Indian policy contained an extensive attack on women's roles, responsibilities, and political participation. For example, the *Indian Act of 1876* assigned fewer fundamental rights to women than to men; most crucially, women were denied the right of full participation in band affairs.[11] Women were not allowed to hold electoral office, to vote for male representatives, or even to speak at public meetings. As the government extended its presence into all aspects of Indigenous peoples' lives through further expansions to the *Indian Act*, women's property rights, economic activities, and social and legal status were all drastically limited.

Perhaps the most crucial legal move through which this disempowerment of Indigenous women occurred was through the question of Indian "Status." The 1869 *Indian Act* not only contained regulations governing all aspects of life on Indigenous reserves, and replaced traditional forms of Indigenous government with "democratized" forms,[12] it also specified the regulations about who was, and was not, a Status Indian. To be Status meant that one was a member of a band, and had access to all of the special services from the government, including housing on the reserve, medical, property, inheritance, educational, and voting rights. One of the regulations stipulated that Status would descend patrilineally, a principle directly opposed to the matrilineal character of many Indigenous bands' traditional social structures. This meant that if an Indigenous man married a non-Indigenous woman, she would gain Status, as would their children. However, if an Indigenous woman married a non-Indigenous man, she and all her children would permanently lose Status. They would be unable to live on the reserve, even if there were a divorce later, would not receive any health care, could not vote in band elections, and so on. The implications of this are obvious—not only did it force women to marry within bands if they wanted to maintain band membership, it also ensured that Indigenous men could marry whomever they liked. It meant that every Indigenous woman was dependent on a man—father or husband—for Status. This particular element of the *Indian Act* was a crucial site of Indigenous women's—and often men's—activism throughout the late 1800s and early 1900s.

Thus the colonization of Indigenous peoples in Canada happened not only through the disruption of traditional political and social structures, but, as part of this, through a fundamental disruption of traditional gender roles and responsibilities. Just as one of the crucial axes of conflict in many bands today is between "traditional" political structures, including hereditary roles and responsibilities for leadership, and "Indian Act" structures of governance, characterized by "democratic" elections that sometimes have less than democratic effects,[13] another crucial axis involves tensions between "traditional" gender roles and those produced by colonial structures. In both cases these conflicts are in large part a legacy of colonialism. In both cases, also, the distinctions and their political effects often become muddled, as when activists such as NWAC are branded as "a bunch of women libbers who fight for their own, individual rights" (Fiske, 1993: 21). An effort to discredit the activists by attributing their ideas to settler (colonial) sources (feminism), this kind of political rhetoric also conceals the historical reality of Indigenous women's positions in their communities. Thus the political effects of distinctions between "tradition" and "colonialism" make these discursive strategies high stakes games.

The effects of the gendered nature of the colonial history of Indigenous peoples in Canada emerged with particular clarity when Indigenous women began to protest their condition in the 1970s. One example of this is described in a collection of oral histories compiled by Janet Silman (1987). In 1977, a group of Maliseet women on the Tobique reserve in New Brunswick began to organize to protest the situation of women on their reserve: property titles to homes were in the names of men, and some men had kicked out their wives and children, who were then left stranded with nowhere to live, unable to get another house. In addition, the band government failed to provide them with other support services. Meanwhile, some of the men remarried non-Indigenous women, who gained Status and lived in the homes of their new husbands. At the same time, any woman who returned to the reserve but was non-Status because she had married a non-Indigenous man (often unaware that this would cause her to lose Status) would find herself unable to receive any support at all from the band. A group of women mobilized, eventually occupying the band offices for over four months, insisting that their needs be met. Their actions were met with extreme resistance, violence, ridicule, indifference, almost everything but action. Not only was the band government unresponsive and in fact aggressive, but other band members were as well. The reserve became completely polarized. Neither federal nor provincial governments, nor national Indigenous organizations would intervene, claiming it was an internal matter. The women eventually focused their efforts on the Status question, realizing that until they had legal and political rights on their own reserve, they would be unable to seriously alter the situation they faced.

The question of Status had already been the site of significant activism on the part of Indigenous women. The issue had been raised a number of times, most recently in a case where two women, Lavell and Bedard, took their complaints to the Supreme Court of Canada (1973). They argued that the regulation of Status under the *Indian Act* should be considered as sexual discrimination under the Canadian Charter of Rights and Freedoms. In response, the Supreme Court argued that it could not use the Charter to overrule the *Indian Act*, which conferred special status and separate government on Aboriginal peoples.[14] Perhaps more important than the decision, however, was what the struggles around it revealed to Indigenous women activists about their leaders. The case proved to be an illustration of the ways in which, as Fiske put it: "The NIB[15] and other male-dominated organizations confronted women's struggles by adopting discourses from dominant society that reflected the extent to which they had internalized the patricentric privileges offered them by colonial society" (Fiske, 1993: 21). The largest pan-Indian organizations went to court to argue against Lavell and Bedard: "engag[ing] the women in a lengthy, bitter confrontation over the nature of 'Indian rights' and 'women's rights,' asserting that women's rights must not be obtained at the expense of self-government powers" (Fiske, 1993: 21). When the Supreme Court ruled against Lavell and Bedard, Indigenous women were left doubly disempowered, with no legal recourse within Canada or through their Indigenous governments.

The Tobique women picked up this history, and, realizing they had no further recourse to address the Status issue within Canada, they filed a formal complaint against the Canadian government in the United Nations (December 29, 1977) on behalf of Sandra Lovelace, one of the members of the group. Lovelace had married a non-Indigenous man, whom she later divorced, only to return to the band and discover that she and her children were non-Status and therefore could not live on the reserve, let alone access any social services through the reserve. After four years of delays by the Canadian government and heavy lobbying by Indigenous women across Canada, the United Nations Human Rights Committee found Canada in violation of the *International Covenant on Civil and Political Rights*, owing to the fact that the *Indian Act* denied Sandra Lovelace the legal right to live in the community of her birth. While this decision was embarrassing for the Canadian government, it could not force the Canadian government to change the Act. The issue dragged on for much longer before the Canadian government finally (in 1985) passed an amendment to the *Indian Act*, Bill C-31, in an attempt to resolve the Status issue.[16]

The National Indian Brotherhood, the largest pan-Indian organization at the time, protested this attempted resolution as well. Rather than arguing, as they had in the Lavell and Bedard case, that Bill C-31 would be an infringement on their sovereignty, they protested it as having potentially assimilative effects:

Denying systematic sexual discrimination in their own ranks, the male leadership alleged its opposition derived from a real fear that western philosophical traditions of individual human rights would undermine the collective identity of Aboriginal peoples and the sacred traditions that bind individuals into a mutually-obliged collectivity.[17]

(Fiske, 1993: 22)

As might be predicted from this opposition, even upon the passage of Bill C-31, the struggles of Indigenous women continued as many band governments either refused to implement the changes or dragged their feet, claiming either that the changes were unjust or that they simply did not have the resources to effect them.[18] Struggles like these characterize the history of Aboriginal women's attempts to have their concerns addressed at the level of federal Indigenous political organization, and provide one context for NWAC's position of opposition to the Charlottetown Accord.[19]

While this history and evidence would suggest a strong legitimacy for NWAC's position, we should be careful before we jump to accuse Indigenous leaders of sexism or condemn Indigenous political structures as inherently patriarchal. Considering the strategic field faced by Indigenous leaders and the nature of pan-Indian political strategies, the challenges posed by NWAC are serious ones. Although some of the responses to NWAC, as to Lavell and Bedard, have exhibited a certain intolerance for Indigenous women's concerns inasmuch as they have attempted to discredit rather than seriously engage these women, this is in part an expression of the depth and stakes of the challenges posed by their claims.

Challenges and implications

The context invoked by NWAC's paper not only provides depth to their claims, it also reveals something of the broader terrain of Indigenous politics, and the role of discourses and practices of sovereignty in shaping this terrain. For example, considering the assimilative history of Canadian policy (the ways in which Canadian legislation was aimed directly at the destruction of collective cultural identities and the forced inculcation of a liberal individualist subjectivity) and considering the potential implications of these concepts gaining a legal foothold against Aboriginal governments (i.e. legal claims to individual property rights leading to dissolution of collective resources), some concern on the part of Aboriginal leaders is clearly understandable. In reaction to the history of forced assimilation, the rise of Indigenous nationalism had been grounded in the promise of not having to constantly resist settler government attempts at assimilation. Challenges to this promise, especially when it seemed to be so close to fulfillment, would hardly be warmly received.[20]

Even more to the point, these challenges potentially raised the specter of more than a limitation of their sovereignty; they raised the specter of losing the moral and legal groundwork for their claims. As with other nationalist struggles, pan-Indigenous nationalism in Canada developed through the practice of sovereignty: through constitution of a shared ontology, expressed in an identity of interests. This was no easy matter, given the diversity of Indigenous groups in Canada: there are hundreds of tribal communities in Canada, scattered over a huge territory, representing at least ten linguistic groups; they have several different legal statuses in relation to the government of Canada;[21] they live with a range of different social and economic conditions: some are located on or have claims to rich deposits of natural resources or large tracts of land, while others are largely urbanized or dispersed; their histories of contact with settlers and the status of traditional economies vary widely, and so on. These differences often led to very different ideas about what policies were most urgent or what strategies should be pursued. Not surprisingly, given the logics of sovereignty, the strategy used to overcome these differences was the production of an identity constituted through opposition to "white" or non-Indigenous culture. Thus in the rise of federal Indigenous politics we can trace the development of an essentialized "Indigenous" identity defined in opposition to all things "white." In this respect, their strategy precisely mirrored that of Thomas Hobbes when he produced the ontology of the modern subject that in turn illustrated the necessity of sovereignty, thus authorizing it, and its violences.

Given that this identity-in-difference provided the authorization of their collective claims, their strategic position was deeply threatened by NWAC's arguments. In asserting that Aboriginal women constitute a "distinct and insular" minority, NWAC not only threw into question the representativeness of the pan-Indigenous organizations. They also threw into question the underlying identity-of-difference that grounded their claims. The story NWAC tells denies the absolute difference between Indigenous and non-Indigenous, instead pointing to shared traits, political and social structures ("patriarchy") that express an underlying continuity. Although these commonalties are expressions or effects of colonialism, their presence nonetheless enables a wedge to be drawn in the strategic alliance, either in the form of arguments that they are not "real Indians" but rather are "just like us" but claiming special rights, or in the form of arguments that they are not adequately democratic, "developed," or "mature" to be considered responsible. Both are clearly expressions of the history of Canadian sovereignty discourse and its embeddedness in the colonial project, but because of this each is still potentially a potent line of critique, especially considering the precarious support for Indigenous self-government.

This is especially true given the assumptions about identity and ethnicity that characterized Canadian negotiators' approaches to indigeneity, assumptions that are clearly recognizable effects of Canadian sovereignty discourse:

> Much of government policy reflects what I call the 'hydraulic Indian' view of ethnicity. This view depicts an Indian or native person as a cylin-

der which, at some unidentified point in history, was full to the top of 'Indianness,' that is, traditional Indian culture. As time passed, and as Indians adopted non-native ways, the level of 'Indianness' dropped to the point where the cylinder now is nearly empty.

(Boldt and Long, 1985: 146)

This essentialized concept of ethnicity was fed by the construction of "Indianness" as all things non-White. Because "Indian" identity/ethnicity rested upon the same terms as their earlier colonization, the "authenticity" of their ethnicity was evaluated by these terms. This measure of authenticity then can be used to discredit Indian political claims based on this essential difference between "Indians" and "Whites":

Racial characteristics and traditional cultural elements such as language, religion, weapons, tools, transport, and clothing were the criteria adopted [by the dominant society to determine who was and was not an Indian]. Aboriginal people and culture were taken to have existed in a pure form before contact, but to have been 'diluted' through interbreeding and acculturation. This erosion of Indian race and culture was used to discredit contemporary Indian claims to aboriginal rights on the grounds that the claimants had ceased to be Indians.

(Jaimes, 1992: 322–23)

This danger forces Indigenous leaders to be constantly reasserting and emphasizing the authenticity of the distinction between Indigenous and non, walking a fine line of arguing that changes and developments—read as indications of "Whiteness" by this measure of ethnicity—shouldn't interfere with legal and political claims. By this measure, NWAC was clearly posing a serious challenge. By emphasizing the effects colonialism has had in terms of the inculcation of colonial ideologies, political and social structures (problems), they potentially opened Indigenous organizations to the accusation that their "distinct" identity claims are fraudulent. Although it was clearly not their intention to argue against the "authenticity" of Indigenous identity, their strategy forced the articulation of legal and political claims away from the production of identity and ethnicity they rested on. This produced a kind of credibility gap for Indigenous leaders, especially in the short term, which is crucial in the context of fast-moving Constitutional negotiations.

However, NWAC's challenge also reveals potential dangers contained within the strategy being pursued by Indigenous leaders. The definition of ethnicity they were working both within and against also potentially freezes Indigenous culture in time, unable to institute the kinds of developmental changes that may be necessary to survive in the world as it is:

This is a truncated and static understanding of ethnicity, one that freezes cultural idioms in some historic moment. It fails to comprehend that

> ethnicity is a process that unfolds over time as groups continually select
> and reinterpret diverse cultural forms around them (Aboriginal and
> non-Aboriginal) in defining themselves as distinct from the larger society.
>
> (Boldt and Long, 1985: 146)

Thus, an essentialized notion of Indianness also—in the effort to assert its
legitimacy—runs the risk of erasing or minimizing the effects of colonialism
on their societies. Because they have to prove their authenticity, measured in
relation to their "pre-contact" selves (or how they were written in Canadian
sovereignty discourse), they have to deny the effects of colonialism (thus
minimizing claims for assistance in addressing these effects). In other words,
these discourses of authenticity themselves become mechanisms of colonization. In a desperate attempt to get the government out, the long-term impact
of colonialism within Indigenous cultures, identities, selves, politics, is concealed. While this might seem to be a minimal danger from Indigenous leaders' perspectives—operating on the belief that success in sovereignty claims
will mean they will have the resources to address these problems—NWAC is
clearly more concerned that the effects of colonialism be taken seriously as
part of the process of moving towards sovereignty. They also want to insist
that responsibility for remedying them remain at least in part with the federal
government.

These challenges posed by NWAC's strategy reveal why their demands are
not easily addressed at the federal level and, thus, why at times they have been
responded to less than gracefully by Indigenous leaders. The response by
Indigenous leaders is telling, though. As NWAC's paper points out, the tendency was to discredit NWAC by rendering them not "real" Indians: "When
Aboriginal women demand sexual equality, we are accused of being feminists. We are accused of dividing our community along sexist lines" (Moore,
1992: 10). This response by Indigenous leaders emerges directly from the
necessity of maintaining a homogenized/essentialized identity to ground sovereignty claims. It also clearly expresses the potential violences of sovereignty
discourse: in order to maintain legitimacy, the sovereign must be able to
maintain a coherent self, and thus a clear inside/outside distinction. In
this context, the inscription of inside and outside—the reproduction of the
sovereignty of the "self"—requires the exclusion—through discourses of
authenticity—of others (Indigenous women) from that self. While perhaps
strategically crucial in the short run, in the longer run it produces a festering
problem—as emerged in NWAC's opposition to the 1992 Referendum.

Most crucially, however, this tension needs to be understood as an effect in
part of how sovereignty discourse has already produced the strategic field in
ways that constrain Indigenous political expression. As their claims (their
very subjectivities) are dependent on sovereignty discourse, they have to produce themselves according to its mold. Always requiring a violent[22] production of "self" and thus "other," this production becomes multiply treacherous
when the "other" (in this case Indigenous peoples) tries to produce itself as

the "self" (sovereign). The multiple differences of situation, history, and ontology amongst Indigenous peoples must be erased or homogenized in order to claim sovereignty on their colonizers' terms. The situation of NWAC in the constitutional discussions thus reproduces the role Indigenous peoples played in the constitution of sovereignty in North America: they mark the edges, constitute the margin. They are the ones who come to mark what is sovereign, precisely by their exclusion—whether self-imposed or forced upon them—from it. This leaves us with crucial questions about the long-term effects of sovereignty discourse. The claim in the past has always been that the violences effected by sovereignty discourses and practices were, as Tocqueville argued, "regrettable necessities," unfortunate but necessary because, without sovereignty, political community is not possible. Such a claim reproduces and strengthens sovereignty, insofar as it reinscribes its role as the very condition of possibility for politics, and thus its constitution as something pre-political. But we should have no small suspicion here for how this claim is deployed. Indigenous groups no less: it has provided the justification for their past treatment.

Indigenous leaders in the negotiations clearly thought it a worthwhile gamble: the potential achievement of self-government was the precondition for resolving and responding to these "secondary" concerns. NWAC was not willing to take this gamble, insisting instead upon the constitution of a different kind of sovereignty, one which might provide a recognition of the complex historical interconnections amongst Indigenous and settler communities constituted through colonialism. A sovereignty which was grounded in this, they argued, would provide a better starting point for self-government. However, this would also require a renegotiation of sovereignty discourse itself: the constitution of a sovereignty grounded in a non-essentialized identity. In the absence of this, either the federal Indigenous claims fail—discredited by the inability to exhibit the appropriate signs of sovereignty—or NWAC's concerns are excluded, and they become the underside or "other" that enables the emerging recognition of Indigenous sovereignty. During the Constitutional Referendum, the strategic field faced by Indigenous politics seemed almost this sharply defined. Thus, insofar as one accepts this either/or expression of political necessity, the defeat of the Referendum, in particular its resounding defeat by Indigenous peoples, appears disheartening.

On my reading, though, the defeat might be read as a defeat of the particular strategy of sovereignty in play, an unwillingness to live by its terms. It thus might facilitate an opening for a rearticulation of sovereignty discourse through indigeneity and Indigenous politics, and vice versa, perhaps opening the possibility of a rewriting of the history of sovereignty's "regrettable necessity." On this reading, rather than seeing NWAC's position as a strategic disaster—a failure to support Indigenous sovereignty at the crucial moment—one might read it as a challenge to a particular form of sovereignty politics. Read this way, what is striking about NWAC's position is the vision of politics they articulate. Clearly sharing a desire for Indigenous communities to emerge from their colonized past, their vision nonetheless is grounded in a concern for the health and viability of their communities rather than an abstract and formalistic legal guarantee of their status as autonomous units. Thus, rather than legal status granted by colonizers being the precondition for the necessary changes Indigenous communities seek, the reverse becomes true. The internal viability of the communities becomes the crucial site of political action. A politics of "inside" dominates, with necessary connections to the "outside" in order to enable these politics.

Of course, even this articulation of politics is grounded in a language of sovereignty, as was clear from NWAC's position paper. Rather than an escape from sovereignty, it provides a potential rearticulation of it that refocuses its meaning and effects in relation to Indigenous communities. Further, this strategy itself is dependent upon the sovereignty strategy already being pursued, inasmuch as it is articulated through and in reference to those discourses. In other words, I am far from recommending that NWAC's political vision supplant the dominant strategies: there is a dangerous element to their discursive strategies as well. As federal Indigenous leaders know all too well and the history of Indigenous–Canadian relations exhibits tenfold, the only reason Indigenous peoples were getting the attention and concessions they were was because of the strength of the sovereignty claim they could mobilize. While NWAC's desire to focus on social problems is crucial, a strong sovereignty claim is quite possibly the condition of possibility for accessing the resources necessary to realize such a focus.

There is thus a dynamic tension expressed by the conflict between NWAC and federal pan-Indigenous organizations. This tension is produced by how sovereignty discourse shapes politics, especially for those—like Indigenous peoples—who have been so clearly marked and located within sovereignty discourse. This tension is a dangerous one, but also, crucially, a productive one. It is an expression of serious contradictions and challenges that are deeply embedded in modern political thought and practices. They thus need to be opened up and worked on rather than "resolved" at a symbolic or formal level. The crucial thing that must be resisted is closure, is the assumption that the struggles expressed by these tensions can and should be contained within existing structures and discourses. To assume this is to seriously underestimate the complexity of the political terrain faced by Indigenous peoples. If my sympathy seems to lean towards NWAC's strategy, it is because they (if only because they are the weaker party) seem to be resisting this kind of closure most strongly, insofar as they are resisting the inscription of a potentially violent version of sovereignty politics. This resistance to sovereignty as a solution and emphasis on a rearticulation of political space express a more promising sense of the politics necessary to engage their situation, suggesting the dynamism Indigenous politics must force upon the articulation of political space.

The development of the discourse on Indigenous women's concerns in the intervening years seems to be an illustration of the positive effects of NWAC's strategy, even though much of this discourse emerged through critiques of their strategy. For example, compare the following analysis, developed recently by Turpel-Lafond, to NWAC's. Turpel-Lafond clearly expresses a negotiation of these tensions that keeps alive a complex political space, one where the possibilities for addressing sovereignty and colonization, gender and tradition simultaneously appear to open up:

> It is essential that you separate two concepts that are in the foreground here so as not to be confused. On the one hand, it is important to understand the position that First Nations women occupy both historically and in the real contemporary sense, in some of our communities, particularly those which are matriarchal, and to appreciate how this position was attacked by the Canadian state. On the other hand, it is essential not to confuse First Nations women's suppressed status as a result of state-imposed legal definitions and institutional structures in the *Indian Act*, with a reaction translatable into a desire to have what non-native women or men have in this society. The former is patriarchy, the latter is paternalism. Both were imposed upon us as communities and as individuals. We do not want continued patriarchy nor do we want paternalistic prescriptions for our future paths. We want to extricate ourselves from both of these debilitating forces. At the same time, it is wholly distracting and irresponsible to place the blame for First Nations women's experiences at the feet of First Nations men. Yet, neither can we exonerate them today when they are shown the context yet decide to ignore it and embrace learned patriarchy.[23]
>
> (Turpel-Lafond, 1997: 71)

This description of the political terrain suggests a more subtle and flexible vision of the possibilities for sovereignty while holding firm on the necessity of some form of self-determination. Insofar as political strategies can be crafted through recognition of this kind of complexity, and sovereignties formed that recognize and negotiate the complex effects of colonialism, we will see forms of sovereignty emerge which resist some of the now familiar violences of modern sovereignty. This would be a considerable achievement. Given the live struggle with this complexity in Indigenous politics at diverse sites, such a reformulation is likely to emerge from their political activities.

The 1992 Referendum did indeed mark the end of a particular form of pan-Indigenous politics, and there is cause for some regret on that front.[24] However, the assumption that this means that "we are back where we started" is not appropriate either. For one thing, it remains clear that a renegotiation of Canadian sovereignty cannot happen in the absence of a consideration of and reconciliation with its colonial past. The magnitude of this project has also become clearer. More importantly, however, it has galvanized Indigenous politics in important ways towards more promising rearticulations of sovereignty. In these rearticulations we will find crucial resources for thinking about the future of politics.

6 Adjudication
Paradoxes of law
and sovereignty

One of the most important recent sites of struggle for Indigenous peoples in Canada has been that of law. To go to the courts—one of the systems through which their dispossession was enacted—for justice might seem somewhat paradoxical, if not quixotic. Success in this context would require convincing the court that the dispossession of Indigenous peoples was unjust even in the colonizer's terms. Further, they would have to convince the court of this within the highly ritualized and tightly controlled guidelines of legal procedure: within the rules set by the court itself. Yet further, they would have to do so in a context where this claim potentially puts the legitimacy of the court itself into question: either the courts were unable to prevent an unjust dispossession of Indigenous peoples, or they actively participated in it. Either way, if the courts accept the claims of injustice, they are implicated in a travesty of justice.

If Indigenous peoples face a considerable challenge when they enter the courtroom, the justice system also faces a formidable challenge when it considers Indigenous peoples' claims. The debate about the roles and responsibilities of the courts in the dispossession of Indigenous peoples has a very long history, going back at least as far as the 16th century.[1] One question framing contemporary debates is whether the colonization of Indigenous peoples was a perversion of the law—the law being used as an instrument of power, to enforce the will of a specific group—or whether it constituted a violation of law—a failure of the powerful to live by their own rules. Put differently, the question is whether the justice system is capable of delivering justice, or only of enforcing the wishes of the powerful. The resilience and polarization of this argument suggest that it is a tension that needs to be unpacked more carefully. It is enabled by the assumption that politics and law are, or at least should be, separate. Law, committed to an abstract, universalizable concept of justice, should not be influenced by the concerns and interests of politics, the more mundane negotiation amongst the competing desires of a population. As we saw in both Hobbes and Tocqueville, this distinction is an effect of sovereignty; it is one of the practices through which sovereignty is instantiated and maintained. For Tocqueville, one of the crucial enabling factors of democratic sovereignty is a shared faith in law, or at least the idea of law. Although law is an expression of the majority will, it is guided by a commitment to a potentially universalizable set of standards that exceed the particular expressions of interests that characterize politics. It thus produces resonance even amongst those disadvantaged by it due to the recourse it provides from the vicissitudes of the majority. However, if law comes to be seen as merely an extension of politics, or of the will of the majority, democratic sovereignty is in jeopardy, as those disempowered in the political arena feel they have no recourse, no leverage to bring to bear on the political. The connection to Hobbes is perhaps apparent: his rendering of ontology and epistemology as pre-political makes them an apparently neutral, naturalized, and universalizable basis for the arbitration of differences without recourse to violence; hence his focus on the definition of terms, the regulation of their meaning and his concern with "madnesse" as an expression of differing conceptions of the meanings of these terms. In the context of the state, law provides a key mechanism for this regulation. For both Tocqueville and Hobbes, then, sovereignty is produced and maintained through a crucial distinction and negotiation between the particular struggles that characterize the negotiation of political power and a broader set of commitments that frame and mediate those struggles.

The claims of Indigenous peoples clearly throw this distinction into question. Their claims suggest that either the courts have been the handmaidens of the majority and unconcerned with justice, or they have significantly misinterpreted what justice is. Either way, a crucial axis of democratic resonance is thrown into question: the institutional expression of justice, or the concept of justice itself. The claims of Indigenous peoples thus potentially pose a serious challenge to the court. To acknowledge their validity is either to admit the courts' participation in a travesty of justice and potentially delegitimate their own institution, or to reconsider the concept of justice itself as it has been interpreted in relation to Indigenous peoples, thus revealing the contestable (rather than universal) nature of such concepts. Inasmuch as they challenge this division of law and politics, and inasmuch as this distinction is constitutive of Canadian sovereignty, Indigenous peoples in this way once again open the question of sovereignty: the legitimacy of Canada's sovereignty story, the legitimacy of the conceptions of justice around which its sovereignty resonates.

Thus legal strategies, just as we saw in Chapter 5 with constitutional negotiations, are embedded in a struggle both within and against practices of sovereignty. The recent court case which has posed this challenge most acutely is *Delgamuukw v. British Columbia*, a land claims case filed by the hereditary chiefs of the Gitksan and Wet'suwet'en First Nations of British Columbia. In what follows, I examine this case in order to illustrate the political terrains produced and negotiated by Indigenous peoples' engagements with law, terrains crucially shaped by practices of sovereignty. As in the previous chapter, the analysis seeks to illustrate both how sovereignty produces and constrains possibilities for Indigenous peoples, and how their engagements with these political terrains rearticulate it, opening new trajectories of political possibility. My analysis here represents a limited foray into a rich field of engagement with law and indigeneity, one tightly focused on sketching an understanding, practice and terrain of politics.[2]

The claim, argument, and context

The situation for most Indigenous peoples in British Columbia is somewhat different from Indigenous peoples in other parts of Canada, in that there were very few treaties signed in British Columbia.[3] There was no formal transfer of land from First Nations to the Queen or the government of Canada. This has meant that legal claims to territory have been pursued differently in British Columbia from the rest of Canada and potentially have very far-reaching effects. This is especially true as First Nations' land claims currently cover most of the land base of British Columbia, and the economy of the province is highly dependent on the extraction of raw materials from this land. The Gitksan–Wet'suwet'en land claim (or the "Delgamuukw case," as it came to be known) was filed in 1984, and went to court in 1987.[4]

As was the case elsewhere in Canada, the 1970s and 1980s had been dynamic times for Indigenous politics in British Columbia. In particular the 1980s saw a series of court cases in which the decisions went further than any previous decisions towards a recognition and definition of "Aboriginal rights."[5] There was the appearance of a steady trend towards recognition of Indigenous claims to land and resources, particularly in British Columbia. In part because of this, the Gitksan and Wet'suwet'en chose to pursue their claims through the courts, and also chose to file a comprehensive claim. Rather than choosing to pursue recognition and definition of a particular (limited) right, such as the right to fish for food, they chose to file suit claiming ownership and jurisdiction of all of their traditional territory (approximately 58,000 square kilometers) as well as the rights to self-government and compensation for lost land and resources (Wa and Uukw, 1989: 1). The scope of their case was significant.

Even more important, however, was the way in which this case would be argued. Consistent with the scope of their case, the Gitksan and Wet'suwet'en felt that the only way they could prove their claim to the land would be to convince the court not only that it had been unjustly appropriated, but that they had a relationship with and a claim to the land that pre-existed contact with settlers. They needed to convince the court that they were sovereign and this sovereignty should be recognized and affirmed. Convincing the court of this, they realized, would require overcoming ethnocentric prejudices embedded in "white" culture and legal doctrine, not least "the tendency to view aboriginal societies as at an earlier stage of evolutionary development" (Wa and Uukw, 1989: 21). In other words, recognition of Gitksan and Wet'suwet'en title to the land involved a fundamental challenge to the sovereignty myth of Canada.

Clearly, this posed a significant challenge for the plaintiffs, as might be predicted from the analysis in previous chapters. Significantly, they recognized this, realizing that in order to be successful at disrupting this ethnocentric view they would have to convince the judge of the validity of their own worldview (ontology). As chief counsel for the plaintiffs put it: "The Gitksan have to show the judge not just the time, but how to make a watch" (Monet and Skanu'u, 1992: 31). In other words, they recognized that within the sovereignty myth of Canada there was no way for them to articulate their claim without them being rendered as primitive societies; they thus had to convince the court that this whole worldview was an inappropriate lens through which to view Gitksan and Wet'suwet'en societies. They proposed to do this by presenting the court with their worldview as part of the evidence for the trial and trying to get the judge to view their evidence through their worldview: "The challenge for this court, in listening to the Indian evidence, is to understand the framework within which it is given and the nature of the worldview from which it emanates" (Wa and Uukw, 1989: 22–23). This worldview is characterized by conceptions of space and time, selves and subjectivities, causality, and so on, that are fundamentally different from the court's (modern) worldview. It is a different ontology, characterized by a different set of enabling distinctions:

> The Western world-view sees the essential and primary interactions as being those between human beings.[6] To the Gitksan and Wet'suwet'en, human beings are part of an interacting continuum which includes animals and spirits. Animals and fish are viewed as members of societies which have intelligence and power, and can influence the course of events in terms of their interrelationship with human beings. In Western society causality is viewed as direct and linear. That is to say, that an event has the ability to cause or produce another event as time moves forward. To the Gitksan and Wet'suwet'en, time is not linear but cyclical. The events of the "past" are not simply history, but are something that directly effects the present and the future. The nature of the continuum between humans, animals, and the spirit world, within cycles of existence, underpins much of the evidence you will hear.
>
> (Wa and Uukw, 1989: 23)

In attempting to understand this worldview, counsel for the plaintiffs warned, it is important to be aware of the particularity of the modern Western worldview, of how this worldview will tend to "read" or attribute validity to truth claims expressed through the Gitksan–Wet'suwet'en worldview:

> Of particular importance to us [non-Indigenous] are such fundamental distinctions between the secular and the sacred, the spiritual and the material, the natural and the supernatural. Many of the distinctions which we make in order to make sense out of the world are absent in the

Indian world-view. It is not difficult to see, therefore, and indeed it is inevitable, that if we apply our distinctions without discrimination and caution to what Indian people say, we will make nonsense out of their evidence. The integration of what to us are discrete and separate parts of life, infuses Gitksan and Wet'suwet'en thinking, and permeates their most important institutions.

(Wa and Uukw, 1989: 24)

Along these lines, particularly challenging—and important—for the court would be the negotiation of the problem of not only the content of the evidence, but the medium of its presentation. As the Gitksan and Wet'suwet'en have oral rather than written traditions, the majority of the evidence presented specifically by Gitksan and Wet'suwet'en peoples was in the form of oral histories, rather than as written records. The challenge this posed to the court, of course, was one of epistemological validity. Although these oral histories were backed up with more familiar forms of "scientific" evidence when possible, counsel argued that the force of the case required that the court accept these histories as valid on their own terms as well: "For the court, however, to deny the reality of Gitksan and Wet'suwet'en history except where it can be corroborated by expert evidence in the Western scientific tradition is to disregard the distinctive Gitksan and Wet'suwet'en system of validating historical facts" (Wa and Uukw, 1989: 39). These are not "just" stories, counsel argued. Rather, they represent a well-defined and carefully monitored system of knowledge. To reinforce this, counsel outlined the Gitksan and Wet'suwet'en epistemological system, and made a strong argument not only for its validity, but for the importance of its recognition by the court. To hear the evidence presented but subject it to evaluation by Western epistemological standards would be to repeat the historical treatment of Aboriginal peoples as "less developed versions" of our selves, rather than recognizing and struggling with the reality of cultural difference (Wa and Uukw, 1989: 40–41).[7]

One of the final concerns the counsel for the plaintiffs raised was the difficulty the judge would face with the problem of time and change, tradition and continuity: the problem of how to reconcile this different worldview with the sovereign assertion that those who do not share the same conception of sovereignty as we do live "out of time" and thus do not "progress." Concerned that the judge, if he did accept their worldview, would then subject it to criteria of "authenticity"—requiring that it remain intact and unchanged today—counsel sought to reframe the problem of history and change. Rather than demonstrating a stagnant form of identity, the Gitksan and Wet'suwet'en presented evidence of both continuity and change. They presented evidence of the dynamic, fluid nature of Gitksan and Wet'suwet'en societies—their historical adaptations to different circumstances, including the arrival of non-Aboriginals—and they used this evidence to argue that these historical adaptations are evidence of the vitality of Aboriginal societies, not evidence of their demise. Crucially, though, the continuity is expressed through a continued relationship to their territory, resources, institutions, laws, and social structures. It is also expressed in their constant and continued resistance to the dispossession of their lands and the lack of recognition of the validity of their societies. This line of analysis provided a basis for the argument for both the continuity of their societies and for their ongoing attachment and claim to their land.

The challenge posed by the Gitksan and Wet'suwet'en case was thus a significant one. They posed a challenge not only to the legal history of their treatment but also to the ontological and epistemological systems upon which the legal system—and modern sovereignty—is based. They were using the authority of law, itself an expression of sovereignty, to demand that the court recognize its own particularity rather than universality. They were calling on an expression of sovereignty to question particular enabling characteristics of their sovereignty. Contained within this challenge was also hope, not least the hope that the challenge might be taken up as an opportunity (Wa and Uukw, 1989: 36). Ultimately, they argued, what they sought was not in any way the rejection of Canadian sovereignty, or the denial of Canada. Rather, quite the opposite: "This case offers you an historic opportunity, based on evidence no other court has ever heard, to render judgment that will move Canada closer to the achievement of a true Confederation which includes its founding Indian nations" (Wa and Uukw, 1989: 89).

The Crown's defense against the claim by the Gitksan and Wet'suwet'en reproduced by now familiar themes about the relationship between the production of Canadian sovereignty and the Aboriginal peoples who inhabited the land previous to this production.[8] The Crown pursued a four-part defense. First, it denied the existence of Aboriginal title, arguing that Gitksan and Wet'suwet'en societies did not exhibit the characteristics of properly organized governments prior to contact.[9] Further, in case the judge decided that there were some recognizable forms of social organization in existence before contact, the Crown argued that there was minimal occupation and no consistent use of the territories they claimed. The only areas they might have consistently inhabited were the village sites near the main river, sites that are largely included in contemporary Reserve lands. If there was any other use of the larger territory, the defense argued, it was random and unorganized. Second, should any form of title have existed at contact, the Crown argued that such title was extinguished prior to or at the point when British Columbia joined the Confederation. Third, if Aboriginal title survived past Confederation, it was voluntarily extinguished when the Gitksan and Wet-'suwet'en (supposedly) accepted Indian reserves, and in their compliance to and benefits from the sovereignty of Canada since then. Finally, rather than pre-existing contact, what social structures and organization the Gitksan and Wet'suwet'en did exhibit were learned from and acquired during early contact with fur traders and government representatives. Further, any distinctive way of life they might have maintained historically had now been replaced by "Indian reserves, cars, public education, Christianity, the wage economy and provincial jurisdiction over hunting and trapping" (Ray, 1990: 14). As they no longer maintained a distinct way of life or relationship to their territory, there was no ground for granting them a distinctive form of title to it.

Thus, while there is a certain symmetry in the issues between the plaintiffs and the defense, there is a definite asymmetry in their engagement with these issues. Given the character of national and international discourses of human rights, cultural diversity, multiculturalism and anti-colonialism, this defense is surprising, to say the least. One would have thought the conditions under which such explicitly racist assumptions could be reproduced no longer obtained.[10] However, the fact that this is not the case speaks worlds about the challenges this claim posed to the conditions of possibility for Canadian sovereignty. The connections between this defense and the assumptions embedded in the history of Canadian "Indian policy," in reproductions of Canadian sovereignty, in Tocqueville and in Hobbes, are all too apparent. One effect of the articulation of this defense was, perhaps paradoxically, a certain elation amongst the Gitksan and Wet'suwet'en and their supporters: a defense with such clear roots in discredited discourses of the past surely could not succeed.[11]

As might be predicted by the scope of the claim, the nature of the evidence, and the depth and complexity of issues at stake in the conflict, the trial was long, complex, and exhausting for all involved. The complexity of the arguments and extent of the difference between the plaintiffs and defense are one reason for this, but also particularly difficult was the negotiation of the problem of the limits of the court as a site for engaging the kind of challenge posed by the case. The court is a site at which the operation of sovereignty is in a sense laid most bare, exposed most fully, not least due to the highly structured context in which all questions are considered. The nature of the plaintiffs' case was such that its presentation required almost constant conflicts around questions such as the admissibility and relevance of evidence. Each of these conflicts, small in itself, posed a challenge to the sovereignty of the court—the question of what ontological and epistemological ground this issue would be negotiated on. Each decision on the part of the judge was an expression or performance of sovereignty, an exercise in the negotiation of limits. The judge was the sovereign: the site of the decision of what would count, what could be heard and what could not. So, paradoxically, although their attempt was to insist upon an alternate sovereignty, their attempt was constantly up against the necessity of achieving permission for their sovereignty from the sovereign as expressed in the judge. This is an indication of how the structure of the court, of sovereignty, produces a series of paradoxes as a response to any challenge to its conditions of possibility. So, for example, often the counsel for the plaintiffs was forced to walk a fine line between establishing the legitimacy of evidence on the terms of the court and asserting the terms of legitimacy of the Gitksan and Wet'suwet'en worldview, of establishing a space for the legitimacy of the Gitksan–Wet'suwet'en ontology within the context of "Canadian" sovereignty, a sovereignty that is itself produced through the rendering of other ontologies as primitive, non-sovereign, illegitimate. There is, of course, much more that could be said about the performances of sovereignty that characterized the courtroom phase of the drama; however, this has been richly discussed by other commentators.[12] The ultimate manifestation of sovereignty in this context, however, is that in the end one judge wrote a decision evaluating all that he had seen in the context of the necessities placed upon him by his position as a subject of the law.[13] It is to this decision that I turn next.

The decision

Chief Justice McEachern's decision in the case, *Delgamuukw v. British Columbia* (1991), was against the Gitksan and Wet'suwet'en in almost all regards. Their claim for ownership and jurisdiction was dismissed; their claim for damages was dismissed, and they received no provision for costs. They were found to be entitled to continued use of vacant or unoccupied Crown land for Aboriginal sustenance purposes, subject to provincial laws, until or unless the province chose to otherwise utilize it. It was a complete rejection of the challenge posed by the Gitksan and Wet'suwet'en. Not surprisingly, this rejection proceeded through and relied upon sovereignty discourse—and all of the double binds and paradoxes that it rests upon and reproduces for Indigenous peoples—as authorization for its conclusions. What follows is an examination of Chief Justice McEachern's rearticulation of sovereignty in response to the challenges posed by the Gitksan and Wet'suwet'en claim as they were discussed earlier.[14]

The first challenge posed by the claim was that the judge would have to reject the ethnocentric assumptions about the "level" of "civilization" of Indigenous societies. The response to this was unequivocal. Directly paralleling the structure of Tocqueville's writing of sovereignty, Chief Justice McEachern begins the decision with an assertion of the "emptiness" of the territory in question:

> The most striking thing that one notices in the territory away from the Skeena–Bulkley corridor is its emptiness. I generally accept the evidence ... that very few Indians are to be seen anywhere except in the large river corridors. ... As I have mentioned, the territory is a vast emptiness.
>
> (*Delgamuukw*, 1991: 12)

Comments on the size, emptiness, apparent "wildness," and "inaccessibility" of the territory continue throughout the decision. This observation lays the groundwork for assertions about the relationship between territory and civilization, as we saw in Tocqueville and will see again later. It also provides the basis for assertions later in the decision that the Gitksan and Wet'suwet'en don't *use* the territory and thus don't have a significant claim to it. The echoes of Locke ring through strongly here, as First Nations' apparent failure to "mark" the territory with appropriate indications of their presence will translate to an inability to claim it.[15]

Having established this groundwork, McEachern C.J. then moves immediately to comment on the Indians' "level" of civilization. At this point, our old friend Hobbes makes an appearance, apparently still a reliable commentator on Indigenous life:

> It would not be accurate to assume that even pre-contact existence in the territory was in the least bit idyllic. The plaintiffs' ancestors had no written language, no horses or wheeled vehicles, slavery and starvation was [sic] not uncommon, wars with neighboring peoples were common, and there is no doubt, to quote Hobbs, [sic] that aboriginal life in the territory was, at best, 'nasty brutish and short.'
>
> (*Delgamuukw*, 1991: 13)

This assertion of the lack of "development" resurfaces throughout McEachern C.J.'s decision: "The evidence suggests that the Indians of the territory were, by historical standards, a primitive people without any form of writing, horses, or wheeled wagons" (*Delgamuukw*, 1991: 31). Without explicitly denying "civilization" of some form, McEachern C.J. clearly reasserts that—despite the fact that the Gitksan and Wet'suwet'en wish to call their societies "civilized"—their "civilization" is not in any way comparable to European civilization:

> I have no doubt life in the territory was extremely difficult, and many of the badges of civilization, as we of European culture understand the term, were indeed absent. Because of the low threshold, however, it will not be necessary for me to quantify the level of aboriginal social organization in the territory at any particular time . . . the descriptions I heard tended to be both idyllic and universal, neither of which terms, in my view, accurately describe what 'happened on the ground' in the day to day life of these people. Life for the Gitksan and Wet'suwet'en has never been idyllic, and universality in practice was seldom seen.
>
> (*Delgamuukw*, 1991: 31–32)

Further, any attempt to assert that these forms of life might be, or have been, desirable is enough to render the speaker's opinion suspect:

> Some of this evidence had a decided complexion of unreality about it, as if nothing had changed since before contact. This affects the credibility of statements which were often repeated that ancestors had been using

these specific lands from the beginning of time, or similar expression. Aboriginal life, in my view, was far from stable and it stretches credulity to believe that remote ancestors considered themselves bound to specific lands.

(*Delgamuukw*, 1991: 56)

While he takes some time to summarize what he understands of Gitksan and Wet'suwet'en forms of social organization, his assertions about the quality of life under these forms of social organization remain unsubstantiated. Clearly if the marks of civilization that Europeans would recognize are absent, this past cannot have been pleasurable or "idyllic" (although the same observation might be made of European societies at the time). The reassertion of the assumption that Indigenous societies were "less civilized" than European ones is not terribly surprising, although the cavalier way in which it was done reveals the failure to take up in any way the challenge posed by the plaintiffs to consider the particularity of Canadian sovereignty discourse.

The second significant challenge posed to the judge by the opening statement was the challenge to view the evidence provided by the Gitksan and Wet'suwet'en in the context of their worldview, with attention to the difficulty of cross-cultural communication and a sensitivity to the ways in which the Western worldview tended to discredit the Gitksan and Wet'suwet'en worldview. Because McEachern C.J. had allowed oral histories to be presented as evidence, there was some hope that this evidence might be taken seriously as establishing both a claim to the land and the validity of the epistemological systems of the Gitksan and Wet'suwet'en. However, Chief Justice McEachern's final position on this type of evidence clearly located this evidence as at best secondary to "scientific" evidence, certainly unable to stand alone: "I am unable to accept *adaawk*, *kungax*, and oral histories as reliable bases for detailed history, but they could confirm findings based on other admissible evidence" (*Delgamuukw*, 1991: 75). His failure to seriously consider the particularity of his own cultural biases, and ontological and epistemological systems is expressed clearly:

When I come to consider events long past, I am driven to conclude, on all the evidence that much of the plaintiffs' historical evidence is not literally true. For example, I do not accept the proposition that these peoples have been present on this land from the beginning of time. Serious questions arise about many of the matters about which the witnesses have testified and I must assess the totality of the evidence in accordance with legal, not cultural principles.[16]

I am satisfied that the lay witnesses honestly believed everything they said was true and accurate. It was obvious to me, however, that they were recounting matters of faith which have become fact to them. If I do not accept their evidence it will seldom be because I think they are untruthful, but rather because I have a different view of what is fact and what is belief.

(*Delgamuukw*, 1991: 49)

With a simple assertion of his own epistemological criteria, and without serious attention to the ways this is embedded in a series of power relations the Gitksan and Wet'suwet'en were attempting to challenge, the judge reasserts a Hobbesian ontology of sovereignty as the necessary and naturalized ground of authority.

The Gitksan and Wet'suwet'en had presented several expert witnesses, in particular anthropologists and historians. The evidence of the anthropologists was especially important to the case, in part because this evidence posed the most serious challenge to the ethnocentric assumptions of the defense (and, as it turns out, the judge) and the most support for the claims by the plaintiffs that their societies should be considered "civilized." The judge's response to this evidence was as clear and absolute as his response to oral histories. Quoting a passage from the American Anthropological Association's "Statement of Ethics" concerning anthropologists' responsibility to the peoples they study, he concluded that the anthropologists were simply biased and rejected their evidence out of hand: "Apart from urging almost total acceptance of all Gitksan and Wet'suwet'en cultural values, the anthropologists add little to the important questions that must be decided in this case" (*Delgamuukw*, 1991: 51).[17] This can be contrasted quite sharply with his treatment of other expert witnesses:

> Lastly, I wish to mention the historians. Generally speaking, I accept just about everything they put before me because they were largely collectors of archival, historical documents. In most cases they provided much useful information with minimal editorial comment. Their marvelous collections spoke largely for themselves.
>
> (*Delgamuukw*, 1991: 52)

This treatment of oral histories and anthropological and historical evidence is particularly revealing of how the rituals of the court—rituals that are practices of sovereignty—enable an apparently arbitrary assertion of authority insofar as it abides by certain legal norms. Anthropologists testifying in the case were up against the kinds of dilemmas discussed in Chapter 3. Because the external authority of the discipline rests upon its reproduction of particular discourses of sovereignty, their challenging of these discourses—their urging of acceptance for Indigenous cultural values, for example—becomes cause for the rejection of their insights. The judge's acceptance of historical and rejection of anthropological evidence is not incidental: to accept the anthropological evidence would have required that he throw many of the assumptions embedded in the decision into question. However, he retains

Derrida

the authority to reject them. In this way, the courtroom context produces the judge as sovereign. As other sovereigns, he is constrained by the necessity of legitimating decisions based on a system of agreed upon authority, but within that system his judgment is protected.[18] Although the later Appeal decision on the case will take issue with McEachern C.J.'s dismissal of oral histories, establishing a more rigorous framework for their evaluation, it upholds his dismissal of anthropological evidence. Evaluations of the credibility of witnesses are part of the job of a judge, and the Supreme court of Canada cannot take issue with a trial judge's conclusions in this regard. If a judge simply finds historical evidence to be more persuasive than anthropological evidence, there is no recourse, despite their relative significance to the case being presented. In this way, the significance of his dismissal of oral histories and anthropological evidence rests not primarily in the evidence it provides of ignorance or racism, but in what it reveals about how practices of sovereignty structure the content and negotiation of legitimate authority. This leaves the Gitksan and Wet'suwet'en in familiar double binds, with their efforts to challenge the worldview of the court rejected on all fronts.

As identified above, one of the most crucial double binds the Gitksan and Wet'suwet'en faced is the bind of authenticity, continuity, and change. Although McEachern C.J. rejected the plaintiff's "idyllic" description of pre-contact civilization, he continues the tradition of evaluating the "authenticity" of the "Indians" according to the extent to which they resemble the image of Indigeneity at contact. He finds the disparity between this image and the people he sees before him grounds to delegitimate their claim:

> The evidence satisfies me that most Gitksan and Wet'suwet'en people do not now live an aboriginal life. They have been gradually moving away from it since contact, and there is practically no one trapping and hunting full time, although fishing has remained an important part of their culture and economy.
>
> (*Delgamuukw*, 1991: 56)

Evidence that the Gitksan and Wet'suwet'en had adapted to changing circumstances is seen as evidence that they have "lost" their "Aboriginality" rather than as evidence of the flexibility and vibrancy of their culture:[19]

> As early as the 1850's the Gitksan, who had not previously seen a horse, quickly became adept at packing for the construction of the Collins Overland Telegraph, for the Yukon Telegraph, for the Omineca and Cassiar Gold Rushes, and for the construction of the Grand Trunk Pacific Railroad in the first decade of this century. At the same time the Indians increasingly participated in commercial fishing at the coast, and in the logging and lumbering industries which became the economic mainstays of the region. Witness after witness admitted participation in the wage or cash economy. . . . Even in their aboriginal pursuits, however,

the plaintiffs do not seem to consider themselves tied to particular territories.

(*Delgamuukw*, 1991: 56)

Thus an "aboriginal" life or "aboriginal pursuits" are defined exclusively as those pursuits that pre-date contact, effectively freezing Aboriginal culture in the past. Later in the decision, the judge will use this apparent departure from "aboriginal pursuits" to constitute potential grounds for the termination of their Aboriginal rights:

Aboriginal rights depend upon long time and, I think, regular if not continuous use of territory for aboriginal purposes. . . . I have no doubt aboriginal activities have fallen very much into disuse in many areas. This was admitted by several Indian witnesses who observed that many of their young people have very little interest in aboriginal pursuits. The aboriginal activities that are being pursued now may be indistinguishable in many cases from the wilderness activities enjoyed by many non-Indian citizens of the province.[20]

(*Delgamuukw*, 1991: 284)

On this reading, then, the effects of colonization on the economic structure of Aboriginal groups become the legitimation for continued colonization. What a hundred years of "Indian policy" has failed to achieve—assimilation—is thus asserted by legal fiat.

Considering all of the above, McEachern C.J.'s position on the sovereignty claim itself is hardly surprising. First, because Canadian sovereignty is the enabling authority of the court, he places challenges to this sovereignty beyond its jurisdiction:

After much consideration, I am driven to find that jurisdiction and sovereignty are such absolute concepts that there is no half-way house.[21] No court has authority to make grants of constitutional jurisdiction in the face of such clear and comprehensive statutory and constitutional provisions. The very fact that the plaintiffs recognize the underlying title of the Crown precludes them from denying the sovereignty that created such title. I fully understand the plaintiffs' wishful belief that their distinctive history entitles them to demand some form of constitutional independence from British Columbia. But neither this nor any court has the jurisdiction to undo the establishment of the Colony, Confederation, or the constitutional arrangements which are now in place. Separate sovereignty or legislative authority, as a matter of law, is beyond the authority of any court to award.

(*Delgamuukw*, 1991: 224–25)

This line of argument clearly renders legal strategies for the pursuit of

Aboriginal sovereignty a waste of time. It also appears to doom First Nations to a choice of either accepting and living with the "reality" of colonization or opposing it in more radical ways, such as taking up arms against it, since: "[s]eparate sovereignty or legislative authority, as a matter of law, is beyond the authority of any court to award." In a series of moves that strongly echo Tocqueville, the judge reasserts the sovereignty myth: although there were probably some primitive peoples running around the land before the assertion of (real, British) sovereignty, their claim cannot be considered as a sovereign one. Rather, a "vacuum" of authority existed before the British came along to fill it:

> I am prepared to assume for the purposes of this part of my judgment that, in the legal and jurisdictional vacuum which existed prior to British sovereignty, the organization of these people was the only form of ownership and jurisdiction which existed in the areas of the villages. I would not make the same finding with respect to the rest of the territory, even to the areas over which I believe the ancestors of the plaintiffs roamed for sustenance purposes.
>
> (*Delgamuukw*, 1991: 222–23)

The right of the British to "fill" this "vacuum," he asserts, is clearly established in the Law of Nations: "In my view it is part of the law of nations, which has become part of the common law, that discovery and occupation of the lands of this continent by European nations, or occupation and settlement, gave rise to a right of sovereignty (*Delgamuukw*, 1991: 81). The Gitksan and Wet'suwet'en, of course, have challenged this assertion that they ever surrendered their sovereignty under the very same Law of Nations. Chief Justice McEachern dismisses this quite out of hand:

> Aboriginal persons and commentators often mention the fact that the Indians of this province were never conquered by force of arms, nor have they entered into treaties with the Crown. Unfair as it may seem to Indians or others on philosophical grounds, these are not relevant considerations. The events of the last 200 years are far more significant than any military conquest or treaties would have been. The reality of Crown ownership of the soil of all the lands of the province is not open to question and actual dominion for such a long period is far more pervasive than the outcome of a battle or war could ever be.[22]
>
> (*Delgamuukw*, 1991: 81)

The assertion of Canadian sovereignty is unquestionable, the judge asserts; it is a "legal reality," the only reality recognized by the courts. End of story.

Some important tasks remain for McEachern C.J., however. Once again, the violence of Canadian history and sovereignty, and the ritual reproduction of this violence, have to be concealed. The trial had exposed and attempted to hold "Canada" accountable for this violence, had attempted to use Canada's justice against itself, to reveal the price of its assertion of self and appropriation of territory. Throughout the trial, McEachern C.J. had resisted any assertion that treatment of the Indians entailed any violence or bad intention; instead any ill effects were unforeseeable or regrettable necessities of an "enlightened policy." The echoes of Tocqueville are apparent in his assertion of this position:

> Being of a culture where everyone looked after himself or perished, the Indians knew how to survive (in most years). But they were not as industrious in the new economic climate as was thought necessary by the newcomers in the Colony. In addition, the Indians were a greatly weakened people by reason of foreign diseases which took a fearful toll, and by the ravages of alcohol. They became a conquered people, not by force of arms, for that was unnecessary, but *by an invading culture and a relentless energy with which they would not, or could not compete.*
> (*Delgamuukw*, 1991: 129; emphasis mine)

Once again, he equated a lack of bloodshed to a lack of violence, ignoring the violence of assimilation:

> What seems clear, however, is that the source of Indian difficulty was not the loss of land for aboriginal purposes. So far as the evidence shows, they were largely left in their villages and aboriginal life was available to them long after the "Indian problem" was identified.
> (*Delgamuukw*, 1991: 129)

And finally, to extinguish any claim for compensation, his assertion: the violence they describe has very little to do with the effects of the colonization of territory and peoples. Rather, it is due to their failure to adapt to changing circumstances, although their adaptations, of course, have already been read as grounds for denying their claims: "[T]he difficulties of adapting to changing circumstances, not limited land use, is the principal cause of Indian misfortune" (*Delgamuukw*, 1991: 300).

Chief Justice McEachern's response to the challenge posed by the Gitksan–Wet'suwet'en was thus exactly the one Tocqueville would have predicted. In response to the multivalent challenge to Canadian sovereignty, he perfectly reproduced that sovereignty. Reading their challenges as throwing into question the relationship between law and politics by insisting upon the injustice of their treatment, he attempted to protect this boundary by reinscribing their treatment as necessary and inevitable rather than unjust. He rejected the argument that there was any injustice against First Nations, attributing their condition instead to unfortunate but unavoidable side-effects of an inevitable confrontation between primitive and advanced societies.

Responses

Criticisms of Chief Justice McEachern's judgment immediately rained in from a variety of perspectives: it rested upon and reproduced mythologies about both Canadian history and First Nations that were false; it reinscribed a historical tendency of courts to confuse justice with power; it rested upon a misuse of precedent, a misunderstanding and misrepresentation of Aboriginal title, and an inappropriate evaluation and use of evidence.[23] Virtually all commentators agreed that the decision was problematic. Of central concern not least was the apparent retreat from the judicial ground gained through recent legal and political developments. The government of British Columbia, meanwhile, bound and published Chief Justice McEachern's *Reasons for Judgment* in book form, distributing it widely throughout the province (Culhane, 1998: 31). The decision was immediately appealed to the Supreme Court of British Columbia, and eventually to the Supreme Court of Canada, to whose decision on the case I turn on pp. 121–135.

There was also some criticism of the legal strategies used by the Gitksan and Wet'suwet'en legal teams in the case.[24] In particular, some analysts expressed concern that the Gitksan and Wet'suwet'en had "asked for too much," in that they had demanded recognition of their "ownership and jurisdiction" rather than making a claim for either a limited form of Aboriginal rights to use the land or a claim for Aboriginal title to the land. This strategy, some legal analysts argued, was misconceived in that it misunderstood the tendency of the legal system to proceed incrementally. The statement of claim was amended in the appeal process in a manner consistent with this criticism (from a claim of "ownership and jurisdiction" to a claim of "Aboriginal title"). However, the response to this criticism by the Gitksan and Wet'suwet'en is significant. As Satsan (Herb George), Speaker of the Office of the Hereditary Chiefs of the Gitksan and Wet'suwet'en, responded:

> The criticism that we had to take was that we were entering a game in which we had no involvement whatsoever with the putting together of that game, the making up of the rules, in the appointment of referees and umpires.
>
> We entered a game that most people believed we could not win. And it's true. We put the institution of justice in this country in a dilemma.
>
> Although we knew what the game was, and what the rules were, we had to take into account that the greatest thing that we were in danger of losing was our very beings as Gitksan and Wet'suwet'en people.
>
> If we were to accept what has now come to be known as the conventional view, if we were to approach this whole issue of our rights in a step-by-step manner, then at the end of the day it may well be that we can gain something small and certain. No. We are Gitksan and Wet'suwet'en people. We like to be that. We want to continue to be that.
>
> (Cassidy, 1992b: 54)

The Gitksan could have chosen to play the incremental game, Satsan continued, but "if we had chosen to play that game the way it was set out, I think that in the end we would more than likely have lost that which is so great to us" (Cassidy, 1992b: 55).

Satsan is explicitly concerned about the effects of legal strategies on the Gitksan and Wet'suwet'en, rather than whether the strategies themselves succeeded or failed. It is crucial, he insists, that both the Gitksan–Wet'suwet'en and the legal system understand and face the magnitude of the challenge posed by the claims of First Nations, and not be satisfied with incremental changes:

> The great tragedy will occur if people believe that common law, as we understand and know it, can't accept something as radical as we were putting forward in our case, and that the argument for our rights must be built step-by-step. The tragedy for me is that if we accept that view, we will sacrifice ourselves as a people while we wait to win.
>
> (Cassidy, 1992b: 57)

His comments reveal a clear sense of both the necessity and dangers of challenging the parameters of the court, of law. Because of their awareness of the challenge they posed, he argues, the Gitksan and Wet'suwet'en, unlike the legal community, were unsurprised by the original decision:

> We asked ourselves: 'What's the worst case scenario? What do we expect?' And we weren't very far off the mark. We just weren't as creative as the Chief Justice was in his use of the wonderful English language. Our scenario was that we lost, because we know, we understand, what we are up against here. . . . I guess one of our chiefs at the outset of the trial put it best when he was asked by someone, 'What if you guys lose?' I don't remember which one of our chiefs it was, but the answer was, 'We're already winning. It doesn't matter what the court says, we're already winning as a people.'
>
> (Cassidy, 1992b: 55–56)

Crucial to these remarks is that for the Gitksan and Wet'suwet'en the court case does not define the parameters of their struggle or strategy: the point is not to win the court case. The court case, rather, is an expression of a much larger struggle.

Thus, their reflections on the initial decision and their approach to the appeal process were characterized by a very different set of priorities than the exclusively legal arguments might suggest. Their efforts were not necessarily to win recognition and status within the legal system as an end in itself:

> What's important for us is that we have become stronger people, much stronger people, because we haven't put all of our wishes for a better

future in the hands of the court. We have done our work amongst our-selves. We have started to pick ourselves up to the point where we'll decide whether or not we have a right. No court can extinguish the fire that burns within us. We'll assert that right, whether they agree or not. Our people are currently undertaking plans and putting in place strategies to move onto our land, to move off those reservations, to start to take care of the land.

That's how we view this judgment. We knew what the outcome would be. *We knew that we couldn't depend on the court, that at the end of the day, even if we won, when we woke up the next day, nothing would have changed in our lives.* We are the most powerless community in North America, and we accept that powerlessness.

What this decision means to us is that we will not be bullied anymore. We will not have somebody else determine what our rights are, to tell me that my right is only to subsist, to tell me that my right is only to fish for food for societal and ceremonial purposes.

We view this judgment for what it is—a denial and a huge misunder-standing and ignorance of the First Nations across this country. It is a failure to recognize the First Nations of this country for what they are and who they are—the First Nations of this land, the owners of this land.

Without that kind of understanding, we do not believe that we will be treated fairly when we come to the table to negotiate with the federal Crown or the provincial Crown. There will be no justice. There will be no equality and no respect.

(Cassidy, 1992b: 56; emphasis mine)

Satsan's comments, as well as the legal and political analyses of the failures of Chief Justice McEachern's decision, provide an important con-text in which to read the Appeal decision. This is not least because they suggest that a reading of the decision itself is not enough to determine the status of the issues at stake. They suggest, in other words, that the Supreme Court of Canada's decision will not define the parameters of the political.

To put it slightly differently, Satsan's comments reveal a way in which the original decision, a "failure" on all counts when measured according to the legal claims it addressed, nonetheless also potentially reveals the extent to which the courts have little control over the effects of the case. In fact, the decision apparently reinforced a crucial sense of self-reliance and political determination on the part of the Gitksan and Wet'suwet'en, a development that in the long run may have a profound effect on the political spaces of Indigenous politics. In other words, the legal strategy revealed, in its "fail-ure," its own limitations: "even if we won, when we woke up the next day, nothing would have changed in our lives." The recognition of the sovereignty of the Gitksan–Wet'suwet'en would, on the one hand, be momentous and perhaps facilitate their political desires; but, on the other hand, it could not grant or fulfill these desires.

When the Supreme Court of Canada's Appeal decision was released, it was greeted with enthusiasm on the part of almost all commentators, both because it overturned the much criticized original decision and because it broke new ground in jurisprudence regarding Indigenous issues, in particular Aboriginal title. In light of this enthusiasm as well as Satsan's comments— which, although they were made after the initial decision, are very relevant to an evaluation of the final one as well—the Appeal decision is obviously important. It is to that I turn next.

The Appeal: paradoxes of sovereignty

In the Supreme Court of Canada's Appeal decision, authored by Chief Justice Lamer, five major issues were taken to be at stake:

> The principal issues on the Appeal, some of which raised a number of sub-issues, were as follows: (1) whether the pleadings precluded the court from entertaining claims for aboriginal title and self-government; (2) what was the ability of this court to interfere with the factual findings made by the trial judge; (3) what is the content of aboriginal title, how it is protected by s. 35(1), and what is required for its proof; (4) whether the appellants made out a claim to self-government; and, (5) whether the province had the power to extinguish aboriginal rights after 1871, either under its own jurisdiction or through the operation of s. 88 of the Indian Act.
>
> (*Delgamuukw*, 1997: 3)

The finding of the Supreme Court was that the Appeal should be allowed, and that there should be a new trial. It found that while the pleadings were properly before the court, there was a defect in them which prevented a determination of the claim to Aboriginal title or self-government.[25] It also found that while the court could not interfere with the findings of fact on the part of the trial judge, the trial judge had used inappropriate criteria to evaluate the validity of the evidence before him, thus his findings could not stand. Because of these findings, and because the trial was too complex for the Supreme Court to use the records to come to a new decision about the above issues, a new trial was ordered. The reasons for judgment went on to outline some of the considerations which should be taken into account in the new trial.[26]

As the issues posed by the Appeal suggest, however, the implications of the Supreme Court's decision will reverberate much more widely than only in the new trial. This is because the case provided the opportunity for the Supreme Court to clarify the jurisprudential issues around Aboriginal title. Since the inclusion in the Constitution of Section 35(1), which recognized and affirmed existing Aboriginal and treaty rights, the necessity of developing Canadian jurisprudence to recognize, define, and protect these rights had become increasingly apparent and was proceeding apace. This case, according to Chief Justice Lamer, was simply the next step in the process of developing this jurisprudence.[27] The most significant implications of the decision flow from its recognition and definition of Aboriginal title, the tests for identification and justification of title, and the guidelines it sets out for the kinds of evidence that may be considered for these purposes. In terms of the Gitksan and Wet'suwet'en, the Appeal decision does not recognize their claim to Aboriginal title, but does set out the parameters under which that claim might be evaluated. Both because these parameters will determine the future success or failure of the Gitksan and Wet'suwet'en claims, and because they will define jurisprudence for all other Aboriginal peoples who make these claims, I begin my analysis with them.

Chief Justice Lamer's judgment is consistently guided by the principle of reconciliation.[28] It reads the inclusion of Section 35(1) in the Constitution as forcing a reconciliation of the prior presence of Aboriginal communities in North America with the assertion of British, and later Canadian, sovereignty over the same territory (*Delgamuukw*, 1997: 79). This reliance on the logic and principle of reconciliation, importantly, shifts attention away from the tangle of assumptions that grounded the original decision. Rather than passing judgment on the historical treatment of Indigenous peoples—requiring engagement with questions about their social and political systems, relative levels of "development," and so on—the emphasis shifts to the question of what procedures should be used now to recognize Aboriginal claims and to reconcile them with existing legal/sovereign discourse. The question faced by the court on these terms is thus not one of competing sovereignties; the sovereignty of the Crown is the assumed ground upon which Aboriginal title comes to have meaning: "Aboriginal title is a burden on the Crown's underlying title" (*Delgamuukw*, 1997: 80). Although it is the prior inhabitation of the land and the pre-existing social systems that legitimate the claim to title, the authority of recognition of that title rests entirely with the Crown/sovereign, and the challenge resides in reconciling these claims with that authority. In other words, because Canada has committed itself to recognition and reconciliation in the Constitution, Canada (the Supreme Court, in this instance) must now develop a way to do this. What is not at issue, however, is Canadian sovereignty.[29]

Thus by comparison with the original decision's refusal to consider seriously the claims to authority of the Gitksan–Wet'suwet'en, the Appeal decision looks much more progressive: it acknowledges that Aboriginal peoples have legitimate claims, that these claims have leverage in the legal structures of the Canadian state, and it takes on the challenge of determining under what conditions and through what processes they can be realized. Crucially, though, the precondition for this approach is the assumption of the sovereignty of Canada. In other words, the Appeal decision does not throw sovereignty into question any further than did the original: it reinforces Canadian sovereignty as the ground upon which the claim to title will come to have meaning. What it does do is consider how to carve out a "special" status within that sovereignty that would acknowledge some of the claims to "difference" of Aboriginal peoples. The principle of reconciliation thus enables an evasion of some of the explicit violences of "civilization" apparent in the first decision, and in Tocqueville, but does so by reinscribing a more firm hierarchy of authority: by limiting the challenges posed by Aboriginal claims and reinforcing the inevitability and neutrality of the ground of sovereignty. The question at stake is not who has sovereignty over the territory in question, but on what terms the sovereign—Canada—will recognize and facilitate the continuation of forms of Aboriginal authority within and contingent upon Canadian sovereignty.

At the centre of the Appeal decision is thus an elegant reframing of the problem as it had been understood in the original decision. Its elegance rests in the simultaneous opening of potential for Indigenous claims and careful bracketing of that potential. The irony is that, unlike the original decision, it actually refuses to recognize the claims as they were posed by the Gitksan and Wet'suwet'en: claims for sovereignty. The decision thus reframes the legal and political terrain for Indigenous peoples, offering them much more than had been apparent before, at the cost of relinquishing or putting into abeyance the totality of their claims. It is an archetypical practice of sovereignty, with all of the ambivalence that should now be familiar. The ambiguity it presents to Indigenous peoples should not be underestimated. It may seem, from what has gone before, that it is a "trap" for Indigenous peoples, in that it clearly requires forms of compromise: in particular in relation to the constitutive ground or ontology that enables authority. But to read it primarily in this way is both strategically and conceptually problematic; it is, ironically, to reproduce the mythology of sovereignty by holding out for a kind of perfection that has never existed, and to potentially reproduce the kinds of closures discussed in Chapter 5. The question remains, though, of how to read it. As with all practices of sovereignty, the effects of this one will rest primarily in its instantiation. It seeks to produce a political terrain, but the character and effects of that terrain will depend upon how it is engaged and negotiated. The initial terms of this engagement are laid out in the particulars of the decision, and the rest of this chapter will explore and briefly evaluate these, seeking to illustrate both the potential and dangers contained within the particular terrain produced by the practice of sovereignty in this decision. It focuses especially on the definition, character, and criteria for recognition of Aboriginal title.[30]

As discussed above, the crucial principle guiding the recognition and defin-ition of Aboriginal title in the decision is that of reconciliation. According to the decision, the process of reconciliation must involve not only a recognition of Aboriginal rights of access to land and resources, issues the court had already developed jurisprudence on, but also pre-existing social and political structures of Aboriginal peoples. Aboriginal title falls into this latter category; it is not simply the assertion of a right to use the land, but the assertion of a complex social and cultural relationship to land, an assertion of a relationship of authority in relation to territory:

> I first consider the source of aboriginal title. As I discussed earlier, aboriginal title arises from the prior occupation of Canada by aboriginal peoples. That prior occupation is relevant in two different ways: first, because of the physical fact of occupation, and second, because aboriginal title originates in part from pre-existing systems of aboriginal law. However, the law of aboriginal title does not only seek to determine the historic rights of aboriginal peoples to land; it also seeks to afford legal protection to prior occupation in the present-day. Implicit in the protection of historic patterns of occupation is a recognition of the importance of the continuity of the relationship of an aboriginal community to its land over time.
>
> (*Delgamuukw*, 1997: 72)

These sources lead to an understanding of Aboriginal title as unique in the legal system, as "*sui generis*" rather than as a variation on existing forms of title, such as fee simple (*Delgamuukw*, 1997: 6), thus reinforcing the necessity of new jurisprudence in relation to it. The characterization of Aboriginal title in the decision reflects this complex background:

> Although the courts have been less than forthcoming, I have arrived at the conclusion that the content of aboriginal title can be summarized by two propositions: first, that aboriginal title encompasses the right to exclusive use and occupation of the land held pursuant to that title for a variety of purposes, which need not be aspects of those aboriginal practices, customs and traditions which are integral to distinctive aboriginal cultures; and second, that those protected uses must not be irreconcilable with the nature of that group's attachment to that land.
>
> (*Delgamuukw*, 1997: 68; see also 6)

A few things are immediately striking about this definition. First, it is crucial that this definition of title does not limit the activities covered by Aboriginal title to those which are constituted as "traditional," precisely because what is being recognized is a set of social and political institutions that shape a relationship to the land. This recognizes the need for dynamism and change. At the same time, however, it contains a fundamental limitation on title: the uses of the land must not jeopardize the nature of the group's attachment to the land. This limitation on title again emerges from the principle of reconciliation, in particular from the necessity of the Constitution to provide protection for Aboriginal title into the future:

The relevance of the continuity of the relationship of an aboriginal community with its land here is that it applies not only to the past, but to the future as well. That relationship should not be prevented from continuing into the future. As a result, uses of the lands that would threaten that future relationship are, by their very nature, excluded from the content of aboriginal title.

(*Delgamuukw*, 1997: 72)

Embedded in the definition of Aboriginal title are thus sovereign obligations, not least the obligation to ensure that the purpose of Aboriginal title is maintained. The meaning and limits of Aboriginal title are thus not determined by Aboriginal political structures, but by the sovereign's perception of those structures and their meanings, the relationships they produce. Although, as the decision emphasizes, the "limitations arise from the nature of aboriginal title," the *meaning* of those limitations is determined by the sovereign:

Accordingly, in my view, lands subject to aboriginal title cannot be put to such uses as may be irreconcilable with the nature of the occupation of that land and the relationship that the particular group has had with the land which together have given rise to aboriginal title in the first place. . . . It seems to me that these elements of aboriginal title create an inherent limitation on the uses to which the land, over which such title exists, may be put. For example, if occupation is established with reference to the use of the land as a hunting ground, then the group that successfully claims aboriginal title to that land may not use it in such a fashion as to destroy its value for such a use (e.g. by strip mining it). Similarly, if a group claims a special bond with the land because of its ceremonial or cultural significance, it may not use the land in such a way as to destroy that relationship (e.g., by developing it in such a way that the bond is destroyed, perhaps by turning it into a parking lot).

(*Delgamuukw*, 1997: 73; see also 7)

In the same gesture as recognition of Aboriginal title, its limits are circumscribed and—more importantly—the authority for determining those limits is granted to the sovereign. The paradoxical structure of the authority the court grants Aboriginal title begins to emerge: on the one hand, it is an "exclusive" right, not limited to traditional uses of the land; on the other hand it *is* constrained by the *sovereign*'s perception of the traditional relationship between culture and land or territory.

The paradoxical nature of this resolution of the question of the authority invested in Aboriginal title resonates throughout the rest of the decision. For example, regarding whether or not Aboriginal title can be alienated, on the one hand: "It is for this reason also that the lands held by virtue of aboriginal title may not be alienated. Alienation would bring to an end the entitlement of the aboriginal people to occupy the land and would terminate their relationship with it" (*Delgamuukw*, 1997: 73). On the other:

> Finally, what I have just said regarding the importance of the continuity of the relationship between an aboriginal community and its land, and the non-economic or inherent value of that land, should not be taken to detract from the possibility of surrender to the Crown in exchange for valuable consideration. On the contrary, the idea of surrender reinforces the conclusion that aboriginal title is limited in the way I have described. If aboriginal peoples wish to use their lands in a way that aboriginal title does not permit, then they must surrender those lands and convert them into non-title lands to do so.
>
> (*Delgamuukw*, 1997: 74)

So, on the one hand, lands held by virtue of Aboriginal title cannot be alienated, as this would by definition be to terminate the unique cultural and social relationship to land that the Constitution has pledged to protect. On the other hand, if the holders of Aboriginal title wish to be free to develop the land as they would be if they were holders of "fee simple" title, they have to relinquish this relationship to the Crown before proceeding. In this case, then, the Crown would facilitate the termination of the special title and relationship to territory, the special relationship to territory the court is obligated to protect. Everything thus hinges on the determination of the parameters of the relationship between any given Aboriginal group and its territory, and this determination is ultimately subject to the authority of the sovereign, not the group. They are, in a sense, free to be who they wish as long as the sovereign agrees that it is appropriate to their special status.

This paradox is compounded further by the analysis of whether Aboriginal title can be infringed upon by federal or provincial governments. The conclusion reached is that it can be infringed upon, although such infringement would have to pass a two-part test of justification. First, it would have to be in furtherance of a legislative objective that is substantial and compelling (*Delgamuukw*, 1997: 88). Second, it must be consistent with the special fiduciary relationship between Crown and Aboriginal peoples (*Delgamuukw*, 1997: 88–89). A test for infringement will always be complex and highly contextual. However, the decision provides examples of what might be valid bases for infringement:

> In the wake of *Gladstone*, the range of legislative objectives that can justify the infringement of aboriginal title is fairly broad. Most of these objectives can be traced to the *reconciliation* of the prior occupation of North America by aboriginal peoples with the assertion of Crown sovereignty, which entails the recognition that "distinctive aboriginal societies exist within, and are a part of, a broader social, political and economic community" (at para. 73). In my opinion, the development of

agriculture, forestry, mining, and hydroelectric power, the general economic development of the interior of British Columbia, protection of
the environment or endangered species, the building of infrastructure
and the settlement of foreign populations to support these aims, are the
kinds of objectives that are consistent with this purpose, and, in principle, can justify the infringement of aboriginal title.

(*Delgamuukw*, 1997: 91; emphasis in original)

Thus, though holders of Aboriginal title cannot develop the land in a manner
incompatible with their relationship to it, the sovereign can. In some cases the
infringement might be justified by giving Aboriginal peoples a greater share
of the benefits arising from the infringement; in some cases it might be
enough to involve Aboriginal peoples in the decision making process, as long
as this is done "in good faith" (*Delgamuukw*, 1997: 92).

Again, then, Aboriginal title is being recognized because of the commitment on the part of the sovereign (in the *Constitution Act*) to reconcile their
previous inhabitation of the land with the assertion of Canadian sovereignty.
This means in principle that the Constitution is committed to protecting
Aboriginal title, even to the extent that it can prevent (by forcing title to be
relinquished) certain uses of the land because they are in violation of what it
perceives to be the relationship appropriate to Aboriginal title. However, this
commitment to protect Aboriginal title is itself limited in that it exists within
a range of other Constitutional commitments. Aboriginal title can thus be
infringed upon when the government can show that this infringement is
for the benefit of a broad section of its population. This argument for
justification is particularly chilling given that the historical infringement of
Aboriginal title in fact has indeed benefited the "general interest" enormously; arguably the Canadian economy has always been grounded in and
enabled by the exploitation of resources which would presumably fall under
Aboriginal title. While the decision might enforce the necessity of "compensation" or "consultation" in relation to these, it definitely does not suggest
that Aboriginal title should presume primacy in these determinations. This
element of the decision thus illustrates the ambiguity of Aboriginal title for
Indigenous peoples: its simultaneous promise and danger. The promise rests
in the potential status and leverage Aboriginal title might grant to Aboriginal
societies, status that might make a significant difference to their capacity
for self-determination. The same gesture, however, appears to leave the
underlying structures of authority—the same structures which have facilitated their dispossession—intact, in fact strengthened insofar as the gesture
of recognition grants a greater level of legitimacy to Canadian sovereignty.

Practice: the terrain of negotiation

The ambivalent potential contained in the decision will be worked out in
practice, most crucially perhaps in the negotiation of the meaning and effects

of Aboriginal title itself. The decision details three criteria for the recognition of Aboriginal title. First, the land must have been occupied by the Aboriginal group at the time when the Crown asserted sovereignty over the land (*Delgamuukw*, 1997: 79). Second, if present occupation is relied on as proof of occupation pre-sovereignty, there must be a continuity between present and pre-sovereignty occupation (*Delgamuukw*, 1997: 83). Third, at sovereignty, that occupation must have been exclusive, although this exclusivity might be shared between two neighboring communities (*Delgamuukw*, 1997: 85). These criteria immediately suggest the crucial role that evaluation of evidence will play in the determination of Aboriginal title, as the evidence necessary to fulfill these criteria often exists exclusively in forms that were to a large extent discredited in the original decision. The parameters of Aboriginal title will prove irrelevant, of course, if the claiming of it is made impossible due to the criteria of evaluation of the claims.

Alert to this problem, the Appeal decision devotes careful attention to the use of evidence in the original decision, in the process setting out the parameters that should be used to evaluate such evidence in the future. It is especially critical of the treatment of oral histories in the original decision. Although supportive of the decision to admit oral histories as evidence, the Appeal decision is critical of the failure to give these histories virtually any weight at all as evidence, except insofar as they could confirm other forms of factual evidence. Chief Justice Lamer points out that the characteristics of the evidence presented by the Gitksan and Wet'suwet'en that McEachern C.J. felt rendered it invalid are characteristics of all oral histories. Thus if his criteria were authorized, Chief Justice Lamer argues, all oral histories would be rendered invalid as evidence. This runs contrary to earlier Supreme Court decisions, in particular *Van der Peet* (*Delgamuukw*, 1997: 60–61). To reinforce the necessity of negotiating the challenges posed by different forms of evidence, Chief Justice Lamer reiterates the necessary adaptation to laws of evidence contained in his decision in the *Van der Peet* case. Not surprisingly, it is the principle of reconciliation that Lamer C.J. turns to in order to guide these efforts, arguing that true reconciliation requires taking into account the perspective of both Aboriginal peoples and the common law, placing weight on each: "[t]rue reconciliation will, equally, place weight on each" (*Delgamuukw*, 1997: 54). What is required, consequently, is an adaptation to the rules of evidence to enable this, and what should guide this adaptation is a sensitivity to the specific characteristics of evidence that emerges from Aboriginal cultures. The aspiration should be to "equally, place weight on each" form of evidence, evaluating Aboriginal evidence as much as possible from "the perspective of aboriginal peoples." This apparently simple aspiration, of course, conceals a truly challenging project: given that the court is enabled by authority grounded in a specific ontology, which already determines its necessary epistemology (as encoded in the rules of evidence), and given that—as we have seen not least from the argument of the Gitksan and Wet'suwet'en—Aboriginal claims necessarily challenge this epistemology, the task of reconciling these two forms of evidence is anything but straight-forward. Giving it serious consideration is certainly possible, but to "equally, place weight on each" might require throwing into question much more than Chief Justice Lamer is willing to allow:

> In other words, although the doctrine of aboriginal rights is a common law doctrine, aboriginal rights are truly *sui generis*, and demand a unique approach to the treatment of evidence which accords due weight to the perspective of aboriginal peoples. *However, that accommodation must be done in a manner which does not strain "the Canadian legal and constitutional structure."*
>
> (*Delgamuukw*, 1997: 54; emphasis mine)

Thus on the one hand the aspiration of Chief Justice Lamer here is clearly on the side of the angels: the court should be respectful of cultural difference and not discount Aboriginal cultures because they do not meet conventional standards for epistemological validity. On the other hand, this aspiration is clearly bounded by the injunction that this project itself should take place within a predetermined ground. This ground, of course, is the ground of sovereignty. In this way this injunction gives the well-intentioned judge a basis upon which to grant unprecedented legitimacy to Aboriginal cultures, epistemologies, claims. At precisely the same time, however, it carefully reserves the authority of the *judge* (who is authorized by a particular ontology) to make that judgment, and limits the ability of any judge to make that judgment in such a way that it "strains the Canadian legal and constitutional structure."

The implications of the reservation of the authority of the judge become clearer as Chief Justice Lamer proceeds. Although the decision in *Van der Peet* requires judges to consider Aboriginal forms of evidence on their own terms, Lamer C.J. is insistent that this does not mean that appellants can challenge a trial judge's findings of fact simply because they disagree with them (*Delgamuukw*, 1997: 57–58). Nor can higher courts. As in this case, if the trial judge has not followed proper procedure in evaluating the evidence, the court can dismiss findings of fact. However, if proper procedure is followed, the findings of fact cannot be challenged (*Delgamuukw*, 1997: 64). This, of course, is what leads him to reiterate these procedures in the decision. However, he is very careful to warn the appellants: "In applying these principles, the new trial judge might well share some or all of the findings of fact of McEachern C.J." (*Delgamuukw*, 1997: 64). In one step, then, Chief Justice Lamer overturns much of what in McEachern's decision was so objectionable: in this case the extraordinary ethnocentrism. At the same time, he does so without denying the *authority* of the judge to come to the conclusions that he did. Much resides, thus, in the practical negotiation of what will count as evidence, and how that evidence will be counted. In many ways, this brings us back to Hobbes: the real substance through which authority is constituted is that of ontological and epistemological resonance: the negotiations at this site will determine much of the meaning of Aboriginal title, and, indeed, of Canadian sovereignty.

Conclusions?

The Supreme Court of Canada's decision on the Appeal, no less than the original decision, thus effects a practice of sovereignty, albeit one that offers considerably more space for negotiation for Indigenous peoples in Canada. In a gesture that should be familiar to us now, it simultaneously opens and constrains spaces of possibility for Indigenous peoples. The spaces that it opens are political, explicitly so. The decision concludes with a statement that, despite the court ordering a new trial in the case, a better arena for the resolution of the issues raised is one of good faith negotiations between all parties:

> Ultimately, it is through negotiated settlements, with good faith and give and take on all sides, reinforced by the judgments of this court, that we will achieve what I stated in *Van der Peet*, *supra*, at para. 31, to be a basic purpose of s. 35(1)—"the reconciliation of the pre-existence of abo-riginal societies with the sovereignty of the Crown." Let us face it, we are all here to stay.
>
> (*Delgamuukw*, 1997: 101)

The decision of the Supreme Court thus reframes the political space of nego-tiation, providing guidance and reference points, while leaving open the range of possibilities within. The decision has resettled the relationship between law and politics here, responding to the disruption of resonance effected first by the claim itself and again by McEachern C.J.'s decision, by reframing the problem, reasserting a possible terrain of resonance.

But how shall we evaluate this terrain? This is a difficult question, and one that will ultimately be worked out in practice. As is emphasized in the analysis above, however, there is considerable reason for caution. Chief Justice Lam-er's (Bull's, Clastres') is a less violent gesture than McEachern's (Toc-queville's), but they can be read as variations on the same theme. While these variations matter, if we focus on them to the exclusion of the practices of sovereignty that enable and link them, we run the risk of missing much of the political terrain we must engage. Most crucially, we run the risk of forgetting the underlying violences effected by practices of sovereignty. This in turn risks a reproduction of them: behind and enabling every Bull or Lamer rests the necessities of a Hobbes or McEachern. Chief Justice Lamer knows he must enforce the legitimacy of the sovereign—the capacity of Chief Justice McEachern to decide—if not all of his decisions.

So is the implication of all of this that the Supreme Court's decision is not a victory for the Gitksan and Wet'suwet'en, that the recognition of

Aboriginal title is not a cause for celebration for Canada's First Nations? To come to such a conclusion would be to oversimplify the situation significantly. The Supreme Court's decision does open new spaces and possibilities for Aboriginal jurisprudence, offering leverage to Aboriginal claims and new legitimacy to some of their arguments. Particularly interesting in this regard is the way that it carefully reinforces the need to struggle with the challenges posed by the ontological and epistemological differences between Aboriginal peoples and the courts. As we know from Hobbes, it is the enforced resonance at the level of ontology and epistemology that has facilitated the worst violences of sovereignty. It is thus difficult to underestimate the importance of the practical struggle over the conditions under which ontological and epistemological claims will be authorized. One of the important successes of the decision, thus, rests in its insistence that this terrain must remain open to negotiation. In this way it resists the closures effected by Hobbes' architecture of sovereignty, which sought to carefully constrain the terrain of politics to the negotiation of relations between preconstituted subjects and the sovereign. Perhaps despite itself, in resisting this closure, the Supreme Court has provided a narrow opening to a negotiation of ontology and epistemology, to the negotiation of the enabling resonance of sovereignty. Further, it urges this negotiation towards the realm of politics, and away from the precise constraints of the courtroom. Potential and danger for Indigenous peoples reside intertwined here, and their balance remains to be worked out. I return to these challenges in Part III.

7 Limits

James Tully and the politics of theory

discussive practice

As previous chapters suggest, Indigenous movements pose challenges to contemporary political theory. Although theorists such as Hobbes and Tocqueville had no direct hand in Indigenous peoples' treatment, the concepts, principles, and logics of their arguments, the political structures they produced, legitimated, and defended, were responsible for shaping and legitimating the treatment of Indigenous peoples. To be clear, a direct line of causality here is less important than the resonances across contexts: political theory expressed and legitimated what was possible and desirable. As such, it is implicated, and is itself a key site of engagement: violences and limitations of inherited concepts and institutions must be revealed and explained, and other visions of what is possible and desirable must be articulated. This is a necessary part of the process of change, and how it is executed matters. Until we can imagine better, less repressive and violent, practices of sovereignty— practices through which we can produce legitimate forms of authority—we will remain trapped within the logics and necessities of those we have inherited.

Many political theorists have recognized and responded to this challenge. Some of the most important trends in contemporary political theory, for example, have centered around efforts to respond to the challenges posed by the institutional accommodation of cultural difference. Whether in the form of a politics of recognition, policies of multiculturalism, a renewed constitutionalism, or a rearticulation of rights discourse or principles of justice, a range of important efforts have been made to articulate principles upon which, or procedures through which, the challenge of cultural difference might be met within the context of the liberal democratic state. While these efforts have opened important new terrain, and have indeed had substantial impact on the formulation of responses to challenges of cultural difference at many sites, difficult tensions and awkward situations continue to arise.

Partly through and in relation to these difficult tensions and awkward situations, this chapter examines the limits of these responses, and the broader implications of these limits. Specifically, it does so through a reading of the work of James Tully, the theorist who has most seriously and productively struggled with the particular challenges Indigenous peoples' political claims pose to attempts to construct more pluralist forms of constitutional democracy. Tully is part of a broader "Canadian" school of pluralist political thought—including Charles Taylor (1993, 1994; Tully, 1994) and Will Kymlicka (1989, 1995, 1998), among others—concerned with problems of regionalism, multiculturalism, and Québec nationalism. Although grounded in and informed by specifically Canadian contexts, their work proceeds in close dialogue with American theorists—such as Benhabib (1995, 2002, 2004), Connolly (1991, 1995, 2005), Rawls (1971, 1993), Sandel (1982), Walzer (1983, 1987), and Young (1990, 2000)—engaged with questions of "difference" in contemporary constitutional democracies. Together, these theorists have had a major influence internationally on the conceptualization of and possibilities for responding to the challenges posed by the institutional accommodation of cultural difference. In what follows, I examine James Tully's work as an illustrative example of the potential and limitations of contemporary political theorists' engagement with the kinds of challenges posed by Indigenous politics. My purpose in doing so is to sketch a terrain of negotiation: to develop a sense of what is at stake in how political theory responds to these challenges.

Contexts of/and political theory

Much of James Tully's work has focused on developing an approach to political philosophy that throws light on the present through contextual studies of the history of modern political thought. Following Quentin Skinner, he pursues close readings of key texts of modern political thought in their historical context (Tully, 1988). Resisting either a strictly textualist or contextualist approach, Tully, like Skinner, claims that the meaning of a text can best be determined by understanding it in relation to the linguistic and political context in and to which the author wrote. By using his historical research to develop a thorough understanding of a text in its context, he also seeks to reveal limitations and advantages of using these texts to frame contemporary problems. In the process, he hopes to open possibilities for thinking differently about our own political dilemmas (Tully, 1993: 1–2). Tully's work thus can be read as an attempt to loosen the contemporary context of political discussion by denaturalizing it, by showing the specifics of how this context has come to be and suggesting ways of recontextualizing political problems. His approach is an attempt to bring together what he sees as the strengths of political philosophy and the history of political thought, using them to complement one another in coming to understand both historical texts and contemporary political questions.

This approach is exemplified in "Rediscovering America: The *Two Treatises* and Aboriginal Rights" (Tully, 1993: 137–79), in which Tully relocates Locke's *Two Treatises* in a historical context that includes Indigenous peoples and politics, using this context to explain and illuminate some aspects of Locke's work as well as to challenge the uncritical use of Locke to frame contemporary discussions of Indigenous politics.[1] Tully argues that while the *Treatises* are appropriate to represent many contemporary political problems, they are insufficient as a basis for discussions of two of them: Indigenous self-government and ecology. In fact, they are not only insufficient, they are also inappropriate because Locke constructs and defines the core concepts of his theory of popular sovereignty—political society and property—in direct opposition to the Indigenous forms of nationhood and property with which he was familiar. By reading Locke's text in its historical context, Tully is able to use historical evidence to argue that Locke misrepresents Indigenous societies, and, further, that the misrepresentation is intentional.

> Indeed, the very manner in which Locke arranged these concepts causes a reader to overlook the way European concepts of political society and property are imposed over and subsume Amerindian nations and property (thus foreshadowing what was to occur to a large extent in practice in the following centuries).
>
> (Tully, 1993: 140)

Tully documents numerous examples of the kinds of information about Native Americans to which Locke had access, and makes a very persuasive case that Locke's was a deliberate misrepresentation for the purposes of illustrating his theories and justifying their dispossession (Tully, 1993: 151). Accurate representation, Tully argues, was not Locke's goal: "In using these concepts in this way Locke was intervening in one of the major political and ideological contests of the seventeenth century" (Tully, 1993: 139).

Tully's article goes on to develop the significance of Locke's misrepresentation in much more depth, both by tracing the effects it might have had in relation to the treatment of Indigenous peoples at various sites and by exploring other texts which represented Indigenous societies more accurately. However, this statement about the way in which Locke's representation of Indigenous societies was shaped—in order to intervene in one of the major political and ideological contests of his time—poses an important set of questions about the politics of political theory, about the relationship between our explicit purposes in writing texts and their broader political effects. For Tully, despite Locke's deliberate misrepresentation of Indigenous peoples, and the devastating effects such misrepresentations have enabled, this misrepresentation does not undermine the value of Locke's work on other counts: it remains appropriate to discuss other contemporary political problems, just not those involving Indigenous sovereignty and ecology. By arguing that the detrimental effects of Locke's arguments on Indigenous peoples should be traced to his misrepresentation of them, rather than to the assumptions that enable Locke's argument or the structures of the argument, Tully effectively rescues Locke's ideas from a much more damaging critique. If the explicit racism and ethnocentrism in early-modern texts is a symptom of a larger problem rather than the source of the problem, Tully's analysis and response can only be partial at best, and carry their own dangers insofar as they function to bury the problem more deeply. So, for example, it could be argued that as the argument put forth in the *Treatises* is constructed in opposition to a (mis)representation of Indigenous communities, thus effectively excluding them and their institutions from consideration in this argument, the use of this argument to frame other contemporary political problems must exclude their perspectives as well. To problematize Locke's views on Indigenous political institutions and ecology is to raise questions not only about the framing of "difference" in pluralism but also about representation and community.

Tully chooses to overlook this latter possibility, instead reading Locke against himself: revealing the misrepresentation and arguing that if we correct it, Locke's argument adequately protects Indigenous peoples, even providing them with justification for defending their rights and property, by force if necessary (Tully, 1993: 175). As this suggests, the intervention effected by his analysis is thus no less political than Locke's original one: he, like Locke, is using concepts in the way he is in order to intervene in one of the major political and ideological contests of his time. In so doing he, like Locke, is reproducing a particular idea about the scope and character of political possibility in contemporary circumstances. This, of course, is true of all contemporary political theory, with disagreements amongst theorists often emerging from differences in their assumed understanding of politics, although they tend to explicitly play out in relation to apparently different themes. In the rest of this chapter, I render Tully's assumed terrain of politics more explicit, in order to raise the question of its political stakes. After all, Tully, like Locke, might effectively "win" his political and ideological contest, but, as was the case with Locke, the contest he wins might have problematic implications for others, including those whose claims he seeks to address. Given that Tully's assumptions about the political are conventional—albeit not uncontested—within contemporary political theory, this may have much broader implications as well.

Strange Multiplicity: decolonizing constitutional dialogue

Closely following Tully's book on Locke is *Strange Multiplicity*, a work more directly framed by concerns of the present, in which he uses a similar method of reading the history of political thought to see his way through a contemporary impasse. This work marks a departure from his earlier work: rather than being primarily concerned with locating a work of political theory within its historical context in order to illuminate its meaning more appropriately and only secondarily using this analysis to shed light on contemporary political dilemmas, his project here is reversed. He begins with a contemporary problem and reaches back into the history of political thought to unearth tools to more effectively respond to it. In so doing, he departs from Skinner's more resolutely historical method, and it is in this departure that some of the problems I seek to identify emerge. Such a reversal raises one of the central problems addressed by Skinner's historical method: the problem of "time travel" or anachronism. It is one thing to argue that putting a text in historical context allows for a "better" (or at least an important kind of) understanding of the meaning of the text, as Skinner does. It is another thing to bring that understanding into the present and deploy it in relation to contemporary political struggles; the present context is, after all, no more transparent than the past. The dangers of anachronism—particularly in relation to assumptions about the space and character of the political—in this context are in part what I seek to emphasize here.

The question to which *Strange Multiplicity* is addressed is: "Can a modern constitution recognize and accommodate cultural diversity?" We are entering into an age of cultural diversity, Tully argues, and it is the political challenge of the day to figure out how to engage the challenges to political institutions and modes of thought that are posed by this. He uses six examples of contemporary political movements to illustrate why the question of the age is posed by the problem of the recognition of cultural diversity. The examples include claims of nationalist movements to be either nation-states or autonomous units; the pressures on existing nation-states to recognize and accommodate larger units such as the EU and North American Free Trade Agreement (NAFTA); claims advanced by linguistic and ethnic minorities within states or larger units for constitutional recognition; "intercultural" demands of citizens, immigrants, exiles, refugees; claims from feminist movements seeking recognition of women's culturally distinct ways of speaking and acting; and, finally, the political claims of 250 million Indigenous people who seek justice and self-government. Although generally these different kinds of political movements are analyzed separately, Tully argues that there are three crucial similarities that enable them to be thought of as forming a coherent challenge to contemporary constitutionalism. First, all these demands for cultural recognition are aspirations for appropriate forms of self-government. Although the *forms* of self-rule will vary, these movements express a shared desire to rule themselves in accord with their customs and ways. Second, all argue that the basic laws and institutions of modern societies and their authoritative traditions of interpretation are unjust insofar as they fail to recognize cultural diversity. Third, the similarity in the ground of both the aspiration to culturally appropriate forms of self-rule and the claim of injustice illustrates the shared assumption that culture is an irreducible and constitutive aspect of politics. Thus, this range of movements poses the question of the day for Tully, and it is a question of governance, of how we can develop forms of governance that recognize and affirm a range of cultural diversity that our current languages and forms of government cannot. The challenge we face is the insertion of the category of "culture" into our institutions of governance, ensuring that our institutions "recognize" this element of politics.

His focus is on whether contemporary constitutionalism, in particular, can be reshaped to recognize this element of politics. He argues that the dominant languages of contemporary constitutionalism have been unable to respond to these calls because of the ways in which constitutional language has developed from early modernity on: with the "Empire of Uniformity" as its goal. However, he argues that these are not the only languages we can call on to address this problem. While the modern languages of constitutionalism were developed during the modern age of imperialism, hence their aspiration towards an "Empire of Uniformity," these languages have also been appropriated in anti-imperial struggles and they have histories that predate imperialism, all of which can be mined for other ways of thinking and talking about constitutionalism that may open more space for the recognition of cultural diversity. In order to engage the problems posed by the "Empire of Uniformity," we not only have to reveal it as what it is, a "partial forgery" that enforces the exclusion of other ways of thinking about constitutionalism, we also have to change the way we do political philosophy. We have to move away from the dominant languages and methods of addressing political problems, which depend upon "monological" reasoning and trace their history to the likes of Thomas Hobbes, and towards the "dialogical" style of reasoning developed by Wittgenstein and illustrated historically by one of Hobbes' interlocutors, Chief Justice Matthew Hale: "The great tragedy of the modern constitutionalism is that most European philosophers followed Hobbes and turned their backs on dialogue just when non-European peoples were encountered and dialogue and mediation were needed to avert the misunderstanding and inhumanity that followed" (Tully, 1995: 116). Tully's project turns to trying to unearth and develop alternate responses to the problem of cultural diversity by assembling other contexts and examples to draw on when talking about constitutionalism, as his reading of Wittgenstein suggests. Much of the text thus draws on these alternate responses to cultural diversity in order to develop a renewed set of conventions for constitutional dialogue, ones that would enable the recognition and satisfaction of the demands posed by cultural diversity.

Read through this history, challenges for recognition today can be seen not as rejections of constitutionalism but as the extension of common constitutionalism, the revival of its anti-imperial aspects. In response to his opening question of whether a modern constitution can recognize and accommodate cultural diversity, Tully concludes:

> [A] contemporary constitution can recognise cultural diversity if it is conceived as a form of accommodation of cultural diversity. It should be seen as an activity, an intercultural dialogue in which the culturally diverse sovereign citizens of contemporary societies negotiate agreements on their ways of association over time in accord with the conventions of mutual recognition, consent and continuity.
>
> (Tully, 1995: 184)

Contemporary constitutionalism is thus just (once we have amended and abandoned the various aspects of modern constitutionalism that tend towards the erasure of cultural diversity) and worthy of engaging "because it furthers the liberty of self rule. Since there is no greater value in Western civilisation, and perhaps in any civilisation, this is no small recommendation for the vision presented here for your consideration" (Tully, 1995: 184–85). Constitutionalism has a long history, and though (or because) it is not grand theory, but rather a rich but humble conversation filled with exchanges from near and far, with choices made and lessons learned as it goes along, it provides a basis for dialogue into the twenty-first century:

> Hence, in this post-imperial view of constitutionalism the value of progress is also preserved and transformed. Progress is not the ascent out of the ancient cultural assemblage until one reaches the imaginary uniform modern republic, from which one ranks and judges the less developed others on the rungs far below. Rather, it consists in learning to recognise, converse with and be mutually accommodating to the culturally diverse neighbours in the city we inhabit here and now.
>
> (Tully, 1995: 185–86)

Tully's vision is compelling. His approach enables him both to launch an important critique of the dominant schools of constitutionalism, and to do so in a way that develops the basis of another way of thinking and talking about constitutionalism. Rather than critiquing these discourses and dismissing their sources, he puts them in their place: a much broader, richer field of linguistic and political possibility than they represent. Perhaps most importantly, he does so without sacrificing the acuity and depth of the critique of the languages of modern constitutionalism.[2] There is no easy way out, no language that is free of imperialism, nor one that is exclusively imperial. Troublesome though they are, these languages are the starting point we—political theorists—must retrieve and incorporate into our negotiations. Until we understand how they have come to be, to frame our conceptions of political possibility, we cannot begin to think or act otherwise.

Reading the political: the assumption of sovereignty

Tully reads the question of the day as that of "the recognition of cultural diversity," and provides a vision of how a constitutional dialogue specifically, and political theory more generally, might proceed so as to enable this. His aspiration is towards a just form of collective self-rule. He argues that in order to achieve this, particular assumptions and conventions that guide modern constitutional theorists must be thrown into question. In the presentation of his own method, Tully argues that any such critical project must hold in place some background assumptions in order to challenge others. In the spirit of his attempt to denaturalize certain assumptions about what constitutes an appropriate constitutional dialogue in order to open possibilities for thinking differently about the problem of difference in contemporary constitutional societies, I pursue the question here of what background assumptions and conventions enable his project, and whether they might productively be thrown into question in order to more effectively address the challenges of the day.

Tully's analysis is enabled by an assumption about the locus and character of the political: the sovereign state is the locus of the political and political activity is expressed primarily through relations of governance.[3] This assumption is evident not only by his focus on constitutional dialogue as the site of response to such a wide variety of demands, but also on his interpretation of the character of those demands: as demands for the recognition of cultural specificity in relations of governance. This assumption is both conceptual—the crucial questions of how authority is constituted, expressed, bounded, and legitimated are all assumed to be resolved—and practical—such a process as Tully recommends is only feasible in a state where sovereignty is already secured. These are conventional assumptions; they are broadly reproduced by much contemporary political theory. Even theorists of pluralism, when they focus on relations of governance as the crucial site for the negotiation of questions of justice or equality, assume the resolution of the prior question of the constitution and bounding of the political space in which this negotiation takes place. Governance, and particularly the character of it (whether it expresses "self"-rule, what forms or modes of justice and equality it reproduces, and so on), is the question of the day, rather than sovereignty, or the constitution and legitimation of authority.

Tully reproduces these assumptions in part for strategic reasons: he, as he identified in relation to Locke, seeks to intervene in one of the major ideological and political conflicts of his time. *Strange Multiplicity* is directed towards audiences not only of constitutional and political theorists of pluralism, but also of policy makers in states such as Canada who are actively seeking to create procedures and mechanisms through which to accommodate the demands of their culturally diverse citizens. In order to intervene in these conflicts, he must to some extent reproduce the background agreement of these conflicts: the assumption of the state as the locus of and precondition for politics. Particularly given his audience of constitutional policy makers in Canada, this seems an obvious and unproblematic decision. However, as Tully persuasively documents in relation to Locke, although Locke's primary purpose was to intervene in an ideological and political conflict that had little explicitly to do with Indigenous peoples, his problematic representation of them was to have far-ranging implications for them, functioning as it did to legitimate policies and practices which were enormously destructive to their cultures, political institutions, and ways of life. In *Strange Multiplicity*, Tully—like Locke—represents Indigenous peoples, as well as other marginalized groups, this time by characterizing their political claims in an effort to craft a response to them. As he details so effectively in relation to Locke, Tully's assumptions about the character of the major ideological and political conflict he seeks to intervene in also shape his apprehension and representation of these claims. Although there might appear to be an obvious distinction to be made between the two—Tully is seeking explicitly to respond to these peoples' plights, Locke was interested in furthering a colonial project—I argue here that such a distinction may matter little in relation to the potential effects of the representation of Indigenous peoples. In what follows I pursue how the assumptions about the political that enable and ground his project shape his apprehension and representation of the claims of marginal groups, and what dangers this might pose to these groups. In the concluding section I will pursue what dangers it might pose in relation to political theory more generally.

Tully's primary aspiration in *Strange Multiplicity* is to respond to the question of whether a modern constitution can respond to the demands of citizens for recognition of their cultural diversity. His primary interest is in the capacities of modern constitutionalism, or indeed of the contemporary state, particularly in light of the challenges facing it. In order to pursue this interest, he had to take an enormously diverse set of claims and distill them down to a common demand: for the recognition of their cultural specificity. Evaluating the extent to which this is a legitimate reading of these diverse phenomena is beyond the scope of this chapter, but some dangers in the maneuver are worth drawing attention to. Perhaps most obviously, the maneuver immediately distills a complex set of demands to a singular relationship—the relationship between citizens and a sovereign authority, or constitutional state. Such a distillation removes from consideration a range of issues or problems which may not be able to appear in this relationship, imposing a very particular scope and character on political possibility. In so doing it also reinscribes a familiar set of assumptions about political subjectivities, so familiar that they are never explicitly spelled out in his analysis. To assume sovereignty in the way he does also assumes who we are as political subjects: we are all autonomous selves "marked" by culture but still sharing the necessity of a sovereign authority through which our differences can be mediated (thus the emphasis on a constitutional resolution). The structure and form of political interaction are thus given, and it is a familiar form, one we have worked from and through since at least early modernity. Perhaps most effectively presented by Hobbes, it is a form that is necessitated by the kind of individuals (he asserts that) we all are, by our common ontology as modern subjects. Because of who we all necessarily are, we require sovereignty in order to achieve our desires. We are thus all ultimately the "same;" we all share a specific identity that necessitates sovereignty. By assuming the sovereign state as the locus of the political, then, Tully reinscribes not only the necessity of the sovereign state, but a particular reading of political subjects as modern and natural.

One difficulty this poses, as we saw earlier in the analysis of Hobbes, is that this ontology—and the "individuals" it produces and assumes—is culturally (historically, materially, geographically, environmentally, and gender) specific, as are the necessities of governance that flow from it. Further, it expresses a culture that is already enabled through a very specific relationship to "other" cultures. As Tully documents, contained within the history of the tradition of Western thought and society are examples of both certain forms of "recognition" of other cultures and sustained and violent attacks upon them, attempts to erase them, ignore them, assimilate them. Tully wishes to draw upon what he sees as the positive history of cultural recognition in order to guide our current thinking, arguing that these are as much a part of our histories as the negative treatments of cultural difference, even though the negative treatments have too often tended to prevail. However, his logic for this can be reversed: the negative treatments are an inherent part of our history as well. Further, from the perspectives of many of the groups to which he seeks to respond, they have been dominant. Presumably, until we understand why this is, and can respond to the question of under what conditions the more positive elements of our traditions will prevail, it might be problematic to assert and universalize this particular set of assumptions about the necessities of the political as adequate to guide our thinking on these matters. So, for example, Tully sees it as a tragedy that at a crucial time in our history (when Europeans encountered the New World) constitutional theorists followed Hobbes' "Empire of Uniformity" rather than Hale's more benevolent vision. But *why* did they follow Hobbes? Don't we need to understand *why* it was that constitutional theory was unable or unwilling to resist the great violences visited upon Indigenous peoples in the past, before we insist that it is adequate to the task of protecting and nourishing cultural difference today?

To answer this question would require throwing into question not only, with Tully, the history of the treatment of "culture" within Western political thought, but also the cultural specificity of the tradition itself and how its underlying assumptions necessarily frame our thinking about "culture." This is not something Tully is concerned to do.[4] Rather, he attempts to counter the problem within the structures enabled by the assumption of sovereignty. Thus he opens the tradition of political thought to critique, but excludes from consideration the possibility that the background assumptions he relies upon already frame the possibilities for thinking about, recognizing and responding to the problems of cultural difference. In other words, he excludes the possibility that these traditions have already been pushed to their limits, that there is a reason that Hobbes has so often won out over Hale, and that his own analysis—like that of Hale—while expressing a vastly preferable ethical position, might fall victim to the necessities of sovereignty. Thus, though he seeks to contest the negative treatment of cultural difference within Western constitutional theory by "bringing culture in" to institutions of governance, he does so without throwing into question the cultural specificity of the assumptions that undergird his own analysis. However, even the possibility of universalizing a more culturally sensitive version of a tradition in which universalism has generally been a cover for the erasure of culture difference remains worrisome. How will we ensure that the culturally sensitive version remains dominant?

Tully's assumption of sovereignty and exclusive focus on governance as the space for the political thus initiate a potentially dangerous game. This is where echoes of his analysis of Locke begin to appear: is it possible that his aspiration to intervene in the major ideological and political conflict of the day shapes his project in ways that render it dangerous to precisely those to whose claims he seeks to respond? Might he, in other words, be reinscribing the problem in his search for a solution?

The sovereignty of political theory

Tully's analysis in *Strange Multiplicity* seeks to challenge crucial conventions and assumptions of constitutional theorists. However, in order to do so, he also relies upon and reinscribes the constitutive conventions of sovereignty, both conceptually (by assuming the problem of authority to be solved) and practically (by assuming the state as the locus of the political). This is not, however, a problem specific to Tully; quite the contrary. Tully's analysis is enabled by and reproduces the conventions that authorize political theory more broadly. It thus depends upon a series of disciplinary and disciplining conventions. I argue in this section that this assumption of sovereignty and the analytical conventions that flow from it have the effect of reinscribing the marginal status of the groups to which Tully seeks to respond, in particular Indigenous peoples, but also some of the other groups. Further, this assumption—insofar as it marginalizes a series of questions that are becoming increasingly pressing—unproductively constrains not only "marginal" forms of politics, but political theory as well.

The analytical constraints that the assumption of sovereignty imposes on Tully's project are most apparent in his reinscription of governance as the space of politics and the authority of political theory over the analysis of politics.[5] Both of these are accomplished through the straightforward assertion of authorial sovereignty, itself an expression of the sovereignty of political theory. Put bluntly, in order to authorize his project (to solidify a shared "background agreement"), Tully must exclude from consideration a range of critiques that might challenge his assumption of sovereignty as the precondition for the political; this in turn is enabled and effected through the reassertion of the necessities of sovereignty. This assumption of sovereignty, and the parallel assumption of modern subjectivity and "recognition" as the question of the day, is vulnerable to a number of critiques, including those that have emerged in analyses of some of the very movements to which Tully seeks to respond, not least in relation to concepts of "recognition"[6] and subjectivity.[7] Tully's explicit engagement with literatures that might raise these kinds of challenges to his project is very brief.[8] In his discussion of challenges to contemporary constitutionalism, he engages with the challenges posed by "postmodernism" and "cultural feminism."

The challenge posed by "postmodernism" he quickly dismisses through an assertion that it leads to a politically unproductive stance. He effects this by adopting a popular reading of "postmodern" challenges, a reading most thinkers who are lumped under this category have gone to great pains to clearly dispute and distance themselves from. He specifically cites James Clifford[9] to illustrate how a "postmodern critique" unproductively "dissolves" the category of "identity" with a depoliticizing effect that forces "postmodernists" into positions similar to conservative theorists. Because Clifford articulates a political space which for Tully falls outside the properly political (that is, because Clifford seeks to draw attention to the ways in which "identity" as a category/subjectivity is constituted through a play of power/knowledge that he argues should be understood as political), Tully reads his analysis as having no political relevance, as, in fact, being dangerously "conservative." In other words, to the extent to which "postmodernists" seek to redefine the space of the political—to render as political the assumptions that Tully's project relies upon—they are neither relevant to his project nor authorized to speak about the political.[10] Such a dismissal relies upon a reassertion of the sovereignty of political theory. As a political theorist, authorized by the conventional assumption of sovereignty, he can rest upon the conventions of political theory to assume the proper space of the political. He need not (cannot) subject this assumption to questioning without undermining his ability to speak authoritatively about his subject. Thus, what the political is and must be is assumed and reasserted rather than subjected to any scrutiny.[11]

His evasion of critiques that might emerge from feminist material is no less dependent upon a reinscription of the sovereignty of political theory. Rather than rendering feminism irrelevant to his project, he "includes" and responds to the concerns of only those feminist positions whose foundational assumptions correspond with his own: "cultural feminists." Tully's summary of the claims of cultural feminists is as follows:

> The claim of cultural feminists, broadly speaking, is not only that women should have an equal say within the constitutional institutions of contemporary societies and their authoritative traditions of interpretation. Because the constitutional institutions and traditions of interpretation were established long ago by men to the exclusion of women, it follows that they should be amended from the ground up, so to speak, in order to recognise and accommodate women's culturally distinctive ways of speaking and acting, so that substantive gender equality will be assured in the daily struggles in the institutions the constitution founds. Making this task even more difficult, women's culture itself is not homogeneous, but multicultural and contested.
>
> (Tully, 1995: 2–3)

He associates a wide range of feminists with this position: Carol Gilligan, Iris Young, Linda Alcoff, Julia Kristeva, Susan Moller Okin, Seyla Benhabib, Jean Elshtain, Maria Lugones, Elizabeth Spelman, Adrienne Rich, and Martha Minow. As a description of a political position that can be called feminist, his account no doubt offers a recognizable portrayal of a confusing landscape. It also explicitly recognizes the diverse and contested character of the landscape that could be imagined from the texts of the authors he mentions, although it could also be said that the authors mentioned significantly exceed the capacity of a term like cultural feminism to describe either their commonalties or the force of their political critique. It should also be noted that this is a category and grouping produced by Tully, through and in relation to his project, rather than a category actively produced or claimed by all of the feminists he mentions. By "including" (at least some) feminists in this way he adds to the legitimacy of his project. However, as is apparent, the feminist position he has chosen to respond to cannot—by definition—challenge his framing of his project.

The selective reading of those challenges to which he seeks to respond in the book is also evident in what he takes as his primary focus: the situation of Indigenous peoples. Surprisingly, Tully fails to address the question of whether "cultural recognition" is an appropriate response to the demands of Indigenous peoples.[12] While the language of "cultural recognition" is certainly present within Indigenous political struggles in Canada, Tully does not consider whether it is or should be read as the primary demand. Nor does he contextualize this demand within the larger struggles of Indigenous peoples, thus enabling an evaluation of what "cultural recognition" might mean in the context of Indigenous struggles. Thus, much as he enacts a sovereignty in relation to feminism by including only those elements of feminism appropriate to his project, the claim that the recognition of cultural diversity is the question of the day, providing an adequate and appropriate reading of not only Indigenous but a wide range of other struggles, is asserted in an act of authorial sovereignty.

His evasions of critiques that might be posed by two significant literatures, and potential critiques embedded in his primary reference point, are thus enabled through a reassertion of authorial sovereignty, in itself dependent upon the reinscription of assumptions about what constitutes legitimate authority when speaking about the political. His reading of "the political" as expressed in his rejection of "postmodernism" effectively enables him to avoid considering the crucial question of whether his reading of these movements is appropriate with reference to their political projects. In particular, the possibility that these various movements might pose challenges that exceed or challenge the framing of the political within his own project is not considered.

What are the implications of this? After all, every intellectual project selectively produces its subjects and frame. I have been emphasizing that Tully's practices in this regard are conventional, and are not particularly problematic according to the conventions of political theory. I draw attention to them for two reasons, each of which I will develop in more depth below.[13] My first concern is that these conventions function to reinscribe a series of political effects; in particular, to reinscribe the necessary "marginality" of particular kinds of political claims. I share with Tully the aspiration to respond to the challenges posed by marginal movements to political theory. However, I suspect that a response to these movements within the existing conventions of political theory runs the risk of reinscribing the marginality of these movements' claims, contributing to the kinds of effects described so effectively by Tully in relation to the work of Locke: our interventions might function to forward particular aspirations contained within the traditions from which we work, but they may simultaneously continue a tradition of reproducing a systematic blindness to their effects on "marginal" groups. My second concern has to do with the future of political theory. If we rely on the conventions of political theory to frame our ideological and political interventions, we always run the risk of anachronism, of crafting solutions to problems of the past rather than responding to emerging political possibility. My argument in the remainder of the chapter is that the assumption of sovereignty that is conventional in contemporary political theory contributes to both of these dangers. An exploration of the first concern completes this section, and the second is taken up in the final section.

There are a variety of dangers posed to Indigenous movements by framing their demands through the assumption of sovereignty, most of them focused on how this simultaneously forces them into a particular political framework that may be inappropriate to their aspirations, and potentially increases their reliance on the state to authorize their political structures. So, for example, to assume that the primary goal of Indigenous peoples is to be recognized by and within the state (in this case Canada) is to already locate and privilege certain visions and possibilities for Indigenous politics. It is, for example, to assume that there is "a," however contested and criss-crossed, cultural "identity" that can be "represented"—even if by many voices—and "recognized" at this constitutional dialogue. As discussed earlier, Indigenous peoples in Canada vary widely in a range of ways: they come from diverse nations, speak hundreds of different languages, have different formal and informal relationships to the Canadian state, and face widely disparate social, ecological, material, and political challenges. In order for these groups to "represent" themselves, a larger identity construction process must go on, based on parameters dictated by the necessity of operating in relation to a structure established by Canada. As we saw earlier, such a process of "identity construction" has already given Indigenous groups much grief. Such a process would also no doubt exacerbate the struggles for definition of firm group identities, and violences within the groups to define and sustain these identities. The trend in recent federal-level Indigenous politics seems to be away from efforts like this: there is a strong feeling that federal-level politics have already taken too much away from communities. Nor is there any widespread indication that a solution at the level of constitutional dialogue is desirable.

To foreground a federal-level process would, in turn, potentially have the effect of strengthening those forces within Indigenous communities that do aspire to such a solution, once again tipping the scales so that the future of each community is in part decided based upon what is best for Canada. This is not to say that such a solution might not help some communities, but the problematic of "Canada" once again framing the possible options for Indigenous communities is all too familiar. In this way, such a project might have the effect of directing scarce resources away from Indigenous communities as leaders struggle to function under the conditions established by the sovereign.[14] Once again the concerns about the health of the communities and the immediate social and material situations that Indigenous peoples face would potentially be put on the back burner. In this way reading Indigenous demands as being for recognition rather than, say, for resources to address the material effects of colonization, potentially has both immediate and long-term effects not only on the allocation of resources within these communities, but also on the future political structures and possibilities for these communities.

By extension, in responding to Indigenous demands insofar as they are symmetrical with those of a range of other groups, the specificity of the situation they face is potentially minimized in an effort to create a solution that is responsive to what is most common to all of the challenges facing constitutional processes. This is especially true within this proposed constitutional dialogue, because Indigenous demands would be considered in a comparative perspective with those of other groups in this "pluralist vision," thus creating an apparent parity amongst the competing concerns. Clearly the ways in which "culture" has been a vehicle for colonization of Indigenous peoples is not equivalent or arguably even comparable to how "culture" functions in the context of, say, feminist struggles. In this pluralist vision, Indigenous groups become simply one of many different groups clamoring for the attention and recognition of Canada. In this context, although they are the most disadvantaged group in Canada, they might appear to be a small percentage of the population making extravagant demands.

Finally, there is the problem that it is unclear, even if a new constitutional dialogue were established in which Indigenous peoples felt they were recognized, whether the Canadian state will have the capacity in the future to be the source of material retribution for the past wrongs of colonization.[15] The danger is thus that such a process would only increase the dependence of Indigenous peoples on federal institutions to solve their problems, in an age where the resources available to do so—let alone the will to commit them in that direction—may not be readily available.

To read Indigenous politics as primarily a demand for recognition, and the reassertion of the framework of sovereignty as the means to address this demand, thus poses a series of difficulties for Indigenous communities. Most specifically, it leaves them trapped as players in a game not necessarily of their choosing, detracting attention away from their efforts to reconstruct and recreate their community-level political institutions and social well-being out of the effects of colonialism. The potentially critical edges of Indigenous movements—the efforts to hold out for a different vision than the one imposed upon them—remain marginalized. Perhaps most worrisome, such a process as Tully recommends also has the potential to legitimate violence against these critical edges: if some Indigenous groups sign on to and legitimate such a project, and there is a commitment on the part of Canadian people to it, those who do not play along will be marginalized even further. Insofar as they appear to reject apparently well-intentioned efforts to address "their" concerns, insofar as they appear to reject "inclusion" in Canada, they become targets for outbursts of angry nationalism.[16]

The dangers posed to other marginal groups by the assumption of sovereignty parallel those posed to Indigenous groups. To illustrate the dangers of the closures Tully's project effects in relation to feminism, one needs only to look back at his treatment of feminism within his argument. Within the history of feminism, the project of "political change" cannot be divorced from the problem of "changing the political", and what this means has always been highly contested.[17] The development of feminist theory and politics has consistently reproduced a tension between the strategic necessity of working "within" structures of politics and the realization that these political structures are themselves gendered in such a way as to render such "inclusion" unsatisfactory to address their demands. This tension has been expressed in many forms: from early struggles between liberal suffragettes and socialist feminists over whether gender or class should be the primary category of organization, to struggles to assert that the "personal" is "political," to more recent struggles over the strategic challenges posed by the political volatility of the identity of "woman."

Tully's reading of feminism is only attentive to one expression of this (one that shares his definition of the political) and thus selectively legitimates one strand of feminism as containing an appropriately political stance. In this way he ignores broader challenges posed by feminism, the extent to which feminist theory has posed the political as a problem, rather than only posing challenges to who gets to be part of it. This selective reading of feminism has at least two potentially dangerous effects: it weighs in and reinforces power relations within feminist theory, selectively legitimating some kinds of feminism as "more properly political," and it reasserts the possibility of political theory selectively reading feminist theory as it wishes, thus effectively disciplining the critical edge of feminist theory, continuing to exclude it from consideration as properly political. That these dangers so closely parallel the dangers to Indigenous politics developed above is an indication of the larger structural issues at stake.

By choosing which feminists to respond to Tully reinscribes assumptions and logics of what is properly political, assumptions and logics that have been subjected to thoroughgoing critique within feminist theory. By ignoring this element of feminist theory, he not only strikes a blow against feminist efforts to redefine the political, by relegitimating the assertion that "we can't ask some questions" without running the risk of disrupting "gains."[18] He also undermines the legitimacy of feminist conversations on their own terms, thus enabling the politics of feminism to be dictated and controlled by dominant assumptions of contemporary political thought.[19] He thus reasserts political theory's ability to define the political, to depoliticize other expressions and concerns with the political. At the same time, he legitimizes the history of political thought, reasserting its centrality and capacity to respond to all contemporary challenges. The effect of this is to leave the "philosophical" critiques posed by feminism without leverage in the world of so-called "real politics," despite his reliance on another version of philosophy in order to make his assertion of the question of the day.[20]

In this way, then, the analytical conventions through which Tully selects and defines his subject and project, conventions he must reproduce in order to establish enough of a shared "background agreement" with the tradition he seeks to criticize in order to enable his critique, are grounded in, enabled by, expressed through, and reinscribe the assumption of sovereignty as the pre-condition of the properly political. This forces his analysis to effect a range of closures which in turn have the effect of reinscribing the "marginal" status of certain forms of critique and practice, particularly those forms of critique and practice which have been most concerned with the political practices of marginalization.

Recognizing the limit(s)

However, there is no easy way out here, for Tully or for anyone else. The tension that I have been tracing through Tully's work is one version of a larger dilemma facing contemporary political theory. It is a dilemma that is being reproduced by the failure of political theorists to take seriously their reproduction of sovereignty as the precondition for the political, and thus to release or reconfigure their own authority to speak about and have a monopoly on the language and construction of the political. The reluctance on the part of political theorists to throw into question the conventional assumption of sovereignty—and the disciplinary and disciplining practices that it rests upon and reinscribes—poses a series of dangers to the future of political theory that need to be taken very seriously. I develop three of them below: first, insofar as political theorists assume sovereignty, they potentially reinscribe the problems they seek to address; second, the conditions under which an analysis that assumes sovereignty will have relevance to contemporary situations may be increasingly rare, and thus political theory may become increasingly irrelevant to ongoing political dilemmas; and, third, the assumption of sovereignty constrains our possibilities for resisting the violences of sovereignty, and thus also our options for thinking differently about contemporary political dilemmas. These dangers suggest the necessity of engaging with the problem of the limits that discourses and practices of sovereignty continue to inscribe on our political thought and practice.

First, then, insofar as political theorists reinscribe the conventional assumption of sovereignty as the necessary, natural, and universalizable ontology of politics, they will remain trapped in the necessity of reinscribing governance as the space of politics. As we saw above, this in turn forces political theorists to reinscribe particular patterns of inclusion and exclusion, patterns that reinscribe the "marginal" status of movements like those of Indigenous peoples and feminists. In this way, political theorists function in an essentially conservative role, effectively retaining their own authority in order to fight the good fight, but, in so doing, also reproducing the terms and conditions of the war. In the case of Tully, he seeks to respond to the claims of "marginal" groups by giving them a voice at the "center": the very constitution of the state. However, in so doing he also reinscribes the state as the center of politics in a way that poses serious dangers to "marginal" groups, functioning to effectively reinscribe the "center/margin" relationship. More specifically, we make constitutional dialogue capable of attention to the demands for cultural recognition, but the preconditions for entering the dialogue force "the margins" into impossible political binds. Put another way, we make the institutions more welcoming, but we preserve the institutions. If these institutions themselves necessarily reproduce the conditions that require the location of "others" at the margins (or the production of others to be margins), this political strategy might produce a victory in the battle but force a continuation of the same old war.

This is the paradox of sovereignty discourse, and Tully is caught in it. To some extent we all are; though many theorists have developed strategies for engaging this paradox in productive ways. Many feminist theorists, for example, have made abundantly clear that there is no "pure" position one can take in relation to "marginal" forms of politics.[21] Any project focused on the possibilities of recognition and inclusion must necessarily reinscribe an account of the limits of inclusion and the practices of necessary exclusion. The crucial point is that the recognition and struggle with this problem of limits—the problem of sovereignty—must become part of our theoretical and political practice, especially insofar as we seek to respond to the challenges raised by contemporary forms of "marginal" politics (political movements that appear as marginal to political theory and seek to challenge the center/margin dynamic). This in turn reveals the danger of Tully's refusal to take seriously those feminists, anthropologists, and "postmodernists" who focus precisely on the paradox of sovereignty in such a way as to enable this limit to be marked, exposed, and engaged by his project. Thus, I want to draw attention to the need to mark the moment where the politics of recognition must recognize its own limits, and to suggest the need to extend Tully's project to include an exploration of its own enabling conditions.

The second danger posed by a continued assumption of sovereignty by political theorists is suggested by a range of recent analyses arguing that the conditions under which the resolutions of sovereignty can define the exclusive space for politics are becoming increasingly rare.[22] In other words, if we assume the resolution of sovereignty as the precondition for politics, political theorists may have increasingly little to say about a range of important contemporary situations. Note the relative silence of political theorists on ethnic cleansing in Bosnia and Rwanda; nationalist struggles in Kosovo; famine, global warming, or other environmental challenges; even the Holocaust, for example, not to mention Indigenous politics. The range of issues that are excluded when one assumes sovereignty as a precondition for analysis render work dependent upon it capable of only a very partial response to contemporary political problems at best, and, further, a partial response that may exacerbate the terms of the problem.

Put slightly differently, the conditions under which a process such as Tully suggests are plausible are extremely rare. In order to extend our analyses more broadly, to be able to consider, for example, what challenges Indigenous or feminist politics do pose not only to institutions of governance but to political theory much more broadly, we must be able to consider what happens, for example, when "culture" has functioned to throw sovereignty itself into question (as, for example, in the former Yugoslavia). We know that "politics" happens outside of relations of governance, but the analysis of "politics" in these other contexts is increasingly appearing everywhere but political theory, and too often without attention to the strengths that could potentially emerge from political theory. Further, the reassertion of the primacy of political theory means that those who attempt to discuss these issues as political are too often rendered without authority to do so.[23]

This in turn leads to the third danger that emerges from an evasion of the problem of sovereignty. Having raised the possibility that the conditions under which sovereignty defines the possibilities for the political may be becoming increasingly rare, it is also important to note that sovereignty has never completely defined the conditions of possibility for politics. Rather, the assertion that it has is part of the mythology of sovereignty, the same mythology that has produced its violences as necessary and natural. As we saw in the analysis of Tocqueville on pp. 39–50, one of the ways sovereignty discourse "works" is by establishing the parameters of possibility: by convincing us that it is the only possible solution to the problem of social and political order (all else is the state of nature). Because it is the necessary and inevitable precondition for social and political order, its violences are simply regrettable and necessary, rather than constituted by and constitutive of its own successes. To the extent that theorists assume sovereignty, they reinscribe this mythology of sovereignty.

The byproduct of this is not only the erasure and legitimation of the historical violences effected on Indigenous peoples and others, but also the erasure of sovereignty's own conditions of possibility, rendering the ontology of sovereignty necessary, natural, timeless. It is precisely this mythology which has facilitated sovereignty's greatest violences: the "Indians" are doomed to disappear for modern theorists such as Tocqueville not because political order was being guaranteed by a shared ontology, but because it is inevitable that the spatial and temporal resolutions of the sovereign state will prevail, and "Savages" must either become civilized or disappear. The same logic legitimated active campaigns of extermination in the United States. A variation legitimates ongoing episodes of ethnic cleansing: a territory must be governed by a shared ontology; "difference" can only be understood and tolerated if distanced either in space or time.

It is also this mythology that renders discourses of sovereignty so difficult to disrupt: they define not only what "is" but what must be, and what the alternatives are: the state of nature, war, savagery. As long as we continue to inscribe these as our only options, we cannot evade the violences that accompany the "achievement" of sovereignty. So, for example, by erasing the economic, social, and political conditions of possibility through the grounding of sovereignty in the production of collective subjectivity, the ways in which relatively "powerful" or "successful" subjectivities (such as the United States, Canada, France, even "Europe") are enabled by and dependent upon the exploitation of resources, raw materials, extractive processes, and the production of corresponding "victim" subjectivities in the rest of the world are also erased.[24] Thus, the powerful subjectivities/sovereignties appear as mythical ideals: autonomous "selves" legitimated by the (mutually reproduced) global sovereignty of sovereignty discourse.[25] This mythology then in turn provokes and legitimates the efforts of others to pursue the same status, too often with unimaginably high costs.[26]

By erasing its material conditions of possibility and naturalizing its violences, sovereignty discourse draws our attention away from considering whether it is an adequate response to changing conditions today, given both its past violences and the present economic, material, environmental, social, cultural, and political situation we face today. Arguably, Hobbes' production of sovereignty, his "solution" to the problem of order he faced in his own times, has been so compelling and powerful in part because he was an especially prescient observer and analyst of his own social and political context. Rather than *assuming* that we face the same problem he did (or assuming that we don't), this question must be posed: a political theory that fails to consider its location within its own social and political context runs the risk of reproducing a particularly dangerous form of idealism. Thus, if we continue to assume that sovereignty is the necessary response to all problems of social modern order, the ability of political theorists to engage with challenges that are relevant to a wide range of contemporary political phenomena is likely to radically suffer.

So, for example, the crucial question that haunts my reading of Tully's text is *why* political theorists and actors followed Hobbes rather than Hale in their treatment of cultural difference. If our history is full of efforts to recognize and accommodate cultural difference, why have they so rarely prevailed?

If we cannot provide an answer for that question, and given that political theorists rarely have any control over the practical implications of their work, presumably there is no reason to believe that a revised constitutionalism will be any more successful at enforcing cultural recognition than was Hale, when push comes to shove. This is a question that, within the assumption of sovereignty, one cannot answer, cannot even engage. To do so would require rejecting the mythology of the autonomous sovereign, examining the conditions of possibility for the assertion of (Canadian) sovereignty, and how those conditions are produced both materially and discursively. It would require taking (Canadian) sovereignty itself as an object of inquiry, revealing the violences that it required and effected. It would require rejecting the mythology of sovereignty and insisting that we must understand its successes and its violences—its promises, necessities, and conditions of possibility—together, rather than seeking only to build on its apparent successes. An engagement with the situation of Indigenous peoples that would respond to these past violences would presumably require a reformulation of sovereignty in such a way as to render these violences untenable. Until we can answer the question of how these violences came about in the past, this possibility remains outside our reach.

These dangers—of potentially reinscribing the problem in our efforts to find solutions, of drifting into irrelevance, and of remaining trapped within the mythology of sovereignty, unable to consider questions of how we must rethink politics given our current conditions—add up to a significant challenge for political theorists. Put yet another way, political theorists have a little bit of power, in that we have a particular kind of leverage on the language and problem of the political, and political theorists should know that a little bit of power is dangerous. We often prefer to utilize this little bit of power for "good" causes, yet we run the risk, precisely through the practices and conventions we use to address these problems, of reproducing or exacerbating the situation we are trying to ameliorate. My concern is that this may be working to constrain both the capacity of political theorists to respond to a range of important political developments and the efforts of "marginal" political movements to introduce crucial critical perspectives on the situations we face.

Part III
Emerging politicizations

Part III

Emerging public relations

8 Rethinking sovereignty
Deleuze and Guattari

Part I of this book developed an analysis of sovereignty as a practice that has shaped political possibility not only for Indigenous peoples, but also more widely. The second traced a series of contemporary struggles with and against sovereignty. It emphasized how practices of sovereignty work through law, politics, and theory to enable and constrain the struggles of Indigenous peoples. This in turn poses the challenge the remainder of the book takes up: how might we engage more effectively with practices of sovereignty? What kind of work does the previous analysis suggest is necessary for those who seek to respond to the past violences of sovereignty, including those visited upon Indigenous peoples? Or, more simply, where to from here?

Hopefully the analysis in Part II has begun to provide hints of this, insofar as each engagement has opened and redefined political terrain in specific ways, enabling responses to aspects of the challenges posed by Indigenous struggles. Although in each case practices of sovereignty have been re-inscribed in ways that constrain this terrain, each negotiation has also redefined the terms upon which sovereignty works, in part by revealing its violences and necessities. The analysis in Part III builds upon these openings, at times returning explicitly to them, to provide a richer sense of the terrain of the political that contemporary theory must begin to engage.

To this end, I turn in this chapter to examine a text by Gilles Deleuze and Félix Guattari: *A Thousand Plateaus*.[1] As with previous texts, I read it as an illustrative example, in this case of theorizing which seeks to engage explicitly with the problem of sovereignty and the political. Deleuze and Guattari are among those thinkers who have struggled with some of the most difficult conceptual and political terrain of the day. Working in the philosophical wake of Nietzsche, Heidegger, and Husserl, and paralleling the work of such contemporaries as Foucault, Derrida, Lacan, Lyotard, and Baudrillard, they have—both separately and together—sought to challenge the central assumptions, questions, and methods of modern philosophy. Crucially, as with many of their contemporaries, they have sought to do so through and in conversation with a broad range of literatures, resisting the disciplining of thought reproduced in much philosophical work. This resistance emerges in part from their struggle with the problem of how to rearticulate the terms of philosophical critique. Recognizing that to criticize a tradition within the terms of that tradition functions to strengthen and reinforce its necessities, they have sought to disrupt not only some of the dominant intellectual and philosophical traditions of the day in Europe, but also to disrupt and rearticulate the roles and methods of philosophical inquiry and critique. Significantly, their broad grounding, their reach "outside" the terms and traditions of philosophy, is thus not a move to an "external" or "transcendent" alternative so much as a struggle against the constant self-production and reproduction of the philosophical tradition, especially as this is expressed in Hegel's all-encompassing logic of negation.

Predictably, then, *A Thousand Plateaus* is a difficult book. Its scope, context, method, and implications all exceed a single analytical line. The question of how to engage it remains an open and productive one.[2] Most analysts have chosen to take on a relatively small slice of their project, a tactic I follow here. What interests me particularly is how this book expresses an effort to write so as to disrupt the conditions of possibility for and apparent necessities of sovereignty. As might be anticipated from my own argument so far, this is not an easy task. We have seen in various strategies of Indigenous politics, and in the work of progressive thinkers such as Clastres, Bull, Tocqueville, and Tully, an effort to evade the violences of sovereignty. We have also seen how, even as each challenges or attempts to evade these violences, each in some way reproduces the conditions of their necessity. It is possible neither to ignore nor to evade sovereignty without implicitly reproducing its violences, and direct attacks on sovereignty simply do so more explicitly. What, then, to do?

As I read it, Deleuze and Guattari's book is one of many recent attempts to develop ways of more effectively engaging with the problem of how we might disrupt the apparent sovereignty of sovereign thought, to rearticulate the conditions that require its violences. I choose to engage their work rather than that of some of their contemporaries because they have a particularly acute sense of the problem of the political as it emerges through and in relation to modern forms of sovereignty, and because they discuss these themes in ways that explicitly engage Indigenous peoples' position within these problems. On their analysis, the violences of modern sovereignty are not exclusively—or even primarily—the result of what has been thought, but of *how* it has been thought, the image or structure of thought itself, the methods and processes of knowledge production, of the constitution of authority. We cannot respond to the violences of sovereignty unless we address the structure of thought itself. Just as *Leviathan* was not simply an argument for new political arrangements, but for new structures and methods of knowledge production as the precondition for these political arrangements, *A Thousand Plateaus* is an argument for a rearticulation of the conditions of possibility for thought and (thus) for the political. For Deleuze and Guattari, this requires that we write a different kind of book, do a different kind of theory, become different kinds of subjects. The next section begins to sketch what might be different about their approach to theorizing; the subsequent one pursues one of their thought experiments in relation to the argument thus far.

Thinking thought: rhizomes and trees

To illustrate part of the challenge posed by rethinking thought itself, Deleuze and Guattari begin by developing a distinction between two images of thought: "arboreal" and "rhizomatic." They assert that Western thought has for too long been obsessed with thought in the image of a tree: a single trunk supporting an array of branches. This model for thought begins with the assumption of a strong central unity and proceeds through a binary logic of division. Through this process it achieves the appearance of diversity, multiplicity, and universality, but this appearance is always dependent on a primary unity. Because of this, Deleuze and Guattari argue, this is a mode of thought that can never apprehend, recognize, or produce multiplicity. It must always authorize itself through a privileging of the same, of an originary unity.

This description of thought bears strong resemblances to the production of sovereignty by Hobbes in the *Leviathan*; remember especially his typology of knowledge. In this image, the meaning of language must cohere around and be guaranteed by a single source of authority: an ontological homogeneity expressed in sovereignty, or in the image of the sovereign. Authority, in this image, is guaranteed by "resonance," by a shared sense of meaning. A failure to resonate, to accept and reproduce the ontological ground as expressed in language, becomes a precondition for the violences of exclusion. It is thus in part a Hobbesian image of thought that Deleuze and Guattari seek to critically engage: "We're tired of trees. We should stop believing in trees, roots, and radicles. They've made us suffer too much" (Deleuze and Guattari, 1987: 15).

Rhizomatic thought proceeds otherwise, is embedded in different practices and forms. The first and second characteristics of rhizomatic thought are that it proceeds by principles of connection and heterogeneity: "any point of a rhizome can be connected to anything other, and must be. This is very different from the tree or root, which plots a point, fixes an order" (Deleuze and Guattari, 1987: 7). Contrast this to the rigid structure of Hobbes' production of sovereignty in *Leviathan*, in which each analytical move depends entirely upon and emerges from the previous one. Once one accepts his ontological assumptions, the rest of his system must follow (here we hear the necessities of violences). No matter how one might will or wish otherwise, "reality" (the ontology of sovereignty) will establish the ground of necessity. The first two principles of rhizomatic thought insist upon a different structure for thought. They do not proceed on a singular linear unity, but insist that points of connection can and should be made anywhere and everywhere. Thought must proceed not by homogeneity, by building on the same, but through logics of difference. Rather than setting up an oppositional ontological ground, or system of necessities—one that might respond to certain violences but would reinscribe and solidify others—and proceeding through the same logics of thought, they suggest the necessity of proceeding otherwise, of resisting the form of thought represented by the tree logic of unity and homogeneity.

The third and fourth principles of rhizomatic thought—multiplicity and asignifying rupture—extend and deepen these challenges. Each emphasizes a different starting point and practice. To begin from the assumption of multiplicity is to deny the possibility of unity or return to origins: "[I]t is only when the multiple is effectively treated as a substantive, 'multiplicity,' that it ceases to have any relation to the One as subject or object, natural or spiritual reality, image or world" (Deleuze and Guattari, 1987: 8). To proceed through asignifying rupture is to emphasize the necessity and importance of disruption, and the impossibility of escape:

> A rhizome may be broken, shattered at a given spot, but it will start up again on one of its old lines, or on new lines . . . Every rhizome contains lines of segmentarity according to which it is stratified, territorialized, organized, signified, attributed, etc., as well as lines of deterritorialization down which it constantly flees.
>
> (Deleuze and Guattari, 1987: 9)

These principles thus resist foundational assumptions of sovereign thought, resist the move to produce resonance around an originating structure or moment, shifting the focus of analysis away from questions that have obsessed much modern philosophy and towards a very different set of projects. They also resist the kinds of spatial and temporal structures that modern thought assumes and that structure the possibilities for thinking: there is no central structure, no single sign system. There is no "inside" to make us feel comfortable—even within the rhizome there are segmenting forces—no "outside" from which to launch our critiques or claim our piety. Their project not only forces us to give up some of the dualisms we have come to see as obviously problematic, but also those upon which many of us have hung our hats, those upon which many "good" political ships have been launched. Both "lines of flight" or movements of resistance and critique *and* their apparent object emerge from the same terrain. The self-righteousness of the unpolluted stance is denied.

How, then, to proceed? Further characteristics of rhizomatic thought provide hints. Rhizomatic thought proceeds not by tracing, but by mapping: "What distinguishes the map from the tracing is that it is entirely oriented toward an experimentation in contact with the real. The map does not reproduce an unconscious closed in upon itself; it constructs the unconscious. . . . It is itself a part of the rhizome" (Deleuze and Guattari, 1987: 12). A map, they argue, remains open, has multiple points of entry, can be adapted, changed or reproduced on any possible site:

[I]t is detachable, reversible, susceptible to constant modification. It can be torn, reversed, adapted to any kind of mounting, reworked by an individual, group, or social formation. It can be drawn on a wall, conceived as a work of art, constructed as a political action or as a meditation.

(Deleuze and Guattari, 1987: 12)

The relationship between the map and the real is thus contested, as is the form of the map itself: the form of thought must likewise be contested, open to reworking as it intersects with other efforts, and responsive to its own constitutive engagement.

But isn't this distinction between rhizome and tree thought, map and tracing, reproducing a simple dualism of the kind they propose to disrupt? Deleuze and Guattari's rhizomatic/arboreal distinction is not designed to replace one with the other: rhizomes not trees. Rather, their rhizomatic thought proceeds by opposition *and* disruption: make rhizomes not trees but beware of the trees inside your rhizomes and nurture the rhizomes in your trees. What they seek is not to invent anew, to think "outside," but to reconceptualize the terms of distinction themselves. Thought must proceed otherwise; it must enact the disruption of the opposition:

Have we not, however, reverted to a simple dualism by contrasting maps to tracings, as good and bad sides? Is it not the essence of the map to be traceable? Is it not of the essence of the rhizome to intersect roots and sometimes merge with them? Does not a map contain phenomena of redundancy that are already like tracings of its own? Does not a multiplicity have strata upon which unifications and totalizations, massifications, mimetic mechanisms, signifying power takeovers, and subjective attributions take root? Do not even lines of flight, due to their eventual divergence, reproduce the very formations their function it was to dismantle and outflank? But the opposite is also true. It is a question of method: *the tracing should always be put back on the map.* This operation and the previous one are not symmetrical.

(Deleuze and Guattari, 1987: 13; emphasis in original)

The crucial element of the distinction is thus that it is not symmetrical. It is not enough simply to "make maps;" one must also disrupt the opposition between maps and tracings. One must always put the tracing back on the map:

That is why it is so important to try the other, reverse but nonsymmetrical, operation. Plug the tracings back into the map, connect the roots or trees back up with a rhizome. . . . The same applies to the group map: show at what point in the rhizome there form phenomena of massification, bureaucracy, leadership, fascization, etc., which lines nevertheless survive, if only underground, continuing to make rhizomes in the shadows.

(Deleuze and Guattari, 1987: 14)

What is desired, then, is not "rhizomes instead of trees," as all rhizomes carry trees within them, but forms of thought that engage, assemble, and disrupt the two, a pragmatics that negotiates between and across in order to think differently, to enable different questions to be posed:

> There exist tree or root structures in rhizomes; conversely, a tree branch or root division may begin to burgeon into a rhizome. The coordinates are determined not by theoretical analyses implying universals but by a pragmatics composing multiplicities or aggregates of intensities. A new rhizome may form in the heart of a tree, the hollow of a root, the crook of a branch.

(Deleuze and Guattari, 1987: 15)

While Western thought has been obsessed with trees, this does not mean that thought is arboreal. What Deleuze and Guattari propose is not a new alternative, an escape or an "outside." Rather, it is an exploitation of what already exists to open up the possibilities of thinking it differently. They propose not new thought, but a rethinking of what and how we have too often come to assume, an effort to notice, exploit, nurture, reinvent and authorize modes of thought that resist the closures that are affected by arboreal thought. The principles of rhizomatic thought are both parasitic upon and disruptive of tree thought, or what I have been calling "sovereign thought."

This still leaves us with the question of how to read Deleuze and Guattari's difficult book. Brian Massumi, translator of *A Thousand Plateaus*, suggests a way to begin: "The question is not: is it true? But: does it work? What new thoughts does it make possible to think? What new emotions does it make possible to feel? What new sensations and perceptions does it open in the body?" (Deleuze and Guattari, 1987: xv). What follows is an exploration of whether Deleuze and Guattari's rhizomatic thought opens possibilities for thinking differently the map I have been producing so far, for rethinking the politics and practices of sovereign thought, for rearticulating sovereignty. A caveat is perhaps necessary here: Deleuze and Guattari's project is much more rhizomatic than my own. It connects to and draws from debates across a very broad range of literatures, organizing momentary skirmishes with each through a constant production and disruption of sites of conflict or intensity (plateaus).[3] My project might be read as a particular mapping project, a redrawing of the landscape of Indigenous politics and political theory, a combination in which the structures of thought take an unusually rigid—and violent—form at times. Yet this remains a map that still must be reconnected to the tracing. In the rest of this chapter I create a map of aspects of their project and of my own, considering how they resonate within and disrupt each other. My hope is that in the diverse overlaps of these processes, ways in which Deleuze and Guattari's text and method provoke possibilities for thinking differently about sovereignty will emerge.

Sovereignty as apparatus of capture

The plateau of Deleuze and Guattari's *A Thousand Plateaus* that I focus on here is number thirteen: "7000 B.C.: Apparatus of Capture." However, consistent with their rhizomatic ambitions, the apparatus of capture appears in and circulates through many different plateaus. Thus, although I begin with one plateau as they have constructed it, it is multiply embedded in their text. In their rhizomatic spirit, I read their plateau partly in relation to Tocqueville's production of sovereignty in *Democracy in America*, showing how their reconceptualization of the ground of sovereignty provides a basis for resisting what Tocqueville assumed and reproduced as the necessary violences of sovereignty. This is important because if Tocqueville is right that these violences are simply necessary and regrettable, a rethinking of sovereignty as an attempt to address them must lead to a dead-end.

Deleuze and Guattari begin by disrupting the assumptions about the differences between "primitive" and "advanced" societies that Tocqueville's analysis reproduced. Whereas Tocqueville produced the operative difference between the "Indians" and settlers as their respective levels of civilization, Deleuze and Guattari, drawing from and ultimately surpassing Clastres, reject such a distinction as being a matter of civilization defined in evolutionary terms. In so doing, they resist the foundational spatial and temporal distinctions that enable Hobbes' as well as Tocqueville's productions of sovereignty. They insist that the story of the world should not be told from within the linear temporal resolutions of the sovereign state. The distinction between "state" and "non-state" societies is not one of succession, of primitive peoples being less-developed versions of ourselves. Instead of characterizing the distinction as one of evolution, they locate the difference between the two in the way that power works within and throughout society. "Primitive" societies, they argue, are not pre-political, lacking formations of power. They are, rather, characterized by a different operation of power:

> Primitive societies do not lack formations of power; they even have many of them. But what prevents the potential central points from crystallizing, from taking on consistency, are precisely those mechanisms that keep the formations of power both from resonating together in a higher point and from becoming polarized at a common point: the circles are not concentric, and the segments require a third segment through which to communicate.
>
> (Deleuze and Guattari, 1987: 433)

Formations of power that are organized in this way function to resist the organization of power characteristic of the state. The state makes diverse points resonate together, it operates through the organization of power into concentric systems of resonance, structures which produce and reinforce the unity and identity of the state (Deleuze and Guattari, 1987: 443). Their description of the operation of power in the state form is in this way consistent with that of Hobbes and Tocqueville: the crucial precondition for state power is the production of identity, of resonance. However, rather than universalizing the terms of that resonance—the particular ontological resolutions of space and time that produce the necessity for resonance—as Hobbes and Tocqueville do, Deleuze and Guattari insist upon the coexistence of different forms of social organization. Not only are these systems coexistent, they argue, they are mutually constituted and dependent. Primitive systems are not early forms of state power; they are specifically organized to deflect the state's modes of organization or resonance.[4] Thus, the production of sovereignty in the interaction between two different kinds of societies cannot be so clearly defined—or preordained—in the evolutionary terms in which Tocqueville writes it. The production of sovereignty is not necessarily linked to an inevitable march of time or a civilizing necessity (though it might be expressed and justified that way). Rather than describing the interactions between the two as motivated by a necessity of evolution and civilization and thus as posing a choice of extermination or assimilation, Deleuze and Guattari write the clash between these two different societies, and the extension of sovereignty on the part of one, as a process of "capture" on the part of the state and resistance by the "primitive" societies. Rather than "primitives" needing to be civilized, the problem that motivates the conflict is that the forms of power that enable the state—precisely because they depend on identity and resonance—cannot tolerate alternative resonances around them. The state forms of power thus consistently strive to force resonance around the state in order to sustain the authority and identity of the state. Thus the state always seeks to "capture" primitive societies, to produce resonance, to produce sovereignty.

Deleuze and Guattari's characterization of the difference between "primitive" and "state" societies thus significantly changes the terms of Tocqueville's description, in that it recharacterizes the narrative of necessity that drives Tocqueville's analysis, shifting responsibility for it to the operation of sovereignty itself. However, their description of the processes and effects of this extension of sovereignty bear remarkable similarity to Tocqueville's. In fact, within Tocqueville's descriptions of the process of sovereignty production in the New World, we can see an almost perfect reproduction of Deleuze and Guattari's apparatus of capture. We see the state needing not simply to destroy the primitive societies,[5] but to appropriate them, to force them to resonate with the poles of the state (which, of course, does effect the destruction of their cultural and political structures, as they are dependent upon different operations of power). The apparatus of capture proceeds not through explicit violence, but through apparently banal practices of organization. For example, Deleuze and Guattari develop an analysis of ground rent as an apparatus of capture. Although an apparently innocuous practice, ground rent striates and organizes people in relation to land, "capturing" possibilities for being on the land. It imposes an agricultural economy, but in the process, not only are possible ways of being constrained, but what land "is" changes (Deleuze and Guattari, 1987: 441). The effect of this is a reconstruction of the possibilities for being, for social organization in relation to space. In this way, the apparatus of capture— through mechanisms and logics of agricultural production—functions to produce resonance.[6]

This description should bring to mind a range of echoes of not only the *Indian Act* legislation in Canada, which focused on the restructuring of Indigenous peoples' relationship to land, but also of Tocqueville's description of the dispossession of Indians in America from their land. In his description, as the state moved ever closer, the Indians' land was not necessarily taken from them so much as made inhospitable to them. The encroachment of settlers onto Indian lands drove away the beasts of prey the Indians lived on, requiring that they over-hunt or hunt indiscriminately, trade and barter to survive. As they struggled, the state sent envoys, they ate and drank together and the envoys set about convincing and compelling the Indians to move further away, enticing them with riches, promises of healthier and richer land and protection from further encroachment (none of these, of course, ever fulfilled) Alternatively, the Indians were offered land of their own to farm; they were "settled." However, this was no more successful as, according to Tocqueville, they became bored and restless with their settled lives, lacking as they did the qualities of civilization which would have made this life appeal to them (Tocqueville, 1990: 342). In this way the violence of their dispossession is attributed to their failure to adapt, to resonate, rather than to the processes through which their possibilities for being on the land were reduced. The apparent lack of violence involved in these processes of dispossession is what enables Tocqueville to claim that "[t]he expulsion of the Indians often takes place at the present day in a regular and, as it were, a legal manner" (Tocqueville, 1990: 340). Their expulsion is apparently not violent, or unjust: it is a consequence of their failure to adapt to the necessities of resonance.

Deleuze and Guattari's analysis provides the context to reveal how what Tocqueville describes as regrettable and necessary is anything but. Yet they would have some sympathy for Tocqueville's choice of how to locate the violence: "Hence the very particular character of State violence: it is very difficult to pinpoint this violence because it always presents itself as pre-accomplished" (Deleuze and Guattari, 1987: 447). State violence is different from other forms of violence precisely because it produces the conditions of its own necessity: "it consists in capturing while simultaneously constituting a right to capture. It is an incorporated, structural violence distinct from every kind of direct violence" (Deleuze and Guattari, 1987: 448). This distinction between state violence and other forms of violence lies in how the state produces the structural conditions of violence:

> State overcoding is precisely this structural violence that defines the law, 'police' violence and not the violence of war. There is lawful violence wherever violence contributes to the creation of that which it is used against, or as Marx says, wherever capture contributes to the creation of that which it captures.
>
> (Deleuze and Guattari, 1987: 448)

This, of course, is precisely the process at work in Tocqueville's text: the production of the sovereignty/resonance of democracy in America required the production of its antithesis: the Indian. To ensure resonance along lines of civilization, the "uncivilized" was produced, and then this lack of civilization was used to justify the violences against them:

> [T]he State can in this way say that violence is 'primal,' that it is simply a natural phenomenon the responsibility for which does not lie with the State, which uses violence only against the violent, against 'criminals'— against primitives, against nomads—in order that peace may reign.
>
> (Deleuze and Guattari, 1987: 448)

In this way the violence of the apparatus of capture, the production of sovereignty, is always concealed through its apparent necessity, with blame shifted to those who receive the violence. The option of "resonance" for the Indians is the option of submitting to the preaccomplished violence of subjectivity: the necessity to become civilized, to resonate. The alternative is life on the borders, subject to the explicit violence of the state.

On this, then, Tocqueville, Hobbes, and Deleuze and Guattari are all in agreement: sovereignty is enabled by resonance, the production of a collective subjectivity. As Deleuze and Guattari put it: "In short, the nation is the very operation of a collective subjectification, to which the modern State corresponds as a process of subjection" (Deleuze and Guattari, 1987: 456). Where Hobbes and Tocqueville write the violences inherent in this project as necessary, if at times regrettable, Deleuze and Guattari illustrate how these apparent necessities are produced. In particular, they emphasize how the apparently banal character of the operation of the apparatus of capture—through processes such as the distribution of land—becomes violent as it reorganizes the possibilities for subjectivity. Their struggle is to denaturalize and denecessitate the ontological resolutions of state thought as articulated by the likes of Hobbes and Tocqueville (and reproduced by modern philosophy).[7] In so doing they not only relocate and redefine what should count as violent, they shift responsibility for the violence to the state, to the production of sovereignty.

Crucial to Deleuze and Guattari's analysis, however, is that the apparatus of capture is never fully successful. Because the possibility of resonance around the "one" always requires an "outside," that which the resonance is compared to (the "savage" in Hobbes' and Tocqueville's texts), resonance can never be fully effected. Every attempted "capture" also produces its own excesses, produces alternative resonances in order to mark and bound its own identity. It is this excess which maintains the limits, the boundaries, the "Others" of the state. Thus the apparatus of capture functions not only to extend and reproduce its own limits (the limits of sovereignty), it also produces that which escapes its coding, or resonance (Deleuze and Guattari, 1987: 448–49). This is why "state" and "primitive" societies must not be considered in a relation of succession: the "primitive" has *always* marked and produced the margins of the state: "Primitive peoples have always existed only as vestiges, already plied by the reversible wave that carries them off. . . . What is contingent upon external circumstances is only the place where the apparatus is effectuated" (Deleuze and Guattari, 1987: 447). Thus, "primitives," "foreigners," the disabled, criminal, or nomadic do not exist as independent self-contained entities that somehow unfortunately become victims of state thought and violence. These categories, subjectivities, are produced as outsides or victims by state thought—the categories have no meaning outside of this context.[8] These categories are produced as the excesses of state thought. As such, they are not "simply" objects or victims. They are, rather, crucial figures: if the state operates through a process of collective subjectification, the outsiders are potential agents capable of much disruption: "What counts is the collective figure of the Outsider" (Deleuze and Guattari, 1987: 469). It is through these figures that sovereignty can be most deeply challenged, as it is upon these figures that its own identity/resonance/ authority rests. What it would mean to challenge sovereignty in this context is anything but straightforward, however. Because sovereignty operates by subjectification through resonance, if these figures come to be recognizable within or to resonate with the majority, they also potentially lose their ability to disrupt the deeper necessities of resonance:

> The power of the minorities is not measured by their capacity to enter and make themselves felt within the majority system, nor even to reverse the necessarily tautological criterion of the majority, but to bring to bear the force of the non-denumerable sets, however small they may be, against the denumerable sets, even if they are infinite, reversed, or changed, even if they imply new axioms or, beyond that, a new axiomatic.
>
> (Deleuze and Guattari, 1987, 471)

The status of "outsiders" is thus complex, and their political terrain nothing if not ambiguous. On the one hand, they are the obvious victims of state thought; on the other they are its Achilles heel—remember that Tocqueville considered the legacy of the Indians and Negroes to pose the greatest threat to America. On the one hand they are disadvantaged by their lack of

recognition by the majority; on the other, the price of recognition—resonance—is the forfeiting of the resistance to resonance which has defined their
identities and what leverage they do have in relation to the majority.[9] On the
one hand, the "majority"—or the option of resonance—offers recognition,
justice, or amelioration of their condition (and the legitimacy of the majority
rests on this promise). On the other hand, the ability of the majority to make
such claims is dependent upon the exclusion and marginalization of those
who mark its edges, its failures. To resonate in this context is to give up what
has defined who one is as a subject, in the context of a wider system of
resonance that will always need someone to be precisely that subject.

Contextualizing the state

This is complex political terrain, and it only gets more so. So far my analysis
has focused on Deleuze and Guattari's revisitation of sovereignty as an
apparatus of capture. Some important questions arise from this examination,
though. First, what provides the context for the production of sovereignty,
for these regimes of subjectification (states)? Although Deleuze and Guattari's
analysis suggests that linear temporal assumptions of sovereign thought are
misleading as a basis for historical or causal explanation, and insist that both
states and "primitives" have always existed, surely they have not always been
the same. Nor do they function as a self-contained system. What, then, comprises context for these dynamics, what shapes, intersects with, and potentially
disrupts them? What kinds of complications should we consider, what rhizomatic connections do we need to make? A crucial one, Deleuze and Guattari
assert, is that the state as a system of collective subjectification operates as
part of a larger system, an axiomatic: the axiomatic of capitalism. "It is in the
form of the nation-state, with all its possible variations, that the State
becomes the model of realization for the capitalist axiomatic" (Deleuze and
Guattari, 1987: 456).

The advent of capitalism on the scene of historical development is relatively recent, however, and Deleuze and Guattari have been making claims
that these state/primitive dynamics extend far further into the past (remember
the title of the plateau: 7000 B.C.). How to reconcile this? They argue that
capitalism itself arises through the effects of the excesses of the modes of
organization of the state, through the ways in which these excess flows produced by the practices and thought of the state cannot be any longer kept
separate or constrained, but instead combine to form the conditions of possibility for capitalism (Deleuze and Guattari, 1987: 452–53). The advent of
capitalism is thus intimately connected to the structures, organization, and
operation of the state, among other things.

But what does this rise of capitalism imply for the state? How does it
change the state as a regime of subjectification? While one reading would
suggest that the rise of capitalism implies that there is no longer a need for the
state (Deleuze and Guattari, 1987: 453), they emphasize the role that the state

fulfills for the capitalist axiomatic. Capitalism may be in some senses anti-thetical to the state, but the state has also come to be the site of realization for the capitalist axiomatic:

> Each of them [states] groups together and combines several sectors, according to its resources, population, wealth, industrial capacity, etc. Thus the States, in capitalism, are not canceled out but change form and take on a new meaning: models of realization for a worldwide axiomatic that exceeds them. But to exceed is not at all the same thing as doing without.
>
> (Deleuze and Guattari, 1987: 454)

To assert that the states are modes of realization for the capitalist axiomatic is not to assert a level of homogeneity or uniformity—or even unidirectional-ity—in this relationship. While all states in some sense become organized in relation to capital,[10] this does not mean that all states take the same form, achieve the same effects, or are interchangeable.[11] Again, the situation is more complex. In any given state the realization of the axiomatic is a tangled complex of passions, histories, resources, forms of subjectification, forms of subjection. As indicated in the above quotation, the ways in which states function as a realization of the capitalist axiomatic depends upon resources, wealth, population, and so on. The details are crucial, in particular in relation to the constitution or character of political possibility at any given site.[12] Also crucial, though, are the general contours, the ways in which some of the conceptual, linguistic and methodological shifts suggested by this sketch of Deleuze and Guattari's thought might shift our analytical focus in particular ways.

For example, just as their resistance to an evolutionary logic for framing the encounter between "state" and "primitive" societies potentially opens space to denaturalize and denecessitate some of the violences contained within the ontological resolutions and structures of modern sovereignty, their characterization of the relationship between the state and capital (as a dynamic realization of an axiomatic) opens up some key questions, particu-larly in relation to contemporary struggles over spaces and practices of politics. While sovereign thought has been defined historically by its relation to its "outsiders"—be they savages, aliens, foreigners, prisoners, women, the disabled, mad—its contemporary claims to legitimacy are embedded in its capacity to provide for its citizens, a capacity in turn embedded in its capacity to realize the capitalist axiomatic. This suggests a political terrain that exceeds the territorial bounds of the state. This in turn challenges the claim—in particular by state thought as expressed in the writing of political theorists and philosophers such as Hobbes—that the state is and must constitute the exclusive legitimate space of as well as the analytic frame for politics. This assertion, of course, provides the basis for the contemporary study of political science. It is thus an assertion deliberately challenged by Deleuze and Guattari's argument about the relationship between state and capital. They go on to explicitly challenge claims about the study of politics grounded in this claim. They suggest that politics is an axiomatic (rather than apodictic) science. Politics "proceeds by experimentation, groping in the dark, injection, withdrawal, advances, retreats. The factors of decision and prediction are limited" (Deleuze and Guattari, 1987: 461). In science, the axiomatic suggests a parallel methodology:

> But that is just one more reason to make a connection between politics and axiomatics. For in science an axiomatic is not at all a transcendent, autonomous, and decision-making power opposed to experimentation and intuition. On the one hand it has its own gropings in the dark, experimentations, modes of intuition. . . . On the other hand, it is in the nature of axiomatics to come up against *so-called undecidable propositions*, to confront *necessarily higher powers* that it cannot master. . . . It is the real characteristics of axiomatic that lead us to say that capitalism and present-day politics are an axiomatic in the literal sense. But it is precisely for this reason that nothing is played out in advance.
>
> (Deleuze and Guattari, 1987: 461)

Contemporary struggles over the political—both its analytic framing and practices—thus constitute a crucial, if undecidable and certainly not predetermined, terrain. To say that this ground is not given in advance is not to say that we have no points of leverage with which to engage it. In this context, they "take stock," introducing sketches of what they take to be the "givens" in the political as a terrain in the struggle over the axiomatic.

Not surprisingly, one of the (seven) key "givens" they sketch in this context involves the terrain of "minority" politics, or the politics of the "outsider," discussed above. They begin by emphasizing that the question of "minority" politics is a crucial one. This, they argue, is becoming the "age of minorities":

> Whether it be the infinite set of the nonwhites of the periphery, or the restricted set of the Basques, Corsicans, etc., everywhere we look we see the conditions for a worldwide movement: the minorities recreate 'nationalitarian' phenomena that the nation-states have been charged with controlling and quashing.
>
> (Deleuze and Guattari, 1987: 470)

Given the historical relationship between state thought and minorities, and given the ways in which states have come to be a realization of the capitalist axiomatic—and thus their ability to improve the quality of life for their peoples, to act on behalf of their peoples, is intimately linked to their capacity to *be* a site of realization of the axiomatic—this dynamic is hardly surprising. That they are so often "quashed" by nation-states is intimately linked to the form and sources of their self-production:

It matters little that the minorities are incapable of constituting viable States from the point of view of the axiomatic and the market, since in the long run they promote compositions that do not pass by way of the capitalist economy more than they do the State-form.

(Deleuze and Guattari, 1987: 470)

Given this, it is not difficult to imagine the conditions under which, rather than being "quashed," these movements might be controlled, in particular through recognition:

The response of the States, or of the axiomatic, may obviously be to accord the minorities regional or federal or statutory autonomy, in short, to add axioms. But this is not the problem: this operation consists only in translating the minorities into denumerable sets or subsets, which would enter as elements into the majority, which could be counted among the majority.

(Deleuze and Guattari, 1987: 470)

This recognition could only be granted, thus, to those groups that could and would agree to particular forms of resonance, to agree to resonate with the state, to become a part of the realization of the capitalist axiomatic.[13] Such a "solution," however, evades more crucial terrain, according to Deleuze and Guattari, and thus will never suffice to address the necessities of violence embedded in the structures of the axiomatic:

But what we are talking about is something else, something even that would not resolve: women, nonmen, as a minority, as a nondenumerable flow or set, would receive no adequate expression by becoming elements of the majority, in other words, by becoming a denumerable finite set. Nonwhites would receive no adequate expression by becoming a new yellow or black majority, an infinite denumerable set.

(Deleuze and Guattari, 1987: 470)

Thus, these groups are perhaps better served by insisting upon their resistance to recognition, by remaining unrecognizable: "What is proper to the minority is to assert a power of the nondenumerable, even if that minority is composed of a single member. That is the formula for multiplicities. Minority as a universal figure, or becoming-everybody/everything" (Deleuze and Guattari, 1987: 470).[14]

Deleuze and Guattari thus accord a privileged status to minorities or outsiders in the struggle against sovereignty, positing a rethinking of sovereignty that requires a renegotiation of the subjectification of the nation-state—a denial of the necessities of this kind of subjectification to the realization of the capitalist axiomatic. We (the "majority" as much as any "minorities") must, in other words, not seek to extend but to disrupt the regime of subjectivity, become other than subjects that can be classified by gender, race, nationality, age, in order to disrupt the regime of sovereignty. Their effort is precisely not to reformulate sovereignty to be more inclusive, but to use its exclusions to demonstrate and reshape its very limits. It is only through this kind of reformulation that we can hope to address the violent necessities of sovereignty. Rather than expanding the terms of resonance, we must refuse to resonate.

The potential dangers of such a strategy—even so sketchily laid out—are immediately troublesome. Considering that many of these "minorities" face such immediately degraded, violent, desperate life circumstances, and considering that potential amelioration of these circumstances—if not their underlying cause—seems to be most likely through recognition by a nation-state, can we in good faith not fight for their concerns to be recognized and addressed? Are Deleuze and Guattari, in other words, suggesting that such strategies be abandoned? They quickly move to counter the apparent absoluteness in their statement. They are careful not to discount processes of political action that push for recognition, for the adding of axioms:

> Once again, this is not to say that the struggle on the level of the axioms is without importance; on the contrary, it is determining (at the most diverse levels: women's struggle for the vote, for abortion, for jobs; the struggle of the regions for autonomy; the struggle of the Third World; the struggle of the oppressed masses and minorities in the East or West . . .).
>
> (Deleuze and Guattari, 1987: 471)

These struggles reveal and expose the more general violences, and sites of contest, of the axiomatic:

> But there is also always a sign to indicate that these struggles are the index of another, coexistent combat. However modest the demand, it always constitutes a point that the axiomatic cannot tolerate: when a people demand to formulate their problems themselves, and to determine at least the particular conditions under which they can receive a more general solution (hold to the *Particular* as an innovative form). It is always astounding to see the same story repeated: the modesty of the minorities' initial demands, coupled with the impotence of the axiomatic to resolve the slightest corresponding problem. In short, the struggle around axioms is most important when it manifests, itself opens, the gap between two types of propositions, propositions of flow and propositions of axioms.
>
> (Deleuze and Guattari, 1987: 471)

Thus perhaps what is most central and important about such movements in the long run cannot be measured by the "victories" they win as measurable according to familiar political standards: representation, standard of living, and so on. We must also be attentive to the extent to which they reveal, disrupt, and address the violences and incapacities and limitations of the axiomatic through and in relation to which our political possibilities are constituted. This suggests the necessity of understanding these conflicts as doing much more than demanding the extension of the benefits of the axiomatic more broadly. The very constitution and processes of the axiomatic will always constrain such efforts. What must also be at stake are a range of broader questions about identity, politics, social organization; about ontologies; about conditions of possibility. Rather than letting states determine the parameters of the questions of unity and diversity, the question must be opened up much more broadly, and these "minority" movements contain important possibilities for this. Crucially, in large part this responsibility for effecting this rests not only with the strategists of these movements, but as much with those who read and respond to these movements. This, then, is to pose a challenge as much to the "majority" as the "minority."

The political terrain they sketch is in this way almost unthinkable: it truly is a groping in the dark, an encounter with undecidable propositions. On the one hand, they effect a rearticulation of sovereign thought, denaturalizing its founding assumptions and practices, especially how these are embedded in the structure of thought itself. Through this they open space to realize its violences, perhaps even to address some of them. On the other hand, they locate this rearticulation within a larger context that denies that these are challenges that can be "solved" within the political contexts we have available to us. They also suggest the potential limitations and dangers of attempting to do so in ways that strengthen that capitalist axiomatic through realization of the form of the sovereign state. Do they, then, suggest contours of an approach to contemporary Indigenous politics? Well, yes and no. They reshape the terrain significantly from the—largely Hobbesian—terrain we have been on so far. However, the effects of this reshaping remain somewhat, and necessarily, suggestive and provocative rather than programmatic. To begin to illustrate what I take to be their implications, I turn next to a rereading of the *Delgamuukw* appeal decision, first discussed in Chapter 6.

Recontextualizing Canada: rereading *Delgamuukw*

Pursuing the strategic and analytic possibilities opened by Deleuze and Guattari's text not surprisingly opens more questions than it provides answers. This is an indication of the success of the text, its capacity to enable us to think differently, to see things anew, even as it may leave us with a sense of both uncertainty and urgency. They suggest that we are embedded in struggles that may not be the ones we presume, and that how we come to understand—to theorize—the contexts we are embedded in is of central political import. But they also insist such theorization cannot be abstract; thus the need to make rhizomatic connections—to moments of axiomatic struggle, not least—in order to seek sources and strategies for disrupting worlds we inherit that we may wish to disrupt but are in danger of implicitly reproducing. They leave us on uncertain terrain, but also perhaps with the urgency and prompt to think otherwise than we have. With this in mind, it seems worthwhile to revisit some earlier terrain we have covered: the *Delgamuukw* appeal decision. The return will aim to sketch a wider terrain of engagement than suggested by the earlier analysis, to provoke a rethinking of what the decision itself reveals, enables, and provokes, in particular about how we might more productively open the question of sovereignty.

At first glance, a reading by Deleuze and Guattari might emphasize how the decision functions as an apparatus of capture by establishing a necessary ground of resonance, a ground that determines the conditions under which any form of "difference" might be recognized, codified, and (dis)empowered. It simultaneously legitimates a particular form of subjectivity and reasserts and reinforces the underlying authority and necessity of resonance with Canadian sovereignty. Further, the conditions under which the recognition might happen involve the strengthening of the function of Canada as an expression of the axiomatic. Aboriginal title can be recognized (must be, in fact, in order to calm the political climate) insofar as it does not interfere with the ability of Canada to act on behalf of the welfare of its population. In other words, the decision ensures that Canada can still facilitate access to the materials necessary to ensure the benefits of capitalism to its population. In this way the decision reinscribes the state as the necessary expression of the capitalist axiomatic. Further, and consistent with this, the decision effectively formalizes those conditions as legal grounds upon which the dispossession of Aboriginal title might occur. This looks a lot like capture.

All of this, however, is not to say that the terrain of the political is unaffected by the decision. As Deleuze and Guattari say: "the struggle on the level of axioms . . . is determining" (Deleuze and Guattari, 1987: 471), no more so than when it disrupts our assumptions, opens new ways of thinking. What has this moment of struggle opened up? The formal status given to Indigenous epistemological and ontological systems in the evaluation of evidence could emerge as a site where the limits of political discourse could be pushed, where undecidable and productive propositions could be pursued. Here we see the criteria for the evaluation of thought itself disrupted: a rhizomatic possibility opened. The relationship amongst land, culture, identity, and authority that is acknowledged in the recognition of Aboriginal title belies particular stories about prerequisites for properly political communities that are popular in political discourse, both past and present, thus opening another set of important propositions. The possibilities that might emerge from the recognition of title also should not be underestimated. Because this title remains constrained by Canadian sovereignty does not mean it will not benefit some Indigenous peoples, open new possibilities for political, social, and economic organization and reorganization.

Further, the explicit codification of the discourse of limits itself refocuses political struggle. The decision, in other words, lays bare the logic of sovereignty as a discourse of limits in relation to Indigenous politics. This clarity has the effect of signaling the parameters for a strategy of "recognition," marking the edges of political struggle in ways that might also be important. The comments of Satsan are relevant in this context: it is crucial to understand what institutions can grant, and what they cannot. If disillusionment with the decision has the effect of redirecting resources away from formal struggles with Canadian political institutions and into community-based rehabilitation, this may ultimately prove beneficial to some communities.[15] In other cases, such an expression of limits may inspire a more aggressive response, an argument for the need to assert sovereignty through whatever means necessary, given that Canada appears unwilling to recognize it. Thus, at first glance, the decision seems to reinscribe familiar paradoxes of sovereignty, appearing both to open new spaces for political activity and to firmly bound these spaces. On this reading the terrain of the decision Indigenous politics remains framed by sovereignty: the potential authorization of Indigenous groups depends upon the extent to which they can produce recognizable political subjectivities. The terms of recognition are intriguingly broadened, and there is potential for disruption of the underlying capture, but the parameters of struggle remain determined by the sovereign.

For those who accept sovereignty's necessities, for those who consider that, despite its violences, it is the best we can hope for and remains the necessary precondition for political life, such a decision might nevertheless be cause for celebration. It establishes a mechanism through which one of the past violences of sovereignty might be addressed and to some extent remedied, and it does so without compromising the integrity or authority of sovereign power. Thus, although it reinscribes Indigenous politics as a familiar and perpetual struggle within and against sovereignty, from this perspective it is our best hope. Hobbes himself might well be counted in this group. However, as indicated by the specter of violence that haunts such an acceptance, this does little to reframe the preconditions for violence embedded in sovereignty discourse.

This brings us to a critical precipice of sorts in relation to the decision in particular, and discourses of sovereignty more generally: it poses the question of whether we can or should throw into question the assumption of sovereignty.[16] Should we, in other words, explicitly or implicitly accept and work from the ground that the decision establishes? It is a precipice that most evaluations of the decision, most commentaries on Indigenous politics, and most political theorists, step back from. Even those who bemoan the limits of the decision tend to emphasize its potential and the strategic possibilities it opens. However, if, as I've been arguing throughout, it is in part discourses and practices of sovereignty that produce the situation that Indigenous peoples are struggling against, should we still step back from the precipice? Should we accept sovereignty's version of its own necessity and (frightening) alternatives, and embrace the decision's rendition of sovereignty discourse as an improvement, perhaps the best we can do for the moment? To accept this is to constrain Indigenous political movements to a negotiation of the margins; more importantly, it is to reassert that the only political game in town is the game of sovereign states. It is to deny the possibility of difference, the multiple, yet again; it is to accept sovereignty's rendition of its own necessity and alternative. It is to reassert a rigid set of possibilities, even as it denies the appearance of rigidity because it tells us that these are our only options, the precondition for everything else.

This is where Deleuze and Guattari's analysis becomes increasingly relevant. They do not dive over or step back from the precipice; they reject it. It is a precipice constructed by sovereignty discourse, which tells us that this sovereignty is the only possible and therefore necessary response to modern problems of social and political organization. However, while Deleuze and Guattari deny the precipice, they do not deny the illusion of the precipice; they insist on the necessity of seeing and thinking through the illusion. They seek to write a text that disrupts this assumption of sovereignty: one which does not reassert sovereignty, but seeks to ask which sovereignty? How sovereignty? What other forms of sovereignty, or authority constitution, might be possible or desirable? What does it become possible to see and think when we disrupt the apparent necessity of what we have inherited? If we take their arguments seriously, we have to challenge a reading of the decision that continues to assume sovereignty as the condition of possibility for the political. We must seek to produce a line of flight from the apparatus of capture; we must think the problem differently. What, then, does their rejection of the precipice imply for a reading of the decision?

While their reading of the apparatus of capture and its tactics for producing resonance has provided insights into how the decision both opens and constrains possibilities, other parts of their analysis suggest different readings. If, as suggested by their analysis of the apparatus of capture as operating both within and against the capitalist axiomatic, we reject the assumption of sovereignty as the expression of an autonomous political subjectivity, other potential readings of the political and analytical terrain of the decision emerge. First, rather than reading the decision as determining the parameters of the political, the decision instead may appear as an effort to reinscribe the possibility of sovereignty, to rearticulate the subjectivity of Canada such that it can retain its authority to bound the political. This reveals the necessity of (Canadian) sovereignty itself becoming an object of inquiry, rather than an assumed precondition for the analysis. From this perspective, rather than the enabler of political subjectivity, the origin of the authority of the political, "Canada" becomes a nodal point for the organization of certain political possibilities, possibilities that hinge at least in part on its capacity to realize the capitalist axiomatic. This draws our attention to new analytic and political possibilities.

So, for example, rather than seeing the decision as reconfiguring the parameters of Indigenous politics: creating a new goal (Aboriginal title) to aspire to, one might see the decision as an expression of the shifting possibilities available to "Canada" as a result of Indigenous activism. On this reading, the decision reveals the subjectivity/sovereignty of "Canada" itself as a site of political contest, susceptible to particular kinds of challenge. In this case it reveals a vulnerability to the kinds of challenges posed by Indigenous peoples: "Canada" cannot live with the story of itself in relation to Indigenous peoples that was told by McEachern C.J.; it requires and is desperately trying to create another narrative to ground its authority. Why can't it live with this story? An answer to that question that is attentive to Deleuze and Guattari's encouragement to locate the state in the context of the capitalist axiomatic requires locating Indigenous demands in the context of the historical constitution of the authority/subjectivity of "Canada," particularly in relation to its past and present political economy. Two things are immediately striking from even a brief glance at "Canada" from such a perspective: first, the extent to which its economy has always been dependent upon the extraction of raw materials for foreign markets, and thus dependent upon and driven by economic forces on a global scale;[17] and, second, the extent to which Canadian national subjectivity has always rested upon the assertion of an essentially Kantian morality, in particular upon the assertion of being morally superior to and more civilized than the United States.[18] From this perspective, then, some of the specific ways in which Indigenous peoples are always already located within the constitution of Canadian subjectivity and sovereignty become clearer. As discussed earlier, not only did the early settlement of Canada (and thus the development of its political economy) depend upon the aid, resources, and support of Indigenous peoples, but Canada has also continuously produced and promoted itself as the land of vast wilderness (Indigenous land) and yet as a "civilized" state. The latter claim has always hinged in part on the superiority of Canada's "Indian policy" compared to the extermination policy practiced by the United States.[19] Indigenous peoples have always been central to and constitutive of Canada's subjectivity, if primarily as its shadow. Further, this perspective reveals a potential kind of political strength in this position.[20] The appeal decision did not happen in a vacuum: the mobilization of Indigenous peoples in Canada has forever changed the possibilities for the "autonomy" of a Canadian sovereignty that seeks to contain them, and thus to erase this history. Yet further, the strength or leverage of Indigenous activism might to some extent depend upon the extent to which Canada cannot recognize, contain, include Indigenous peoples. The political force of Indigenous people might, as Deleuze and Guattari suggest, rest on the possibility of remaining to some extent indenumerable sets, forcing undecidable propositions upon Canada. The political implications of the institutions of Canadian justice being "put in a dilemma," as Satsan claimed, are intriguing and potentially important.

This also, however, reveals the ways in which this vulnerability of Canadian sovereignty is contingent upon the relationship between Indigenous demands and the capitalist axiomatic: Canada's sovereignty hinges in part on its capacity to retain its status as an expression of the axiomatic. The mobilization of Indigenous peoples has threatened that, in part because of the ways in which Indigenous claims are intimately tied to the resources necessary to sustain Canada's capacity to realize the capitalist axiomatic. Indigenous peoples would be wrong to assume that their successes are expressions of the legitimacy of their political subjectivity in and of itself: it too is an expression of its location within and negotiation of the capitalist axiomatic; in particular, their potential to impede—by way of legal and political discursive strategies, both at a state and international level[21]—access by the axiomatic to material resources.

By disrupting the assumption of "Canada" as the precondition of the political, and the decision as the expression of sovereignty, suddenly we are also forced to reconsider the framework within which we view Indigenous politics. This is not a game with two players—Indigenous peoples and Canada—seeking to renegotiate the distribution of power between themselves. Quite the contrary, Indigenous peoples and Canada are similarly constituted expressions of political possibility. Each is the expression of a collective subjectification: messy, criss-crossed, limited, and constituted in relation to a series of possibilities that exceed the simplistic rendering of an autonomous, "sovereign" subjectivity. Does this mean that these constitutions of political possibility have no independent agency, relevance, or significance? Quite the contrary. Rather, it means that instead of assuming that the terrain of the political is bounded by these two subjectivities, characterized on the one hand as a zero-sum game between them and on the other by each subjectivity's self-negotiation in relation to its constituents, we must redirect our attention to the conditions of possibility for, as well as possibilities and dangers of, these subjectivities themselves. These, further, can only be accessed by changing the context of analysis as described above, by insisting that both the subjects of our theorizing and our theorizing itself not float above and obscure their material contexts. It directs our attention to those sites where articulations of subjectivity are rubbing shoulders with negotiations over the flow of resources, for example.[22]

In this way, Deleuze and Guattari's analysis prods us to shift the context for our own reading of the decision—at least momentarily—encouraging us to ask different questions of it than those it seeks to frame for us. The sketch above is impressionistic at best: a line of flight towards what another analysis might seek to explore, but in this way it gestures towards not just an alternate reading of the decision, but an alternate reading of what is at stake in contemporary Indigenous politics, contemporary Canada, and thus towards a different terrain of the political. A rigorous pursuit of this line of analysis would no doubt identify a range of sites and struggles as politically crucial in ways that we cannot see or anticipate if we assume the terrain of the political to be bounded by sovereignty. Chapter 9 begins to take up this challenge.

9 Rethinking Indigeneity
Remapping the political

Deleuze and Guattari's analysis disrupts and reconfigures the assumed philosophical contexts through which we come to understand and shape our worlds. Not least, they throw into question the space of the political as produced by Hobbes through practices of sovereignty. Their challenge is to see things anew, to loosen the hold that modes of thought and inherited understandings impose upon our imaginations and our theorizing, and so to create new possibilities for understanding and responding to our worlds. Crucially, however, this is not work that they can do on our behalf: we are left with the necessity of doing the same kind of work on our own immediate contexts. Also crucially, this is not work that can be done primarily in and through the abstractions of philosophical tradition. Deleuze and Guattari leave us with the imperative not only to theorize differently than we have been taught, in particular to think rhizomatically, disruptively, creatively, but also to connect in particular to struggles over axioms, and the axiomatic.

Chapter 8 considered how this kind of analysis might open possibilities for thinking differently about the *Delgamuukw* appeal decision. This chapter takes up Deleuze and Guattari's challenge by making a rhizomatic connection to how some Indigenous scholars have articulated the political terrains they see Indigenous peoples facing. Again the analysis here is anything but exhaustive.[1] It seeks to identify a few key themes and challenges articulated by these authors, and to elaborate upon how these might be taken up by contemporary political theorists. It thus extends the critical work of the analysis developed throughout this text towards the challenge of doing theory under contemporary circumstances. Central to the analysis is an effort not only to challenge the limits of inherited traditions, to understand how practices of sovereignty have produced and constrained our sense of what is possible, but also to pursue such work through connection with, and being responsive to, those who have experienced the undersides of these traditions most persistently. In other words, the point here is not to invent new political terrain for the sake of it, however satisfying, comforting, or elegant such a project may be. The point is to theorize so as to enable and authorize political terrains that are responsive to the violences of our inheritances, and thus that contain possibilities for imagining different futures. The point is also to extend and authorize other imaginings of the future than that of the traditions we have inherited and that continue to frame possibilities across the globe. We need to imagine through, against and other than Hobbes' sovereignty, towards other configurations of knowledge, authority, subjectivity, and order: towards other practices of sovereignty.

Rethinking subjectivity, and politics *even identity*

Deleuze and Guattari's provocation to rethink subjectivity and its material preconditions finds expression in the work of contemporary Indigenous writers. Even a quick glance at contemporary Indigenous writing—from literature to theory, poetry to polemics—reveals a consistent engagement with the treacherous political terrain of subjectivity. This is hardly surprising, given the persistence of subjectivity as a site of political intervention under colonialism. Also not surprising, then, is that Indigenous writing on subjectivity is often informed by extensive engagement with wider literatures of anti- and post-colonial struggle. Although they share with the latter literatures the rage at the violences of colonialism and the urgency and complexity of responding to these violences, Indigenous engagements with them refract their core questions, adapting them to their own complex and diverse situations. In so doing they create a political terrain informed by the captures effected of previous anti-colonial struggles, not least in the achievement of the state form, of sovereignty.[2] Resisting the closures of sovereignty, however, requires inventing a politics more appropriate to Indigenous struggles, in the context of a field of politics defined by sovereignty. This is a dynamic site of engagement by Indigenous scholars and activists.[3]

A compelling example of this engagement is the work of Taiaiake Alfred, a Kanien'kehaka scholar and Director of the Indigenous Governance Program at the University of Victoria. Alfred's work stands out in part because it explicitly seeks to inspire and direct Indigenous peoples towards a revisioning of political possibility. He is an uncompromising critic of much of what constitutes "aboriginal politics" in Canada:

> Conventional and acceptable approaches to making change are leading us nowhere. Submission and cooperation, which define politics as practiced by the current generation of Onkwehonwe [original peoples] politicians are, I contend, morally, culturally, and politically indefensible and should be dismissed scornfully by any right-thinking person and certainly by any Onkwehonwe who still has dignity.
>
> (T. Alfred, 2005: 20)

His frustration can be traced in part to the ways in which the drive for sovereignty has shaped and constrained Indigenous politics, and he argues powerfully against the very concept of and aspiration towards sovereignty. Not only is sovereignty an alien and problematic concept for Indigenous peoples, it also leaves them trapped in a game whose terms are deeply biased against them (T. Alfred, 1999: 59). His description of the impact it has had on Indigenous politics echoes familiar themes:

> By allowing indigenous peoples a small measure of self-administration, and by forgoing a small portion of the money derived from the exploitation of indigenous nations' lands, the state has created incentives for integration into its own sovereignty framework. Those communities that cooperate are the beneficiaries of a patronizing false altruism that sees indigenous peoples as the anachronistic remnants of nations, the descendants of once independent peoples who by a combination of tenacity and luck have managed to survive and must now be protected as minorities. By agreeing to live as artifacts, such co-opted communities guarantee themselves a role in the state mythology through which they hope to secure a limited but perpetual set of rights. In truth the bargain is a pathetic compromise of principle. The reformulation of nationhood to create historical artifacts that lend legitimacy to the political economy of the modern state is nothing less than a betrayal.
>
> (T. Alfred, 1999: 60)

For Alfred, the political situation in which Indigenous peoples find themselves is thus as much a legacy of colonialism as the condition of their communities. At the very least, this kind of politics offers little to them in their efforts. Not only do state-led political processes deliberately distract Indigenous peoples from the core challenges they face, he argues, but these processes also function to recolonize them insofar as they increase Indigenous belief in and dependence on the state. A fundamentally different kind of approach is needed to address Indigenous peoples' situation.

A key starting point for articulating a different approach is the demystification of sovereignty itself:

> [S]overeignty is not a natural phenomenon but a social creation—the result of choices made by men and women located in a particular social and political order. The unquestioned acceptance of sovereignty as the framework for politics today reflects the triumph of a particular set of ideas over others—and is no more natural to the world than any other man-made object.
>
> (T. Alfred, 1999: 62)

His rejection of sovereignty, and his critique of much of what constitutes contemporary Aboriginal politics, however, does not imply a rejection of politics. On the contrary:

> It is a *political* vision and solution that will be capable of altering power relations and rearranging the forces that shape our lives. Politics is the

force that channels social, cultural, and economic powers and makes them imminent in our lives. Abstaining from politics is like turning your back on a beast when it is angry and intent on ripping your guts out. It is the *kind* of politics we practice that makes the crucial distinction between the possibility of regenerative struggle and what we are doing now.

(T. Alfred, 2005: 20; emphasis mine)

What he seeks to do in much of his work is to rearticulate the political, to trace pathways forward for Indigenous people that are capable of addressing their situations in ways that the formal political terrain they engage in does not.

But what does this politics look like? His articulation of the political is—as would be expected—complex and nuanced. It is also emerging: his writing is characterized by a provocation to dialogue and debate, to action, to new forms of leadership. That said, there is much that is specific in his provocation. One of the striking aspects of it is his emphasis on subjectivity—both individual and collective—as a key site of engagement, as perhaps the core of a new politics. His focus on subjectivity emerges from his analysis of colonialism as the core challenge that must be addressed, and in particular colonialism as it has shaped Indigenous peoples themselves. Although much of Indigenous struggle is against colonialism's legacy of dispossession, disempowerment and disease, he argues, colonialism also leaves a more insidious legacy: "Yet a parallel truth—and in most cases it is almost unspeakable—is that the injustice and sickness are perpetuated and compounded from within. . . . Although 'they' began our oppression, 'we' have to a large degree perpetuated it" (T. Alfred, 1999: 34). A new politics must thus begin by a renewal of the self: "Personal and collective transformation is not instrumental to the surging against state power, it is the very means of our struggle" (T. Alfred, 2005: 28). Much of Alfred's second book, *Peace Power Righteousness: An Indigenous Manifesto* (1999), articulates what this means in more nuance and detail. He is particularly attentive to the challenge of leadership, emphasizing both its importance for Indigenous communities and the appropriate character and focus of leadership, what it requires of the individual, what it gives to communities. One of the striking characteristics of his description is its resistance to oppositional forms of subjectivity: his is not a story of colonizer–colonized, or even one where characteristics of leadership are articulated through contrast with dominant "white" models. Quite the contrary, he is rigorous and skillful at grounding his vision of leadership in Indigenous traditions and realities, evaluated by its responsiveness to the communities it emerges from. His articulation proceeds in part through incorporating the voices of many scholars and activists in conversation, broadening the terms and perspectives on what constitutes leadership. Again the intent is provocative: the challenge he puts on the table is that of recovering and inventing what it means to be Indigenous.

This challenge is taken up more recently in an essay Alfred co-authored with Cherokee scholar Jeff Corntassel, titled "Being Indigenous: Resurgences against Contemporary Colonialism."[4] In it they extend the argument that the most important challenge facing Indigenous peoples today is that of recovering and reinventing themselves, of learning and deciding what it is to be Indigenous: "The challenge of 'being Indigenous', in a psychic and cultural sense, forms the crucial question facing Indigenous peoples today in the era of contemporary colonialism" (Alfred and Corntassel, 2005: 597–98). They contrast this with the agenda imposed upon Indigenous peoples by institutions and processes of colonizing governments. These practices, as suggested above, force Indigenous peoples to define themselves through and in relation to legal and political categories that are not their own, that reinscribe their colonization even as they appear to offer security through protection of limited aspects of their desired ways of being. Alfred and Corntassel recognize the difficult situation many Indigenous peoples are in: their choice to participate in these processes is often one of desperation as they struggle to survive in the midst of poverty and violence. Nonetheless, they insist, such processes are having the effect of producing Indigenous peoples: "who identify themselves solely by their political-legal relationship to the state rather than by any cultural or social ties to their Indigenous community or culture or homeland," leading them to be only "incidentally Indigenous" (Alfred and Corntassel, 2005: 599).

They argue that it is this identification as Indigenous, this sense of self, community, tradition, and culture, that must be recreated:

> We do not need to wait for the colonizer to provide us with money or to validate our vision of a free future; we only need to start to use *our* Indigenous languages to frame our thoughts, the ethical framework of *our* philosophies to make decisions and to use *our* laws and institutions to govern ourselves.
>
> (Alfred and Corntassel, 2005: 614)

Much of the article is dedicated to an exploration of what this consists of, what models are appropriate to characterize its key processes and characteristics. A central guiding theme is "self-conscious traditionalism," an effort to learn about and from original teachings and orienting values of Indigenous cultures. This is not an abstract engagement; it is a re-engagement with what exists, an adaptation of it to what is needed, a respect for the past and the present. They place special emphasis on the importance of language, history, ceremony, land, and, especially, relationships—kinship networks not only with family, but with all beings: "Clearly, it is the need to maintain respectful relationships that guides all interactions and experiences with community, clans, families, individuals, homelands, plants, animals etc. in the Indigenous cultural ideal" (Alfred and Corntassel, 2005: 609). As the emphasis on relationships suggests, although "being Indigenous" begins with the individual, it by no means ends there:

Indigenous pathways of authentic action and freedom struggle start with people transcending colonialism on an individual basis – a strength that soon reverberates outward from the self to family, clan, community and into all of the broader relationships that form an Indigenous existence. In this way, Indigenousness is reconstructed, reshaped and actively lived as resurgence against the dispossessing and demeaning processes of annihilation that are inherent to colonialism.

(Alfred and Corntassel, 2005: 612)

The desire is to create a broad social and political movement, one capable not only of challenging state power, but more importantly of reinvigorating and realizing the central institutions, beliefs, values, and practices that define what it means to be Indigenous. The aim is to create a movement that brings Indigeneity into being, rather than seeking recognition or permission from elsewhere to be Indigenous. To be clear, this is not primarily a "soft" politics, all about reconnecting, healing, and learning. There is a sharp edge to it as well, clearly articulated by Alfred in particular:

I believe there is a need for morally grounded defiance and non-violent agitation combined with the development of a collective capacity for self-defense, so as to generate within the Settler society a reason and incentive to negotiate constructively in the interest of achieving a respectful coexistence.

(T. Alfred, 2005: 27)

As they articulate their vision of being Indigenous, it becomes clear that they are framing an aspiration rather than something that is accessible to most Indigenous communities (Alfred and Corntassel, 2005: 610). However, an aspiration is no small thing. Their argument for what ethical and political vision could guide a resurgence able to address the situation of Indigenous peoples suggests a very different future than many imagine for Indigenous communities. Although they see no neat model or precise steps for individuals or communities to take to pursue this vision, they do see "identifiable directions of movement, patterns of thought and action that reflect a shift to an Indigenous reality from the colonized places we inhabit today in our minds and in our souls" (Alfred and Corntassel, 2005: 613). They present these as mantras, to be put into practice by each person in their own way, responsive to the particular circumstances they encounter. I reproduce them in full:

- *Land is Life* – our people must reconnect with the terrain and geography of their Indigenous heritage if they are to comprehend the teachings and values of the ancestors, and if they are to draw strength and sustenance that is independent of colonial power, and which is regenerative of an authentic, autonomous, Indigenous existence.

- *Language is Power* – our people must recover ways of knowing and relating from outside the mental and ideational framework of colonialism by regenerating themselves in a conceptual universe formed through Indigenous languages.
- *Freedom is the Other Side of Fear* – our people must transcend the controlling power of the many and varied fears that colonial powers use to dominate and manipulate us into complacency and cooperation with its authorities. The way to do this is to confront our fears head-on through spiritually grounded action; contention and direct movement at the source of our fears is the only way to break the chains that bind us to our colonial existences.
- *Decolonize your Diet* – our people must regain the self-sufficient capacity to provide our own food, clothing, shelter and medicines. Ultimately important to the struggle for freedom is the reconstitution of our own sick and weakened physical bodies and community relationships accomplished through a return to the natural sources of food and the active, hard-working, physical lives lived by our ancestors.
- *Change Happens one Warrior at a Time* – our people must reconstitute the mentoring and learning–teaching relationships that foster real and meaningful human development and community solidarity. The movement toward decolonization and regeneration will emanate from transformations achieved by direct-guided experience in small, personal, groups and one-on-one mentoring towards a new path.

(Alfred and Corntassel, 2005: 614)

Embedded in the mantras are gestures towards a politics that is almost unrecognizable. This is not a politics articulated through modern state sovereignty, although it expresses an ambition not so different from Hobbes: an ambition to create the preconditions for a shared order; an autonomous, internally resonant core of authority and resilience. Like Hobbes, it is a politics embedded in the production of a shared subjectivity, as well as the relationships, practices, and institutions that would allow that subjectivity to flourish. Importantly, though, this is a subjectivity whose substance and definition are becoming, not given, and whose contours are not articulated oppositionally, except to colonialism. In this way it suggests and argues for different practices of sovereignty, holding out the possibility of a sovereignty not grounded in Hobbes' necessities. It is a politics that also echoes parts of Deleuze and Guattari's analysis: this is not an agenda for recognition, for becoming a denumerable subset of the state. While it also does not appear to be a program for remaining imperceptible, to a certain extent it expresses this: it expresses a desire for self-definition as a prerequisite for engagement. It seeks to repoliticize areas of Indigenous life for Indigenous peoples by showing how acting on these grounds—on subjectivity, identity, knowledge production, and so on—is not only political but is the very means of their struggle. But their struggle, their politics, is to be understood differently than they imagine it to be.

In this way it also expresses a challenge to political theorists. It explicitly rejects core concepts of political theory as culturally specific and deeply problematic for Indigenous peoples. It also rejects much of the substance of contemporary theorizing, in that such theorizing has shaped and authorized the kinds of political programs and processes to which both Alfred and Corntassel attribute much of the blame for the dissolution of possibilities for being Indigenous. This is not to say that it lets political theorists off the hook: quite the contrary. The political terrain that Alfred and Corntassel seek to mobilize is not one that will be comfortable for the state: "The mythology of the state is hegemonic, and the struggle for justice would be better served by undermining the myth of state sovereignty than by carving out a small and dependent space for Indigenous peoples within it" (T. Alfred, 1999: 58). The aspiration here is not only to become self-sufficient, but to do this so as to enable the self-determination of Indigenous communities, and this is something with direct implications for the state:

> The state relegates indigenous peoples' rights to the past, and constrains the development of their societies by allowing only those activities that support its own necessary illusion: that indigenous peoples today do not present a serious challenge to its legitimacy. Thus the state celebrates paint and feathers and Indian dancing, because they reinforce the image of doomed nobility that justified the pretence of European sovereignty on Turtle Island. Tribal casinos, Indian tax-immunity, and aboriginal fisheries, on the other hand, are uncomfortable reminders that—despite the doctrine of state sovereignty—indigenous identities and rights continue to exist.
>
> (T. Alfred, 1999: 59)

As such, it also has direct implications for citizens, for individuals, for politics more widely, especially—but not exclusively—for those of us who live on colonized land.[5]

What does a political theory that responds to these imperatives look like? What political theory can help "to create a meaning for 'sovereignty' that respects the understanding of power in indigenous cultures" (T. Alfred, 1999: 54)? That, indeed, can contribute to "a spiritual revolution, a culturally rooted *social* movement that transforms the whole of society and a *political* action that seeks to remake the entire landscape of power and relationship to reflect truly a liberated post-imperial vision" (T. Alfred, 2005: 27; emphasis in original)?

Rethinking knowledge, and politics

Other Indigenous scholars take up the challenge of charting a political terrain rather differently from Alfred and Corntassel, not surprisingly. It is a diverse conversation. As might be gleaned from the analysis above, one of the most dynamic sites of conversation has been around Indigenous knowledge: its loss, its value, the need to protect, invigorate, authorize, and extend it. This conversation has emerged in part from a growing recognition of the distinctiveness and value of these knowledge systems, and from the subsequent development of international regimes to protect/exploit them.[6] Another aspect of it has focused on the integration and authorization of Indigenous knowledge systems in relation to contemporary governance practices: ecological, legal, social, and political. That knowledge is a key site of engagement should not be surprising, of course, but the suddenness and force of attention directed to Indigenous knowledge systems—by everyone from the pharmaceutical industry to ecologists, lawyers to social workers, anthropologists to mining corporations—has put them under tremendous pressure, even as it has also appeared to offer some benefit to some communities. As the analysis above suggests, the recovery and strengthening of these systems is absolutely vital to Indigenous survival; what is less clear is whether and how the attention directed towards them now will contribute to this. By taking a small slice of the diverse conversation on these matters, I explore below a terrain of engagement it might suggest to political theorists.

The political terrain activated by a focus on Indigenous knowledge systems has been a central focus of Chickasaw/Cheyenne scholar James (Sa'ke'j) Henderson. He shares with Alfred and Corntassel a strong commitment to revitalizing these knowledge systems as the key to Indigenous empowerment: "[W]hen one aspires to decolonize Aboriginal people, these neglected lifeworlds contain the authority to heal Aboriginal identities and communities. Restoring Aboriginal worldviews and languages is essential to realizing Aboriginal solidarity and power" (Henderson, 2000a: 252). However, his vision of the political terrain this activates appears to differ in important ways from theirs. For Henderson, the path towards revitalizing Indigenous knowledge systems necessarily passes through engagement with Eurocentric knowledge: "On the various paths to decolonization, colonized Aboriginal people must participate in Eurocentric society and knowledge" (Henderson, 2000a: 248). While this participation is enabling, it must also eventually be renounced: "To speak initially, they have to share Eurocentric thought and discourse with their oppressors; however, to exist with dignity and integrity, they must renounce Eurocentric models and live with the ambiguity of thinking against themselves. They must learn to create models to help them take their bearings in unexplored territory" (Henderson, 2000a: 249–50). The purpose of the engaging with dominant knowledge systems is—perhaps paradoxically—to be able to re-engage Indigenous knowledge systems and adapt them in ways that will make them more effective in resisting colonial forces: "Educated Aboriginal thinkers have to understand and reconsider Eurocentric discourse in order to reinvent an Aboriginal discourse based on heritage and language and to develop new postcolonial syntheses of knowledge and law to protect them from old and new dominators and oppressors" (Henderson, 2000a: 250). The challenge here is multifaceted, if not unfamiliar. This is a route of engagement charted by other post-colonial theorists such as Gandhi, Fanon, and Memmi, important guides—along with many Indigenous scholars—identified by Henderson. Thus, although Indigenous scholars must use the techniques of colonial thought, he warns that they must also "have the courage to rise above them and follow traditional devices" (Henderson, 2000a: 250). The challenge of "harmonization" of these modes of thought provides the focus for Henderson's work.

Henderson's work is thus something of a pastiche.[7] He draws strategic lessons and hope from the patterns of Eurocentric thought, tracing ways that large-scale changes in systems of thought have emerged from the inability of current systems of thought to address the challenges a society faced. He draws upon Hegel to remind readers that "the history of European thought and culture is an ever-changing pattern of great liberating ideas that inevitably turn into suffocating straitjackets" (Henderson, 2000a: 251). In the essay I have been drawing from, he uses this reading of European thought as a backdrop against which to identify some of the challenges facing the articulation of Indigenous knowledge systems, as well as some of their general characteristics. In other essays, he works more systematically within and against European thinkers, considering their value to and compatibility with Indigenous knowledge systems, as well as probing their own limitations and closures.[8] In so doing, he has two ambitions. The first is to establish recognition of and respect for the authority of Indigenous knowledge systems: "Thus, it is fundamental to any Aboriginal emancipation that existing Aboriginal worldviews, languages, knowledge, customary orders, and laws must be validated by Canadian institutions and thought" (Henderson, 2000a: 252). The second—at times apparently contradictory—ambition is to facilitate the capacity of Indigenous peoples to learn about themselves in and through their own languages:

> Aboriginal peoples cannot know who they are through the structure of alien languages. They cannot read about themselves in books or reports written in alien languages. Since they do now know who they are, they remain trapped in another context and discourse that others have constructed on their presumed negative values.
>
> (Henderson, 2000a: 252)

This apparent contradiction is contextualized when Henderson turns his attention to some of the key sources Indigenous peoples might turn to in order to rediscover and revitalize their worldviews: ethnographic research. Because of the systematic ways in which ethnographers objectified and formalized Indigenous worldviews, returning to these texts in order to re-invigorate Indigenous knowledge requires sustained critical re-engagements:

> Because the classic works do not present clear or fair interpretations of Aboriginal worldviews, Aboriginal people have had to suggest a total revision of anthropological and social analysis. . . . We have had to use social analysis to attempt to reverse the process: to dismantle the ideological in order to reveal the cultural (a peculiar blend of objective arbitrariness and subjective taken-for-grantedness). The interplay between making the familiar strange and the strange familiar is part of the ongoing transformation of knowledge.
>
> (Henderson, 2000a: 255)

This kind of critical engagement is vital, Henderson argues, precisely because of the ways in which the representation of Indigenous worldviews is part of the process through which possibilities for being Indigenous are constrained. "The timeless aspect is a Eurocentric attempt to limit the future—another way of forcing Indigenous culture to accept the inevitability of imitating European modes of thought" (Henderson, 2000a: 256). Indigenous scholars, he urges, can and must do better than this. They must not simply oppose Indigenous worldviews to European ones, but work through and against European knowledge systems to create the possibility for Indigenous worldviews to appear and flourish.

Henderson's analysis thus emphasizes the value of critical work across Indigenous and Eurocentric knowledge systems, of seeking not only to revitalize Indigenous worldviews, but to carve out space for them to be realized and respected. Crucially, the need for respect is not only by European thought, but in order to create a way for Indigenous scholars to reclaim knowledge produced about them by European researchers. It is thus a nuanced terrain of engagement, and one that will be familiar and comfortable to most political theorists, especially those familiar with post-colonial thought. It resonates not least with the work of political theorists seeking to create a space for Indigenous knowledge systems within existing traditions of political theory, such as that of Tully discussed above.[9] It is the approach perhaps easiest for theorists to engage, the most obviously relevant to political theory.

The question of the broader political terrain into which this critical work on Indigenous knowledge fits remains implicit, although the terrain that is hinted at is that of struggles over the wider legal and institutional protection of Indigenous knowledge. This, of course, is a terrain characterized by many of the same strategic pitfalls identified in the analysis above. While such engagement is vital, indeed determining, we must be worried about the broader contexts it potentially strengthens and enables. Many dangers lurk here: the possibility that the recognition and institutional formalization of Indigenous knowledge systems may ultimately strengthen the state, and perhaps the formal status of Indigenous peoples, while their communities continue to struggle to survive; the worry that ultimately the parameters of recognition of these knowledge systems shape them such that their "difference" is reduced to an essentially depoliticized one; the worry that ultimately the capitalist axiomatic reshapes Indigenous knowledge, and communities, to participate in its realization.[10] By the same token, the stakes of a failure to engage this intercultural political terrain of knowledge precisely at the moment when the forces of the axiomatic are seeking to codify this terrain at the global level—through international patent agreements, for example—are very high indeed.

Perhaps what appears as a strategic gulf between the two political visions presented thus far might in this way be primarily a question of tactics and emphasis, in the end, with Alfred and Corntassel more concerned about the lived experience and reinvigoration of knowledge systems and Henderson more about the contexts in which those will be authorized more widely. Not that it makes either achievement any less pressing or challenging. Nor does it reduce the challenge to political theorists: what contemporary kind of theorizing might be responsive both to this complex interplay between different forms of knowledge embedded in colonial relationships, and to the difficulty of negotiating this interplay in the context of the enormous pressure at all levels to exploit, protect, renew, and codify indigenous knowledge systems? The need here is urgent: we have ways of doing political theory once the organization of the terrain of knowledge and politics is effected through assumptions of sovereignty—that would be much of what counts as modern political theory. Indigenous struggles clearly require more than this: what political terrain can we theorize that is responsive to this challenge?

Rethinking research, and politics

An important context for Henderson's work—but one which also extends it beyond the familiar realms of political theory—is provided by Maori (Ngati Awa and Ngati Porou) scholar Linda Tuhiwai Smith. Smith's work focuses less on "knowledge" per se than on research: its contexts, assumptions, methodologies and practices, and their implications for Indigenous peoples. By shifting the focus in this way, she extends the realm of engagement to the lived experience of and contexts for knowledge, its dynamism and significance in the context of Indigenous peoples' lives and futures. Her book—*Decolonizing Methodologies: Research and Indigenous Peoples* (L.T. Smith 1999)—is explicitly written for Indigenous researchers seeking to contextualize and guide their own efforts, although it has much to offer to non-Indigenous readers as well, and not only to those who explicitly seek to work with Indigenous peoples or communities.

Decolonizing research, Smith argues, extends beyond adapting research methodologies, to a reconsideration of the understanding of knowledge production and the act of research itself. It requires at the outset understanding the history of the relationships between "research"—formal and informal processes of knowledge production, including everything from casual observation to travelogues, ethnographies to statistical collections—and Indigenous communities. Not surprisingly, it is a bleak history, leading many Indigenous communities to harbor deep suspicions about any activity under that label. This is not a history or a reaction that Smith seeks to overcome or deny—it expresses both the lived experiences of Indigenous communities and also a realistic assessment of the extent to which research processes have not only not helped Indigenous communities but have usually been used to generate additional grounds for controlling and manipulating them: "At a common sense level research was talked about both in terms of its absolute worthlessness to us, the Indigenous world, and its absolute usefulness to those who wielded it as an instrument" (L.T. Smith, 1999: 3). Responding to this history requires more than simply being more respectful researchers, more than asking different research questions or producing different kinds of knowledge; it requires rethinking what and who research is for, what the status of the knowledge produced through research processes is and should be, what the role of knowledge production in society has been and should be.[11] It requires a recreation of research itself as a process through which the very important questions Indigenous peoples have can be asked and answered. This is the scope of the challenge engaged by Smith in her book.

To deal with these questions, the book ranges widely. It begins by delving into the history of research and Indigenous peoples, identifying the assumptions about knowledge, history, society, space, and time that shaped colonial research into and understandings of Indigenous peoples, and the impact of this research on the shaping of possibility for Indigenous communities. It contextualizes the current understanding of research by Indigenous communities in this history, and then goes on to pose the question of what research might be important to Indigenous communities and why. It goes on to explain how research contexts and practices began to change as a consequence of the social movements of Indigenous peoples, the internationalization of their concerns, and debates within academia as influenced by anti-colonial, anti-imperialist, feminist and critical theory. It then turns to an exploration of what challenges are posed by articulating an Indigenous research agenda, emphasizing both research processes, particular challenges that arise within them, and case studies of emerging research projects, approaches, and methodologies. It concludes with an extended case study of the development of Kaupapa Maori research: an approach that seeks to develop research and researchers who are grounded in and capable of responding to the needs of Maori communities.

The picture of research that emerges from this engagement is one that will be almost unrecognizable to many in its reformulation of positivist research assumptions. What it has effected, however, is a restructuring of the precise and careful separation of knowledge and the political established by Hobbes. Hobbes argued for an order in which abstract standards of objectivity produce the necessarily singular ground of resonance, of shared authority, and the space of the political is kept carefully separate from this, bounded by the relationship between pre-formed citizens and their sovereign. Smith's argument reveals the violences effected by this approach, and argues for one in which the process of knowledge production and verification is subject to and responsive to the community from which it emerges, rather than to the abstract ontological and epistemological criteria of modern sovereignty:

> Kaupapa Maori research is a social project; it weaves in and out of Maori cultural beliefs and values, Western ways of knowing, Maori histories and experiences under colonialism, Western forms of education, Maori aspirations and socio-economic needs, and Western economics and global politics. Kaupapa Maori is concerned with sites and terrains. Each of these is a site of struggle . . . They are selected or select themselves precisely because they are sites of struggle and because they have some strategic importance for Maori.
>
> (L.T. Smith, 1999: 191)

This statement expresses a challenge that appears surprisingly straightforward, even as it is anything but. It expresses a research agenda that is self-consciously embedded in its social and political context. In one respect, what she recommends is not so different from the research agendas she argues against, the very standards of modern academic research: these research agendas, too, arose from within a particular cultural, social, and political context and were designed to respond to the needs of that context. A key difference, however, resides in the Hobbesian moment, the moment when that particular agenda is—precisely through practices of sovereignty, in order to enable the sovereign state—asserted to be not particular but universally true and relevant. At that moment, as the political is bounded and the particularity of the ontological resolutions that enable it is erased, the terrain upon which Indigenous difference could be perceived, understood, and responded to became that of sovereignty. We have seen the long-term implications of that for Indigenous peoples. Thus it is not surprising that at the core of an Indigenous resurgence is the assertion of a self-defined research agenda, one that inevitably—in the face of constant (hypocritical) critiques about the "limitations" and lack of "objectivity" of such a research foundation—self-consciously politicizes the process of and context for knowledge production itself.[12] Reclaiming the political character of knowledge production, denying the universality of the systems of knowledge production that it is articulated in response to, is an absolute precondition for knowledge production that expresses anything other than the terrain for Indigenous peoples produced by and through Hobbesian practices of sovereignty.

However, this agenda offers no panacea. It suggests, rather, a work in progress that struggles against some very real constraints and limitations, not least those imposed by contexts that should now be familiar, such as how expectations for research themselves are increasingly being shaped by the demands of market forces:

> Reconciling market-driven, competitive and entrepreneurial research, which positions New Zealand internationally, with the need for Maori to carry out research which recovers histories, reclaims lands and resources and restores justice, hardly seems possible. This is why the debates around self-determination and the Treaty of Waitangi have been significant.
>
> (L.T. Smith, 1999: 189)

In the struggle for research funding—much of which in New Zealand, like Canada, comes from the state—the different interests expressed in the research approach developed by Smith expresses put it at a disadvantage. It also reveals in stark terms one of the broader political terrains of knowledge production. Although the research agenda Smith is arguing for shares a core characteristic with that she is arguing against (that research should be embedded in and responsive to the particular needs and worldviews of its community), the research agenda she is arguing against, the one that has come to dominate and indeed to constitute what counts as research in much of the world, expresses—however imperfectly—the needs, desires, and world-views of a very powerful community indeed: the modern state as the expression of the capitalist axiomatic. In this context, insofar as the question remains of the extent to which any particular Indigenous community define their needs and worldview in ways that are consistent with the realization of the modern state as the expression of the capitalist axiomatic, their efforts to direct their own research agenda may run up against some very rough ground. This emphasizes, as Smith argues, the central importance of the achievement of forms of self-determination, of the capacity to develop and pursue research agendas responsive to Indigenous peoples' questions.

These are not primarily abstract concerns. They cannot be resolved at the level of ontology, epistemology, or universal values. And as such they pose very real challenges to contemporary political theory, much of which has persistently assumed the terrain of the political to be bounded by sovereignty, and thus has assumed and reinscribed the space of the political in ways that exclude precisely the terrain that Smith seeks to foreground. On the terrain of knowledge production itself the broader struggle over political possibility continues to rage. The criteria for what counts as desirable and high-quality research are central to this struggle: the terrain of the political extends here. A political theory that is not responsive to this simply cannot be responsive to the concerns of Indigenous peoples. That said, figuring out how to be responsive to it is a challenge, requiring not only a consideration of the assumptions that ground its own practice, but also a consideration of how this practice can and should be embedded in current circumstances.[13] Smith's book is intended for Indigenous researchers, but compels a response from a much wider readership.

Rethinking law, and politics

One of the key sites at which the challenges suggested by the three previous
sections will be negotiated is that of law. That the terrain of law should be
deeply intertwined with that of politics should not come as a surprise to
readers this far into the text. Although there are resources earlier in the text
to contextualize this challenge, conceptualizing it as a terrain of engagement
for Indigenous peoples and political theorists remains necessary. One of the
key Indigenous voices seeking to engage this challenge is that of Anishinabe
legal scholar John Borrows. Borrows' approach and engagement both
echoes and contrasts with those above. He is driven by the same aspiration
of seeking to authorize and enable Indigenous communities and knowledge
systems, particularly in relation to the operation of law in Canada. His
major text to date, *Recovering Canada: The Resurgence of Indigenous Law*
(Borrows, 2002), develops a powerful argument not only for the necessity of
integrating Indigenous law into the substantive operation of the legal system, but also for how such integration could proceed. Similar to Alfred and
Corntassel, and as suggested by the title of his first chapter, "With or Without You: First Nations Law in Canada," he begins from the assumption of
already-existing and substantive Indigenous legal traditions, and from the
necessity of these traditions coming to govern the communities who gave
them birth. In addition, he seeks to forward the question of whether and
how these traditions might—or might not—come to be articulated in relation to and participate in the governance of Canada, in particular but not
exclusively at those sites where Indigenous and settler Canada intersect. In
his words:

> These principles must be allowed to influence the development of law in
> Canada. When First Nations laws are received more fully into Canadian
> law, both systems will be strengthened. As both an Anishinabek and
> Canadian citizen, it is my hope that Canada will not disregard the prom-
> ise of respect that Canadian law holds for First Nations. Canadian legal
> institutions will soon determine if First Nations law will continue with or
> without them.
>
> (Borrows, 2002: 27; footnote references omitted)

His belief in the vitality of First Nations' legal traditions guides the text
forward. It offers a strong vote of confidence to the systems of law and
knowledge themselves, their appropriateness and adequacy to the task
of governing First Nations communities, as well as what they can offer to
Canadian law more widely. This confidence gives the text a much different
tone and focus from others examined thus far, significantly if subtly shifting
the analytical and political terrain.

Another key difference in his starting point is that he explicitly foregrounds
and emphasizes the diversity across and among Indigenous peoples, globally

but also—importantly—in Canada: "First Nations are as historically different from one another as are other nations and cultures in the world" (Borrows, 2002: 3). This diversity, expressed through different languages, social, political, and spiritual customs and conventions, guides each nation in relation to its distinctive circumstances, and is the grounding for the diverse, specific legal relationships. "The diverse customs and conventions which evolved became the foundation for many complex systems of law, and con- temporary Canadian law concerning Aboriginal peoples partially originates in, and is extracted from, these legal systems" (Borrows, 2002: 4; footnote references omitted). His project thus originates in the complexity and diver- sity of Indigenous societies, and he makes little attempt to generalize across or about them, in some contrast to other authors. This diversity, as we will see below, is their strength, and the necessary starting point for their intersection with Canadian law. Emphasizing it as the starting point neatly evades the challenge of homogenizing Indigenous communities, and the violence that would require.

Although Canadian law in relation to Aboriginal peoples originates in part from these Indigenous legal systems, it also of course emerges from other legal sources: British and American common law, and international law. Just as is the case with Indigenous legal systems (and wider systems of knowledge, as we saw above), "these legal systems are similarly grounded in the complex spiritual, political, and social customs and conventions of particular cultures, in this case those of European nations" (Borrows, 2002: 4). Thus, he emphasizes, Canadian law concerning Aboriginal peoples originates in this culturally mixed, diverse collection of legal sources. Crucially, however, most legal analysis has failed to recognize the importance of Indigenous sources, facilitating the inappropriate application of European law to First Nations, and the neglect of their legal traditions. Too often, Borrows argues, the assumption has been that these traditions are inevitably in conflict, thus implying that one system must dominate. This has led courts to dismiss the relevance of First Nations law, relying exclusively on common law. Borrows argues that such an approach is neither necessary nor appropriate. Not only are there precedents of Indigenous customs and conventions being incorpor- ated into Canadian law, but the Supreme Court of Canada has reinforced this potential by defining Aboriginal rights in such a way that these diverse sources can be harmonized:

> While it is true that legal doctrines from Britain, the United States, and the international community (or, for that matter, First Nations) have had a persuasive influence on the development of Canadian law, the body of case law dealing with Aboriginal issues is, in the end, 'indigenous' to Canada. Thus, while Canadian law dealing with First Nations may bor- row legal notions from various Aboriginal and non-Aboriginal cultures, it is also a uniquely Canadian amalgam of many different legal orders. It is therefore incumbent upon Canadian judges to draw upon Indigenous

legal sources more often and more explicitly in deciding Aboriginal issues.

(Borrows, 2002: 5; footnote reference omitted)

Much of what follows in Borrows' text is almost a "how-to manual" to assist the legal system to incorporate Indigenous legal sources more frequently and effectively, as well as a sustained argument for what such incorporation has to offer not only to Indigenous peoples, but also to improving the capacity of existing legal structures and procedures to respond to other contemporary challenges. Borrows illustrates how Indigenous stories contain and express legal traditions, carefully explaining how they might be understood and applied in this way and considering the particular challenges this poses. He also considers how Indigenous knowledge and experience can inform legal processes and enrich democratic practice in other ways, such as by ensuring their participation in environmental planning processes. It is a solidly argued and richly nuanced analysis, substantively engaging and negotiating many of the challenges to relying on Indigenous law which previously appeared to many to be insurmountable. Crucially, it does this primarily by firmly reminding the legal community about what the law is, and what they as lawyers, judges, and analysts actually do. The analysis identifies existing mechanisms in place to facilitate engagement with Indigenous legal traditions, and effectively contextualizes concerns that such a task is too difficult, dangerous, or otherwise problematic:

> It is evident that the distinctive elements of Indigenous legal reasoning present challenges in communicating and applying First Nations law. Yet, such intellectually challenging work is found in all legal reasoning processes. Answers to tough legal questions are not formulaic or self-evident; they require hard choices concerning the appropriate inferences to be drawn from the facts and cases in any dispute.
>
> (Borrows, 2002: 21)

Although Borrows recognizes that there are challenges to moving legal practices in this direction, he insists that these are not insurmountable, and asserts the legal, political, and pragmatic value of doing so. The analysis is rich and engaging, suggesting a terrain of legal engagement that has the potential to significantly reshape how law responds to and shapes possibilities for Indigenous peoples.

What is most striking about the analysis is its simultaneous awareness of the colonial past of and context for law, and its sharp insistence that other relationships between law and Indigenous peoples are possible, indeed are nascent in existing legal practice. It is something of a cheeky text, in fact, although its rigor and the sharpness of its analysis belie this reading. Interestingly, somewhat unlike the texts analyzed above, this is a text that is not primarily directed to Indigenous readers but to the legal profession. As such, it avoids some of the strategic tensions analyzed earlier: Borrows is not articulating a strategic terrain for Indigenous peoples, but rather for those seeking to respond to their concerns within the field of law. This to some extent also allows Borrows to evade challenges of the kind put forward by Alfred, challenges about where the focus of Indigenous peoples should be, and the dangers of believing too much in colonial institutions to respond to Indigenous concerns:

> Of all these myths, the greatest is the idea that indigenous peoples can find justice within the colonial legal system. People who have studied history know that it teaches a lesson about the law: 'in periods of calm the law may shape reality, in periods of change the law will follow reality and find ways to accommodate and justify it.' The myth is designed to induce tranquility even in the face of blatant injustice. The task is to force turmoil, force the law to change, create new parameters, and make indigenous goals an integral part of the new reality.
>
> (T. Alfred, 1999: 83)

Borrows' text is not necessarily in conflict with such a view of law, despite its difference in tone and focus. On the contrary, it seeks precisely to create some turmoil, to push the law to change, to guide the legal responses to pressures created elsewhere in ways that have the potential to make Indigenous goals an integral part of the new reality. Borrows in this way opens a productive terrain of engagement to the legal profession, suggesting a kind of engagement to allow it to reconsider its inheritances. However, it is a strategy that remains constrained by its target: insofar as the pressure is there to encourage law to take up his challenge, it has a better chance of success. He is clear throughout the text that his challenge might not be taken up, that "Canada" may choose to reject the insights and potentials offered by Indigenous legal traditions. And although he asserts strongly that Indigenous legal traditions will continue "with or without" Canadian engagement, unless Indigenous communities are able to recover, strengthen, and renew their legal traditions through their application to contemporary circumstances, it is difficult to see how this will happen. If it does not happen, of course, then Canada will not have the opportunity to draw from these traditions: these are traditions held by and inseparable from the peoples themselves. Borrows argues that they neither can nor should be codified in such a way that they can be activated other than through engagement with their holders. In the end, then, not only is his argument not necessarily in conflict with Alfred and Corntassel's, in many ways its realization may be parasitic upon their work.

Borrows' text is an appealing one, not least because it forwards an argument that we have the nascent skills and traditions we need—at least within the field of law—to trace ways forward that are responsive to the situations of Indigenous peoples. Despite its appeal, though, it remains haunted not only by Alfred's assessment of the limits of law in times of turmoil, but also by the limits revealed even in Canadian law's more progressive moments, as suggested in the analysis of *Delgamuukw*, above. As we saw in that context, the flexibility of practices of sovereignty apparently offers much to Indigenous peoples, but the problem of limits, their determination and realization, and their violences remains. We have seen frequent and explicitly violent reassertions of this in Canada's recent past, and there is no doubt that they will recur.[14] This is not a problem that can be theorized away; it is perhaps the central political problem, and keeping it at the heart of our theorizing will be necessary if we wish to maintain the relevance of political theory.

Rethinking theory, and politics

Each of the authors above seeks to characterize and respond to the political terrains he or she sees as most vital for his or her communities and for Indigenous peoples more widely. In the process, each frames a particular kind of intellectual and political project, or, perhaps more precisely, each theorizes the political challenges slightly differently. They represent a small slice of a very diverse field of conversation: other scholars would lead us to different political terrains, although those above represent core themes and issues that recur across these diverse conversations. Although the analysis above has emphasized interlinking themes, it is also important to remember that despite the many shared challenges faced by Indigenous peoples their approaches are necessarily nuanced in response to the very real differences in their circumstances. These nuances express strategic and tactical judgments that communities face and that will be vital in shaping their futures. The latter reality suggests both a sustained role for political theory, and a substantial point about the implications of the theorizing we do in relation not only to their communities, but the other communities to which we implicitly or explicitly write. Political theory, no less than any other kind of research, expresses and is responsive to the needs of particular communities, whether consciously, critically, effectively, or not.

Many of the violences of political theory identified in this text have arisen precisely from the assumption of needs shared across all communities, and of the appropriateness of one tradition—emerging from a particular historical moment as experienced by a relatively specific community—to articulate and respond to these needs. Crucially, this practice did not arise in the abstract, but in order to facilitate the political project of creating order and stability, and thus any challenge to it implies and reflects similar challenges to political life more generally. Hobbes' production of sovereignty as both necessary for and constitutive of community is an archetypical expression of this, nuanced by his self-conscious production of the universality of the shared needs. Most other modern theorists have lacked even this level of self-consciousness. Crucial to the analysis developed by the scholars above is their attempt to seize back control over their communities' capacity even to articulate, let alone respond to, their own questions, concerns, and needs in response to their own understanding of who they are and wish to be, and of the context in which they exist. This forces upon political theorists today an engagement with the conditions under which "we" can and should theorize, the question of "for whom" and "for what project" we believe we are authorized to speak. It forces the question of what needs are shared, and how these can be articulated in ways that do not reproduce the violences expressed in and facilitated by Hobbes' production of sovereignty. It forces an engagement with what we had come to assume were the safe assumptions: about knowledge, subjectivity, and the need for particular kinds of shared authority. It exposes these assumptions for what they are—assertions enabled by force and perpetuated by violence, even as they resulted in peace and prosperity for many. It also reveals the stakes of engaging with these assumptions.

Consequently, facilitating the "entry" of Indigenous peoples to this conversation by seeking to adapt existing conversations to their concerns is simply wildly inappropriate. At the very least what is required is a more systematic critical interrogation of the conditions under which this conversation was authorized and thought to be sufficient. But what is suggested beyond that is also crucial, and intriguing: what kind of theorizing, what assumptions, practices, and projects are appropriate in the wake of this critique? Because there are still many challenges, political challenges, today. We live in contexts that must be understood, in which we must shape responses, visions, and trajectories. How we come to understand and respond to the contexts we live in will contribute to shaping future possibilities. The Indigenous scholars above write in and from contexts where the need to seize hold of an understanding of their contexts and a capacity to act in relation to them is urgent. What is striking to me in their analyses is precisely the openings they suggest in this regard, the range of political challenges they identify as the terrain of necessary theoretical work, work that implicates the terrain of political theory that we have inherited, and thus that implicates us political theorists. They suggest starting points, not to solve "their" problems, but at the least to begin to articulate the limits of the traditions we have inherited, and to consider what new points of connection and collaboration might be possible. What forms of authority constitution, what practices of sovereignty, are appropriate to engage with these concerns, given these inheritances and facing these diverse contexts?

To put the challenge somewhat differently, what kind of theory and practice is appropriate to Indigenous peoples is for them to articulate. What this will offer to political theory is rich and important. What remains clear, however, is that there is a lot of work to do in political theory even for that to become a reality: Indigenous self-determination requires systematic work within and against our inherited traditions, even as it compels us to begin to theorize differently. The challenges Indigenous scholars are putting on the table go to the heart of the constitutions of authority and the space of the political that have been produced and reproduced through practices of modern sovereignty, which authorize and frame modern political theory. We must be willing not merely to adapt existing systems, but to participate in rethinking the ontological and epistemological grounding of them. In so doing, we will be rethinking the political. As Borrows suggests, this is happening now in many places—not only Indigenous politics—the only question now is whether it will happen with or without us.

10 Conclusion

Leviathan's angels and the future of political theory

My argument has ranged far and wide, but continues to return to Hobbes' paradigmatic account of how political authority could be reconstituted after the collapse of hierarchical structures of ecclesiastical authority. Hobbes' production of sovereignty is not only particularly elegant and acute, but also tremendously revealing about the nature of contemporary political struggles. In particular, his production of sovereignty reveals how modern political authority has come to be constituted through grounding it in a shared ontology but excluding the constitution of that ontology from consideration as political. By locating the realm of the properly political as the negotiation of relations between preconstituted subjects and a sovereign—in relations of governance—Hobbes effectively stabilizes politics in the form of the modern sovereign state. Sovereignty—the ground of legitimate authority—is produced in the realm of the pre-political. The violences of its production are rendered necessary and inevitable, rather than open to scrutiny or contestation. According to the discourses of sovereignty, all political claims must be framed and interpreted within the framework of governance, rather than posing a challenge to its constitution. Thus, although Hobbes himself explicitly reveals and acknowledges the particularity of the constitution of sovereignty—the processes through which the shared ontology and subjectivity of the citizens are produced and guaranteed—the structures through which he made them appear as natural and necessary have remained stronger than perhaps even he could have anticipated.

The elegance and strength of this formulation are impressive; so too are its violences. Insofar as this shared ontology has been seen as the necessary precondition for social and political order, the violences through which it has been produced, and continues to be reinforced, have too often been overlooked or legitimated as necessary and inevitable. From our contemporary perspective, we can critically reflect upon the violences effected and legitimated by Tocqueville's texts or early Canadian "Indian policy;" we can recognize and condemn them as inappropriate. However, we have too often focused on the particular violences, rather than the processes, practices, and discourses through which such practices were rendered legitimate at the time. So today we condemn the practices of taking young Indigenous children from their families, forcing them into residential schools to become properly "civilized," dispossessing them of family, culture, land. However, we are far more reluctant to throw into question the sovereign state as the assumed ground and frame for the political, even though it is this assumption which has contributed to the apparent necessity of and legitimation for such violences. As the naturalized precondition of the properly political, sovereignty functions to reinscribe itself as the limit condition.

The contemporary situation of Indigenous peoples, I have argued, needs to be understood in part as an effect of these discourses, as an effect as much of their successes as their failures. Despite their continuous production and reproduction as marking the outsides of these discourses, and their experiences as victims of it, Indigenous peoples have had no choice but to appropriate these same discourses in their own struggles for political subjectivity. That they have done so, and have sought to express versions of political possibility that do not resonate with the terms of their colonization, is clear enough evidence that these discourses and practices of sovereignty are not always and everywhere the same, either in form or impact. However, they have histories, institutional and discursive instantiations, and these frame and constrain practices of sovereignty. Thus, forced to appropriate discourses that are enabled by the exclusion and delegitimation of their identities, ontologies, and forms of social and political organization; struggling to articulate a vision of difference within a political discourse in which all differences are reduced to identity by locating them spatially or temporally; seeking to resist the violences necessitated by the discourses they have appropriated, these movements have faced and sought to negotiate political terrain characterized by resilient tensions and double binds. Despite their flexibility and malleability, the specificity of their instantiation at any given site, the discourses and practices of sovereignty continue to reinscribe themselves as the limit condition of political possibility, and to shape all options for political forms and expressions. Even those who have struggled most fiercely to evade these necessities, to reconstitute them, to resist their violences, still struggle to rearticulate them in progressive ways.

I have argued that while these discourses and practices have enabled what is most stable and successful about modern political institutions, they have also required and facilitated their greatest violences. These failures must be understood as necessary effects of their conditions of possibility. As Hobbes argued, we are fallible creatures, and our self-makings will always be cobbled together, fragile and imperfect, however necessary they remain.[1] Given this aspect of Hobbes' argument, I think even he would be amazed at the strength of the discourses and practices of sovereignty whose contours he traced. I think, for example, that he would find alarming the violences those discourses have facilitated, and would have been one of the first to protest their capacity to motivate people to give—and take—lives on their behalf.[2]

When Hobbes formulated *Leviathan* in an attempt to provide a basis for ending the violence of civil war, he reached for an "outside," a difference unknown, powerful and distant enough to signify and produce a commonalty, an identity, amongst the peoples of England. By marking this "outside" with peoples an ocean away, he could hope to distance the expression of violence, to shift it away from an "inside," away from neighbors, hoping in turn to enable peace, prosperity, stability. From a contemporary perspective, we can accuse him of racism and condemn the "distant" violences his use of this metaphor has been used to justify. However, holding him responsible for these violences accomplishes very little, serving as it does to conceal the social, political, and economic forces of which *Leviathan* was an expression.

To condemn Hobbes for his explicit racism thus does not access the problem that we must engage. Rather, we must come to grips with what his production of sovereignty illustrates: the assumptions, discourses, and practices that enable the forms of social and political organization in which we live have in turn enabled and legitimated enormous violences. Further, they depend upon these violences, and thus continue to reinscribe them. More dangerously, these assumptions, discourses, and practices also constrain our possibilities for thinking otherwise about contemporary challenges to our forms of political and social organization. Given that our social, political, and material contexts are all significantly different from those of Hobbes, and—arguably—in a period of rapid change, this latter danger may be the most pressing. In other words, Hobbes used a distanced "other" not in an attempt to sanction violence but to enable peace at home, "inside" the nation. However legitimate a response that was or was not in Hobbes' time, it is increasingly obvious that it is not today. There is no "other" that we can distance, and no "self" we can pretend is innocent of its violences.

Yet despite the mounting evidence of the violences of this mechanism of identity production, on the one hand, and the reformulation of the spatial and temporal conditions under which its idealization might have made some modicum of sense, on the other, we remain in part trapped by its appeal and necessity, longing for Hobbes' solution in a world where even (especially) Hobbes would see that this solution itself has come to construct the problem we face. Much as struggles to re-establish a shared ecclesiastical system of authority—in an earnest belief that it would bring peace—were driving people to inconceivable violences in Hobbes' times, so struggles to establish the ideal of "self-rule" or sovereignty continue to drive inconceivable violences today. The evidence that something must change is mounting. What this involves is much less obvious.

This problem is exacerbated by the fact that sovereignty is not simply an abstract characteristic or attribute of the modern state, but is in fact embedded in the discourses and practices through which we constitute and legitimate authority much more broadly. As we saw in the analysis of disciplinary boundaries in Chapter 4, the resolutions and practices of sovereignty are constitutive of the conceptual frameworks we use to understand the world. These frameworks thus express and reproduce its necessities in the practices through which we apprehend, explain, authorize, and act in the world. Modern subjectivity is inseparable from discourses and practices of sovereignty. The ontology of sovereignty is both our enabling and our limit condition; it expresses the resolutions through which we imagine and produce political possibility. Any attempt to engage with the violences of sovereignty is thus also an engagement with our own conceptual limits, with the assumptions that enable our understanding of political possibility. It can be effected only through immanent critique: there is no "outside" from which to render an "alternative." We can imagine, and perhaps even produce, divided authorities or shared authorities; we can debate over jurisdictions, "levels" of government, and so on, but only to the extent that sovereignty is already resolved. These may ameliorate a given expression of the limits of sovereignty, but they do not necessarily engage with the underlying problematic. To the extent that the underlying resolutions of sovereignty still produce a particular ontology as limit condition, the expression and effects of the violences of sovereignty are likely to remain familiar. This is perhaps most clearly illustrated by the analysis of the *Delgamuukw* decisions in Chapters 6 and 8: although they grant some form of space for a non-resonating ontology, it is a space that is clearly bounded by the necessities of modern sovereignty, the necessities of resonance with the state as the realization of the capitalist axiomatic.

Realizing that there is no "outside" does not have to lead to the conclusion that we are doomed to repeat the necessities of sovereignty, however. On the contrary, it enables the significance and strength of an immanent critique to emerge. Although there is no "outside" to the discourses of sovereignty, to open them up as a problem, rather than assuming and remaining constrained by their versions of necessity, itself reveals crucial possibilities. This is illustrated most clearly by Deleuze and Guattari, whose analysis can be used both to realize the dangers and possibilities contained within Aboriginal title, and to open possibilities for reconceptualizing and indeed recreating the political terrain of Indigenous politics more widely. Through their analysis, especially combined with the writings of Indigenous scholars, we can begin to see how many strategies pursued within contemporary Indigenous politics are also effecting important rearticulations of political possibility, opening possibilities for theorizing the political differently, for rearticulating the necessities embedded in practices of sovereignty. They stretch the boundaries of existing political institutions and assumptions, opening possibilities for disrupting the necessities and violences of the forms of collective subjectification produced by sovereignty discourse. What is crucial is that political analysts, theorists, and strategists do not foreclose consideration of the difficulties and limitations that these strategies also express, that we do not reinscribe the limit condition in such a way as to repeat the closures whose effects we seek to address. By engaging these discourses rather than assuming them, we can access resources to resist familiar closures that Indigenous political movements are struggling against, suggesting possibilities for responding differently to their challenges; indeed, for understanding their challenges differently.

It is this question—of how we might understand the challenges Indigenous political movements pose in ways that do not reinscribe the closures and necessities of sovereignty—that has perhaps most insistently driven the preceding analysis. It is crucial that the complexity of the terrain faced by Indigenous politics as an effect of sovereignty discourse is not simplified, foreclosed, or used to disable these movements. As emerged in the analysis of the challenges posed by the Native Women's Association of Canada to the processes of constitutional reform, or in the Gitksan–Wet'suwet'en's challenge to the Canadian legal system, or in the writings of Indigenous scholars in the previous chapter, it is precisely in their complexity, in how they do not "fit" within the terrain of politics as produced by sovereignty, that the promise of these movements rests. This is a complexity that we cannot respond to—cannot even recognize—if we assume sovereignty as the ground upon which their challenges must be interpreted and engaged. As Deleuze and Guattari suggest, the challenge posed to us by Indigenous political movements is not simply one of the need for the "inclusion" of a "disadvantaged" group of citizens, or even the need to "recognize" their "differences." Indigenous movements pose and are up against a range of far more serious problems, problems that converge to challenge Hobbesian accounts of the political possibilities that enable a modern politics. Insofar as we are willing to consider their challenges in this light, to open the paradoxical terrain of sovereignty discourse and resist its violences and necessities, we will not only be able to more effectively respond to the demands of Indigenous peoples, we will open the possibilities for thinking differently about the political challenges we all face.

Drawing from the preceding analysis, I want to emphasize four primary conclusions regarding contemporary Indigenous politics. Each has implications for how political theorists engage these movements, as well as "marginal" forms of politics more broadly. These implications, and the conclusions they are drawn from, also—not surprisingly—point to the centrality of the challenges posed by Indigenous politics to the assumptions and practices of sovereignty that are deeply embedded in our contemporary conceptions of political possibility. They reinscribe the need to critically engage with how these assumptions and practices currently constrain our ability to engage with contemporary political dilemmas. They also, perhaps even more importantly, suggest the possibilities that might be opened up when these assumptions are challenged.

The first conclusion is that Indigenous peoples and politics do not exist "outside" of modern politics, as movements to be "added" to existing structures and practices of politics. Rather, Indigenous peoples—their subjectivities, forms of social and political organization, resources—are a constitutive element of modern politics, modern subjectivity, modern conceptions and expressions of political possibility. The struggle at this point is not to "include" them, but to figure out how we can reconceptualize our own conceptual frameworks and institutions such that they do not depend upon the prior location of Indigenous peoples as the doomed "margins" of modernity.

Since at least the time of Hobbes, Indigenous peoples have retained a crucial status in the constitution of the conditions of possibility for modern politics, on a range of different registers. First, Indigenous peoples have occupied the material resources necessary to the development of modern state forms. Global capitalism, and by extension the modern sovereign state, could not have developed as it has without access to and exploitation of the resources claimed by (and that previously sustained) Indigenous peoples.[3] Perhaps more crucially, Indigenous peoples have bounded the individual and collective subjectivities that have constituted modern political and social organization; they have provided the "other" that has enabled the modern.[4] They have functioned as the "angels" of modern subjectivity and political theory, marking the edges of possibility: our most treasured sense of who we might be—the Noble Savage—and our most dreaded fear of who we might become—barbarian. Through these renderings, and on the minds, bodies, territories, resources, cultures, hopes, and fears of these peoples, modern political institutions have played out their own constitutive paradoxes, alternatively idealizing and punishing the angels for "our" own failures. A reading of Indigenous peoples' past and present situations, in other words, tells us much more about "us," about the effects of distinctly modern political subjectivities and institutions, than about "them": the peoples these institutions and subjectivities have consistently proven incapable of either acknowledging as anything other than a mirror version of ourselves, or granting enough space for them to recover from the onslaught of modern European cultures. Crucially, though, this is information that we need in order to respond to or facilitate the aspirations of Indigenous political movements. Without it we cannot hope to apprehend and reformulate the violences that our own practices and discourses of sovereignty perpetuate.

To reject a reading of Indigenous peoples and politics as "outside" of modern political discourse and practice has several practical consequences, in terms of both the challenges faced by Indigenous movements and the challenges they pose to contemporary political theory. First, the problem Indigenous peoples face is as much one of attaining political space for (even partially) "non-resonating" ontologies as it is an immediate set of economic, social, and political necessities. In other words, their apparent "exclusion" is not arbitrary, but necessitated by modern political discourse and practice. Thus, to address their situation requires both critical work on those discourses and efforts to engage with their material circumstances. This is apparent in the statements of the Indigenous scholars engaged above. Inasmuch as this possibility is foreclosed by the assumptions that ground modern ontologies, a response to Indigenous political movements requires a rearticulation of these (modern) subjectivities and ontologies, of our own limit conditions. It requires not only tampering with our political institutions, but a change in how we establish and legitimate political authority. This, in turn, requires that we create political institutions that do not rest upon the assumption of the (Hobbesian) modern individual.

By implication, then, the challenge for contemporary political theorists is not merely to address Indigenous politics by seeking to include them in existing political institutions and practices. What is required is a more serious reconsideration of the preconditions for and effects of these institutions. So, for example, notably absent here are recommendations for how Indigenous peoples should proceed in their struggles, or any general recommendations for institutional responses to these struggles. Although some suggestions in these directions might be gleaned from parts of my analysis, I am acutely aware that others are in much better positions than am I at this point to make such recommendations. What I hope—above all—that this book has illustrated is that the most important contribution a political theorist in my position might make to the struggles of Indigenous peoples is to disrupt the particularly damaging and oppressive conceptual frameworks they are struggling against, to render difficult or impossible the conditions under which these frameworks might be used to authorize further violences. I take this position not to demean or belittle other very important contributions political theory can make to these struggles, but to insist that political theorists first and foremost take responsibility for their own participation in reinscribing as necessary the conditions that Indigenous peoples seek to disrupt.

To assert this may appear to condemn political theorists to tasks both arcane and abstract. However, as we saw in Chapter 7, to dismiss critical work on the limits of our understanding and conceptions of the political as vague, merely philosophical, or not adequately or properly "political" is to reinscribe the limits produced by sovereignty—limits that crucially frame the possibilities and dangers for Indigenous politics—as necessary and natural. It is also to flee from at least two important questions: why it is that political theory and institutions have been unable to live up to the ideals through which they legitimate themselves, and whether these ideals remain adequate given the social and political context of our day. To ignore these questions as abstract is not necessarily to focus on the "real issues" at stake. The challenge for political theorists is not only to come up with concrete "solutions," but to consider how the very traditions we are working from are challenged by the problems faced by Indigenous peoples. This requires no less than a critical consideration of the practices and subject matter of contemporary political theory: a reinvention of political theory, not through flight from but through serious critical work on the traditions and conventions that authorize our work. On this point, I am in complete agreement with scholars like James Tully: although we differ in our methodologies for such critical investigation, we share a commitment to keeping alive the conversation about the political stakes of political theory.[5]

This leads to my second conclusion. Insofar as Indigenous political movements are coming to terms with what it means to be framed as marginal by dominant political institutions and discourses, and are seeking to envision futures and possibilities for themselves other than those framed within modern political discourses, these movements share crucial commonalities with other forms of marginal politics, including some feminisms, many anti-colonial nationalist movements, and some environmental movements. Indigenous peoples are not the only "others" of modern political thought, and the late 20th century is full of a range of parallel struggles with the closures and exclusions of modern political discourse. As discussed in Chapter 1, these movements are all facing similar aporias and paradoxes. All are coming to terms not with recognizable identities but with the constitution of specific marginal identities as both their precondition for entrance into modern political discourse and their limit condition. This suggests the importance of feminist struggles to and in relation to Indigenous political movements, the importance of recognizing the extent to which they are participating in a shared struggle to resist the options framed in terms of marginality, even as they will also at times find themselves on oppositional political ground: many women have also benefited from Indigenous colonization, and, as we have seen, gender in Indigenous communities remains politically salient.

This suggests both a broader challenge to and resource for contemporary political theory. The critical work on practices of exclusion and marginalization, on the limits and violences of modern subjectivity, on structural and institutional productions and expressions of power, on racism and sexism—all remain inadequately engaged by contemporary political theory insofar as these concerns have been perceived and responded to as demands of the "marginal" for "inclusion." While this work confronts and expresses many limits that are shared by and familiar to political theorists, it also contains serious challenges to practices that are too often reproduced by contemporary analysts of politics. In particular, as we saw in Chapter 7, to the extent that political theorists fail to engage with the challenge within these literatures to their own practices of authorization, they continue to reinscribe the marginality of these movements and thus reject rather than respond to the most difficult and important critiques they forward. These critiques not only deserve more serious consideration, they also—if read in their complexity—suggest a rich terrain of possibility for contemporary political theory. As suggested by Deleuze and Guattari, to allow these challenges to interrogate discourses and practices of sovereignty opens the possibility of thinking through and otherwise than the limits of political possibility inscribed by sovereignty discourse.

This in turn leads to my third conclusion: these movements must not be read and reinscribed as "marginal;" rather, they pose challenges that go to the heart of modern political transformation. They are struggling with the same questions, problems, and tensions as those at the apparent "center." The struggles of Indigenous peoples are focused around the reconstitution of political spaces, possibilities, and identities; with problems of how to establish and maintain socially, materially, economically, and environmentally viable communities; with the promises and dangers posed by contemporary changes in the forms and processes of capitalism; with the tensions of "difference" (sexual, cultural, generational, ideological) both "within" and "without" their communities. In short, though they appear to be merely "small" communities struggling with "self-interested" problems at the margins, their struggles are at and with the limits of political possibility, limits that frame all other struggles as well. The same is true of many feminist struggles.

Thus, rather than assuming these limits and seeking to "include" the "marginal" movements in what is "really" going on, we must take seriously the expressions of political critique and possibility that are emerging from these movements on their own terms and on shared terms, opening the possibility that they reveal and engage problems that we don't already understand or have not already solved. In other words, we need to create a situation in which their struggle is not always only to retain or secure marginality. Insights regarding what this might involve, again, are contained within the political struggles and theorizing emerging from these movements, particularly in their engagement with processes of authorization of subjectivities, communities, and practices. We must engage with their struggles within and against sovereignty as the constitution of political possibility. To the extent that we assume the political, and thus reinscribe the marginality of their struggles, we necessarily constrain our reading of these movements, and thus render ourselves unable to engage with and build on their insights and struggles. If we can figure out how to respond effectively to Indigenous women's concerns about self-government, or to the challenges—in all their complexity—posed by the Gitksan–Wet'suwet'en, we will have made strides towards the reconceptualization of political possibility necessary to respond to a range of other contemporary political challenges we face.

Finally, and again by extension, my fourth conclusion is that Indigenous politics is one expression of a rethinking of the political (of sovereignty), of the refusals and renegotiations of the limits of modern politics in the modern state. It is also one that already has much to offer political theorists. Political theorists must not engage Indigenous political movements out of compassion or generosity for the oppressed, or even exclusively because they are implicated in the critiques posed by these movements, but because these struggles are crucial to contemporary politics. They provide rich insight into the practices, processes, limitations, and possibilities of modern politics as well as of contemporary social and political conditions. Political theorists, in other words, should engage them because an understanding of them, particularly their critical engagements with and reconstitutions of political authority, is absolutely crucial to doing political theory today. We cannot assume sovereignty, focus on governance, and say much that matters about contemporary politics, because in so doing we reproduce assumptions that are everywhere being thrown seriously into question. Indigenous politics illustrate this with some clarity, and they are only one of many sites at which this is becoming increasingly clear. To the extent that political theorists continue to inscribe governance as the central question of politics, in so doing defending their inscription of themselves as the central analysts of politics, they will continue to drift into areas of increasing irrelevance on the one hand, and reinscribe dangerous limits on the other, limits whose effects are apparent in violent conflicts around the world today.

I, like Tully, Deleuze and Guattari, and many others, thus think that Indigenous political movements pose the question of the day, but I am not sure we even know what this question is with much precision, let alone have an answer to it. My analysis suggests that a reconstitution of the political that addresses the historical violences of sovereignty must involve a rearticulation of subjectivity and sovereignty, and this must happen in a context of understanding them not as givens, but as complex social, economic, political, and material productions. Reconstituting the political in relation to these challenges is perhaps the most important political work of our times. Indigenous peoples are positioned in a way that is absolutely crucial to this, but we cannot assume we understand why, what this means, or what we can learn from an engagement with their struggles.

A response to Indigenous politics, then, requires at the very least an understanding of the magnitude of the challenge they pose, and how deeply embedded "Indigeneity" is in the constitution of modern subjectivity and sovereignty, in modern conceptions and practices of politics. They have never—since contact—been "outside" the parameters of our own self-constitution. Since their "discovery" by Europeans, Indigenous peoples have functioned in the role of angels, mediating between modern subjectivity and its limits, extremes, possibilities. As a projection of our hopes and fears, "they" have inscribed for us who we must be and why, and what possible spaces we must live in, what violences we must commit. This means that an engagement with them must involve a re-engagement with these same questions. The necessity of responding to the challenges posed by Indigenous peoples is as much about reimagining ourselves—politically, socially, individually—as it is about carving out some new kind of political status for them. It requires opening up as political a broad range of practices that some would like to close off, but which can by definition never be resolved. The issue at stake is whether we try to hold the fort and retain these closures in the face of the violences they continue to enact, or struggle with the undecidable propositions that constitute contemporary politics and see where to go from here.

In this struggle, the angels of political theory play a crucial role, insofar as they bring a critical perspective on assumptions that the beneficiaries of Hobbesian sovereignty are all too likely unable to see. Indigenous peoples' struggles pose a challenge that political theory cannot back down from without reinscribing the violences of sovereignty; they pose to us some of the necessary work of our times.

Notes

1 Introduction

1 For the latter argument, see especially Chatterjee (1986).
2 I am thinking here of texts such as Elshtain (1981), Hartsock (1983), and Pateman (1988).
3 Texts organized around this question include, for example, Shanley and Pateman (1991), Hirschmann and Di Stefano (1996), Shanley and Narayan (1997).
4 On the former, see, for example, Irigaray (1985), Butler (1990, 1997), Butler and Scott (1992), Braidotti (1994). On feminist epistemology, see Hartsock (1983), Harding (1986), Haraway (1989, 1991), McClure (1992). On rethinking the significance of emerging forms of feminist activism, see Grewal and Kaplan (1994), Scott, Kaplan, and Keates (1997).
5 While this complexity has been one of the strengths of feminist theory, it has also contributed to some of its current stalemates; in particular, to at times counterproductive debates over what forms of theory or practice should count as properly political, insofar as they appear to run the risk of disempowering the political subject precisely as feminist movements began to achieve political subjectivity for more women. For my analysis of the broader implications of these debates, see Shaw (2002).
6 A very partial list would include: Laclau and Mouffe (1985), Lefort (1988), Connolly (1991, 2005), Hirschmann and Di Stefano (1996), Laclau (1996), Magnusson (1996), Archibugi, Held, and Kohler (1998), Cheah and Robbins (1998), Linklater (1998), Rancière (1999), Butler, Laclau, and Zizek (2000), Ingram (2002), Palonen and Walker (2003).
7 See the conclusion of this chapter for a note on terminology (p. 13), including a definition of Indigenous peoples.
8 This is the characterization that frames much of the literature explicitly concerned with Indigenous politics, especially in North America. See, for example: Deloria and Lytle (1984), Boldt and Long (1985), Jaimes (1992), and Boldt (1993). Although they have rarely taken seriously the *sovereignty* claims of Indigenous peoples (instead considering them as either rights claims or demands for recognition), political theorists have also tended to engage Indigenous political movements within this conceptual framework. See especially: Kymlicka (1989, 1995), Tully (1995), Ivison, Patton, and Sanders (2000), Ivison (2002). Within international relations theory, Indigenous peoples' claims have also often been apprehended as rights claims, again without much engagement with how this understanding limits the critical force of Indigenous peoples' claims.
9 This characterization leads one to post-colonial literatures, especially those focused on nationalism as an ambivalent political discourse for colonized peoples, and on the politics of post-colonial subjectivities. On the former, see especially

Chatterjee (1986, 1993); on the latter, see Memmi (1957), Fanon (1963), Césaire (1972), Nandy (1983).

10 This characterization potentially leads one towards development literatures, literatures on environmental sustainability, and literatures on the "local" effects of "globalization."

11 I am speaking here of the "we" of the largely Anglo- or Euro-American social science disciplines generally, and of the discipline of political science more specifically. However, these disciplines are expressions or manifestations of power relations that are more broadly constitutive of political possibility, and thus this "we" has broader resonances as well, not least more generally across academic communities. Although Indigenous peoples arguably are physically absent from states such as the United Kingdom, they are crucially present in the political imaginaries and discourses of these states. See, for example, Pagden (1993).

12 This argument is forwarded most explicitly in critiques of development paradigms. See, for example, Sachs (1992), Escobar (1995), Tucker (1999).

13 On this, see Wilmer (1993), Brysk (2000), and Niezen (2003). For an analysis of the role of its international articulation on the formation of Indigenous identities in Mexico, see Jung (2003), although her analysis contrasts with the Canadian case.

14 Many scholars and activists would claim their status has not been resolved in the United States, either, only repressed. See, for example, Churchill (1995, 2002).

15 This is especially apparent in Ivison, Patton, and Sanders (2000).

2 Hobbes

1 For an extended analysis of how this has come to be the case, see Bartelson (1995, 2001).

2 My reading of Hobbes is indebted to Flathman (1992, 1993, 1998), although it remains in some tension with his. There are also some echoes here from Hindess (1996).

3 This kind of analysis has been pursued by such authors as Pagden (1993) and Tully (1993, 1995). A parallel analysis of representations of women in the history of political thought has been more extensively pursued; see, for example: Okin (1979), Elshtain (1981), Coole (1988), Pateman (1988), Phillips (1991).

4 Hobbes, of course, did indeed mean "men." I follow his use of gendered language here as I think it is important to keep alive the sometimes discordant resonances between the text and our (various) current sensibilities.

5 The importance of a distinction at this level emerges in such books as Brody (1981), or in the differences in understandings of treaty negotiations, as described by Fumoleau (1973) or Brown and Maguire (1979). It will also emerge in the discussion of *Delgamuukw v. B.C.* in Chapters 6 and 8.

6 Again we see here the kind of subtle move which can function to privilege certain forms of speech or certain users of speech: the abuses of speech (Hobbes, 1968: 102) include inconstancy of language use, use of metaphorical language, use of language to lie, deceive. This is a constant tension in the history of Indigenous/ non-Indigenous interactions: the use and understanding of language, both in terms of invalidating forms of expression of Indigenous peoples and in terms of privileging those who control language: e.g. treaty negotiations. Hobbes, of course, would accuse not only "Indians" for "inconstant" use of language, but the treaty makers for its abuse. Nonetheless, it is clear that a common ground between the two groups based on this definition of the use of language has not been achieved.

7 There are a number of excellent texts that explore further the ways in which epistemology functions to produce and exclude difference: regarding gender, see Harding (1986) or Trinh (1989); regarding the man/beast distinction, see Haraway

(1989); for the primitive/man distinction, see Pearce (1967) or Berkhofer (1979); for particularly colonial relationships, see Fanon (1963) or Said (1979). These are only a few of an enormous range of works on this question.

8 This assertion is then followed sometimes by a move to place those not "us" out of space and/or time, as we'll see below. Or, as Wittgenstein describes, this assertion also paves the way for the violence of persuasion (1969: 81).

9 This is why Quentin Skinner's (1996) analysis of how Hobbes works both with and against Renaissance conceptions of rhetoric is of more than specifically historical interest. Skinner argues at length that while Hobbes initially resists relying on such rhetoric, *Leviathan* embraces it both in form and substance. But while Skinner's is the most detailed account of Hobbes' reliance on rhetoric, and thus the most sustained critique of those who overemphasize Hobbes' commitment to scientific reason, he is only one of a long line of commentators who draw attention to Hobbes' own awareness of the conditional and bounded character of his reasoning.

10 I call them "others" because they are mentioned as specific subject positions in order to illuminate a particular characteristic of the Subject: Man. See, for example, p. 125 regarding women and children, pp. 141–47 for the mad, p. 157 for those from other continents, and we will delve into the "savage" ahead.

11 This is an argument anyone familiar with the history of Indigenous peoples in the United States or Canada will recognize, as it was often used to justify ill treatment. See J.R. Miller's (1991: 122) description of Indians' "failure" to respond to capitalist market incentives as the fur trade spread west. Rather than providing more fur to meet the demands of an increasing market, they tended to provide enough fur to supply for their own needs and stop trapping. This bewildered and frustrated the Hudson's Bay Company men, leading them to speculations that bear significant resemblances to Hobbes' below, speculations later used to justify disciplinary practices in order to cultivate appropriate "desires" (passions).

12 In this sense, Hobbes' production of the state might be read in relation to Nietzsche's argument about the shadow of God: though rejecting divine authority as the basis for civic authority, Hobbes is very careful to render his formulation of civic authority compatible or resonant with structures of divine authority, thus drawing from the authority of these structures. Likewise, the resonances of Foucault's (1980, 1990) analysis of the reluctance of political theorists to "cut off the head" of the monarch are apparent here. The contemporary implications of the failure to challenge this form of authority—the way that it directs the focus for the "political" away from practices of what Foucault calls "governmentality"—are part of what drives my analysis here.

13 But only in terms of their level of historical development, not as essentially different. See, for example, the quotation that opens this chapter (p. 18). This writing of difference is thus dependent upon the underlying assertion of identity: that all men are ultimately the same, which in turn legitimates claims that the colonizers—as they are further advanced on the path of history—know what is best for the "savages." I engage this tension further below, especially in Chapter 5.

3 Violences of sovereignty

1 This line of analysis has been developed by Connolly (1995) more specifically in relation to the potentialities and limitations of pluralism as a response to the contemporary political claims of marginalized peoples. My analysis is indebted to his, although it shifts the focus from the dynamic of identity/difference towards the related problematic of sovereignty as a condition of possibility for political community. This difference in focus is motivated by the differences between the discourses used by Indigenous and other marginal peoples to articulate their claims,

in particular by Indigenous peoples' appropriation of sovereignty rather than identity as the discourse through which they have articulated their political claims. This difference suggests challenges to the practice of pluralism that Connolly's analysis is not explicitly concerned to engage.

2 Hobbes does not appear in Tocqueville's text; however, Rousseau—who works within the same sovereignty problematic as Hobbes—does. Although the affinity between Hobbes and Tocqueville is more important for my purposes, a case might be made that Hobbes' work also—mediated through Rousseau—exerts a more direct influence on Tocqueville than I am concerned to claim here.

3 This is Tocqueville's term, which I will use throughout as its resonances are significant.

4 This doubled representation of "Savages" is one that continues throughout the history of and is crucial to the production of the United States and Canada, and indeed was crucial to the project of modernity more generally. See, for example, Pearce (1967), Berkhofer (1979), Todorov (1982), Rogin (1987), Takaki (1990), Campbell (1992), Francis (1992), Pagden (1993), Churchill (1994), Barkan and Bush (1995). It is a familiar process as part of the dynamic of colonialism in other contexts as well. See, for example, Memmi (1957), Fanon (1963, 1967), and Césaire (1972) as well as a range of more recent commentators such as Said (1979, 1993), Spivak (1988a, 1988b), and Bhabha (1990). For a provocative struggle with the terrain of subjectivity this creates, see Denis (1997).

5 See Chapter 5 of Locke's *Second Treatise of Government*.

6 This, of course, is untrue. Though European-style agriculture was not practiced, the "Indians" were skilled agriculturists, and it is largely due to their willingness to share their skills with settlers that settlers were able to survive (Weatherford, 1988). The Lockean echoes that are apparent in this quotation surface frequently through Tocqueville's analysis. For excellent analyses of the relationship between Indigenous peoples and Locke's writing, see Tully (1993) or Arneil (1996).

7 However, all negotiations with Indigenous groups on the part of the federal government were formally carried out as relations between nations, which belies Tocqueville's stark writing of them. Their status was not as "obvious" as he makes it appear.

8 Other commentators who have developed similar arguments about the relationship between sovereignty and environmental practices include Tully (1993), Knobloch (1996), and Kuehls (2003). See Connolly (1995) for a more detailed analysis of the relationship between territory and identity in Tocqueville.

9 There have been long-standing disputes about the pre-contact population of the Americas, and thus the scale and character of the subsequent depopulation. For analyses that contrast significantly in both style and substance, see Churchill (1997) and Henige (1998).

10 The discussion of religion occupies 14 of the 19 pages in the section.

11 Because of the focus of my argument, I do not examine the history of settler–Indigenous interaction in nearly the depth necessary to understand the specifics of Indigenous politics or histories. Fortunately, there are many others who have done so, and my work builds on theirs. See especially: Jones (1982), Trigger (1985), Berger (1991), Miller (1991), Dickason (1992), Wright (1992), Richardson (1994), and Carter (1999). For rich engagements with the particular challenges Indigenous peoples pose to "doing" history, see: Martin (1987), Brown and Vibert (1996). The telling and retelling of these histories is a crucial part of the renegotiation of sovereignty that indigenous politics requires and is enacting. These histories challenge and rewrite the narrative identities of each nation, thus creating new political possibilities.

12 See, for example, Berger (1991, especially 32–34).

13 Significantly, in the same year, the United States turned jurisdiction for Indian affairs over to the Department of War.
14 This Proclamation was initially designed to protect "Indians" from losing land and was motivated in part by the necessity of maintaining peaceful relations with them, which gives an idea of their importance to colonial governments. It is also an often overlooked cause of the American Revolution, after which it was no longer respected in the United States. It remains a key document in Indigenous peoples' legal struggles in Canada.
15 See also Tobias (1976: 13–24).
16 See Leslie and Maguire (1983) for a more robust history of the *Indian Act*.
17 This, of course, was a policy imposed on Indigenous peoples in other countries, including the United States (Churchill 2004) and Australia (Human Rights and Equal Opportunity Commission, 1997), another indication of the ways that the practices of sovereignty were reproduced across different contexts.
18 See the Royal Commission on Aboriginal Peoples' final report for a summary and analysis of both the history and contemporary struggles around residential schools.

4 Sovereignty and disciplinarity

1 My analysis here is indebted to Ashley and Walker (1990a, 1990b).
2 Thus, while I seek here to draw attention to particular practices of sovereignty discourse expressed in disciplines of anthropology and international relations, this is not intended to imply that these disciplines are exclusively responsible for this problem. This analysis could productively be extended to the social sciences much more broadly. An analysis of economics, sociology, and geography would be equally revealing.
3 This argument is developed in Chapter 3 of Walker (1993).
4 See, for example: Knight (1988), Kreober (1994); International Centre for Human Rights and Democratic Development (1996), Brysk (2000), Niezen (2003), Keal (2003).
5 See especially Snow (1921), Green and Dickason (1989), Williams (1990), Anaya (1996), Venne (1998), Thornberry (2002).
6 She deals with this by engaging the shift from sovereign state to other actors and forms of political community in the international arena, but does not problematize deeper assumptions about sovereignty or the past story of international relations as told from the perspective of and in relation to structures of sovereignty.
7 This is illustrated in relation to international law in Williams (1990).
8 The examples of this are many: from the exclusion of Indigenous communities in texts such as Bull's, to the role of the doctrine of *terra nullius* in authorizing practices of imperialism and colonialism that ultimately led to the creation of such international actors as the United States, Canada, and Australia.
9 See, for example, Pearce (1967) and Berkhofer (1979). More recent variations on the same theme include Francis (1992) and Churchill (1994).
10 To not *assume* sovereignty, but rather to problematize it as an historical discourse and set of practices, requires a range of significant analytical shifts. What this might mean, enable, or look like is the problem that motivates my analysis here. Again, I am relying heavily on the historical and conceptual ground developed by Bartelson (1995, 2001) and Walker (1993) to focus my efforts.
11 Suggestions of what this might look like can be found in Higgins (2004), whose rich analysis of the relationship between Indigenous peoples and the Mexican state is framed provocatively in relation to the discipline of international relations, although its substantial engagement with the discipline is minimal. Were his

approach to be more widely engaged by scholars of international relations, it would indicate a substantial shift in the discipline, one with considerable promise for Indigenous peoples.

12 Some might protest that using a relatively old text to initiate the analysis of each discipline is unfair in that it misrepresents the evolution of each discipline. Again, though, my intention here is not to represent either discipline so much as to illustrate a series of conceptual practices and challenges. Although most anthropologists, especially, would be very critical of the substance of Clastres' arguments, negotiating the conceptual challenge he confronts has proved to be a long-term struggle without satisfactory resolution, as revealed below in the discussion of a more recent text.

13 This, of course, is a temporal problem very familiar to international relations theorists, trapped for so long in the "status of the state debates." See Walker (1993: chapter 5) for a more detailed reading of this debate.

14 We will see how this assertion is reproduced and works against First Nations in the discussion of the Gitksan–Wet'suwet'en sovereignty case in Chapter 6. For an anthropological account of this conundrum, see Clifford's essay "Identity in Mashpee" (Clifford 1988).

15 Ironically, in light of his attack on ethnocentrism, Clastres also reproduces a variety of versions of it in his own text. Most noticeable in this regard is his treatment of gender. Although I think that this is a symptom of the same problem for which I am criticizing Clastres, there isn't space to unravel his treatment of gender here.

16 The book I will be engaging next is an excellent example of the richness of this field: Gledhill (1994). See also Balandier (1970), Vincent (1990), Gellner (1995).

17 This conversation has expanded exponentially; some contributions to which I am indebted are Asad (1973), Fabian (1983), Marcus and Fischer (1986), Clifford and Marcus (1986), Clifford (1988), Trinh (1989), McGrane (1989), Manganaro (1990), di Leonardo (1991), Marcus (1992), Thomas (1994). For analyses more specifically focused on the role of anthropology in public policy related to Indigenous peoples in Canada, see Dyck and Waldram (1993).

18 The impact of these developments/conversations is also constrained in that they remain of interest almost exclusively to anthropologists. Thus although it is perhaps one of the more interesting sites of thinking about the political, political scientists and international relations scholars are virtually never forced to engage with it (unless they need to consult an "expert opinion" on a conflict that seems to concern culture or ethnicity), nor do they generally choose to. More on this below.

19 In particular, in relation to assumptions by non-anthropologists about what anthropology is and should be, as much as by the practices of anthropologists.

20 See also pp. 9–10, where he sketches a history of the discipline, a history framed by the assumptions of what other disciplines believed anthropology should be doing.

21 It is this particular bind that anthropologists who are sympathetic to Indigenous political movements run up against most acutely, as will be documented in Chapters 5, 6 (especially) and 7. It is my reading of how both anthropologists and Indigenous peoples seemed to encounter the same impossible double binds—for example struggles around "authenticity"—when entering the political realm that first directed my attention to the political effects of disciplinary boundaries.

5 Resistance

1 See, for example, Boldt and Long (1985), Sanders (1985), Tennant (1990), Boldt (1993), Mercredi and Turpel (1993), Smith (1993), Richardson (1994), Miller (2004).

2 For analyses of the legal and political relationships between Indigenous peoples and the Constitution in Canada, see especially: Asch (1984, 1997), Dyck (1985), Clark (1990), Cassidy (1992a), Cairns (2000), Macklem (2001), Borrows (2002).

3 "Aboriginal" is the term used by the federal government to refer to Indigenous peoples, and thus has usually been the term of choice in federal-level Indigenous politics. I follow that usage in this chapter.

4 For a summary of the proposed reform, see Boldt (1993: 94–108).

5 While NWAC was the largest and most well-organized Canadian Indigenous women's organization at the time, it was by no means the only one, nor do I have any basis for evaluating how broadly representative it was of Indigenous women's concerns. There was certainly a lot of debate about whether or not it was a legitimate expression of the majority of their views; however, it is clear that they did represent a significant number of Indigenous women.

6 The four groups that were funded were the Assembly of First Nations (representing Status Indians), the Native Council of Canada (representing non-Status), the Métis National Council, and the Inuit Tapirisat of Canada.

7 However, it was ultimately accepted in a compromise move: the Charter would apply, but governments could opt out on matters concerning cultural identity through a "notwithstanding" clause.

8 This passage poignantly illustrates the political implications of Judith Butler's argument about the meaning and practice of the universal (Butler *et al.* 2000: 11–43, 137–82).

9 See, for example, Nandy (1983, 1994), Spivak (1988a, 1988b), Chatterjee (1986, 1989), Chow (1990), Sangari and Vaid (1990), Mohanty *et al.* (1991), Parker *et al.* (1992).

10 For an excellent analysis of how a disruption of gender roles was crucial to the colonization of the Huron and Motengnais communities, for example, see Anderson (1991).

11 For more information on the history of gender in Indian policy, see Jamieson (1978, 1986), Green (1985), Silman (1987), Turpel (1989), Fiske (1993), Moss (1997), Nahanee (1997), (Turpel-Lafond (1997).

12 Political structures were "democratized" on a modern, European model, emphasizing individualized political subjectivities, representation, and property regimes. While there is an extensive debate about the contribution of North American Indigenous political systems to this model, what is beyond question is that many of the institutions and practices of governance of these groups contained internal logics and practices of legitimation that have considerable affinities with "democracy." What is also beyond question is that these institutions and practices were not recognized and respected as such.

13 These conflicts are complex, very important, and nearly impossible to generalize. In some cases the "traditional" leadership is a very progressive anti-colonial force; in other cases the elected or "Indian Act" leadership is. In most cases the distinction is not nearly so clear cut as this. There are several different case studies or analyses of how these issues, essentially the effects of colonialism, play out; see, for example, York (1991, 1999), Boldt (1993), G. R. Alfred (1995), T. Alfred (1999).

14 This, then, is the background for the argument about whether the Charter should apply to Aboriginal governments or not. Aboriginal leaders saw this as a victory in that it reinforced the idea that their governmental structures should have a separate status from Canadian ones. Ironically, of course, the *Indian Act* is an act of Canadian legislation. Nonetheless, this decision was seen as a confirmation of their sovereign status.

15 The National Indian Brotherhood, the predecessor of the Assembly of First Nations, the most prominent pan-Indian federal-level organization.

16 See Green (1985) for an analysis of the changes contained within Bill C-31. As may be obvious, deeply embedded in this case are some of the same logics and paradoxes of sovereignty revealed in the larger narrative: the UN couldn't "force" Canada to change its law; that would be a violation of sovereignty. However, Canada is in general acutely sensitive to external criticism of its human rights record—it is crucial to its international political practices—and so was more likely to respond to pressure in this regard than other—also "sovereign"—countries.

17 Here we see the roots of NWAC's concern that Aboriginal governments would put "community rights" ahead of women's sexual equality rights.

18 The federal government refused to provide adequate resources for many reserves to accommodate the sudden influx of women and children who regained their Status through Bill C-31. There are many discussions of Bill C-31, the impact it has had on Aboriginal communities, its success or failure. Examples include Green (1985), Boldt (1993), Chiste (1994), Alfred (1995), Moss (1997), Nahanee (1997).

19 It is important to emphasize that there have been many other forms of Indigenous women's activism, some more effective. Part of my argument is that these particular kinds of impasses/struggles are produced by the discursive political context in which the action takes place. Thus, rather than making an argument about the inherent sexism of male Indigenous leaders or the patriarchal structures of Indigenous politics (each of which might be important concerns, though I am in no position to consider them here) I am attempting to show how the strategies themselves—in this case the reliance on sovereignty discourse particularly—produce these kinds of conflicts. I hope this becomes clearer below.

20 This itself is an expression of a particular kind of idealism on the part of Aboriginal leaders, a belief in the sovereignty myth: that sovereignty itself was the precondition for solving all of their woes.

21 There are Status, Non-Status, Métis, and Inuit; some bands have treaties with the government, others do not, and so on. Each of these "identities" has specific formal and informal relations to government. For an analysis of how these differences affect political goals and vision, see Boldt and Long (1985, part 1).

22 "Violent" in the sense of requiring the imposition of dualistic categories on realities that are more complex, which in turn shapes and frames the possibilities of those so defined.

23 For other engagements with the challenges and possibilities faced by contemporary Indigenous women, see Allen (1986), Monture-Angus (1995), Anderson (2000), Ackerman (2003), Anderson and Lawrence (2003), Lawrence (2003), Mihesuah (2003).

24 It also marked the end, or a significant pause, in attempts for Constitutional reform in Canada as a response to a range of other challenges, not least Quebec's threatened secession.

6 Adjudication

1 See, for example, Hanke (1959), Williams (1990), Anaya (1996), and Thornberry (2002).

2 Although I do not do justice to it here, this rich field of engagement provides the kind of depth—historical, empirical, and theoretical—necessary to negotiate the terrain I seek to sketch. Citations throughout the chapter suggest resources in this regard.

3 The background I provide here is brief both because of space and because this history is well documented elsewhere. See, for example, Fischer (1977), Tennant (1990), and Harris (2002) for detailed histories of Indigenous politics in British Columbia; Cassidy (1992b) for background more specific to the *Delgamuukw* case.

4 For a very readable introduction to some of the context for the case, see Glavin (1990).
5 See Tennant and Slattery in Cassidy (1992b) and Kulchyski (1994) for more detail.
6 One of the effects of the dualistic grounding of sovereignty is that the presentation of one side of the dualism in any complexity often forces the "other" side into a homogenized form, as the history of the representation of Indigenous societies exhibits. Thus the characterization of Western worldviews is likely to seem a caricature of non-Indigenous ontologies—in the interest of establishing the legitimacy and independence of one worldview, the commonalties, linkages, etc. are minimized. The negotiation of "samenesses" and "differences" forces a freezing of each "identity" into a formalized framework, even if only for a moment, which in turn has a series of important political effects. This effect of sovereignty will become very important in future negotiations of these issues. Read in relation to the ontology of sovereignty that Hobbes produces in *Leviathan*, however, this characterization of "Western" worldviews doesn't seem so far off.
7 This challenge is being taken up across a range of contemporary sites, including law. See, for example, Kawharu (1989) and Borrows (2002).
8 My analysis here draws on the opening statement of the government's position (contained in the Proceedings at Trial, no. 250, 10 July 1989) and relies on two slightly different analyses of the Crown's case, Ray (1990) and Culhane (1998). Both the province and the federal governments mounted cases against the plaintiffs, but their cases were similar enough that I will summarize them together.
9 This is the *terra nullius* defense, the assertion that the land was unoccupied by recognizable societies. This defense has been consistently used and challenged in legal decisions throughout Commonwealth countries, for example in the *Mabo* case in Australia. For more information, see Patton (1996a, 1996b), Reynolds (1996), Sharp (1996). For an astute analysis of the broader implications of *Mabo*, see Rowse (1993).
10 For a description and analysis of the trial and decision that highlights the racist elements of the Crown's defense, see Monet and Skanu'u (1992).
11 It is in part the shock and amazement that flooded British Columbia when it did that inspired Dara Culhane's (1998) rich analysis of the case. Her question became: how could such a defense succeed? How could a contemporary Canadian court reproduce such a blatant injustice? Although this question is not so far away from my own, her argument proceeds through a micro-discursive analysis of discourses of anthropology and law. It thus reveals an enormous amount about the operation of power through discourses of "Aboriginality" in anthropology and law in the courtroom. My own argument, I think, suggests a larger context into which these insights might be productively inserted. Her argument is framed through the distinction between law and politics, and her analysis is focused on showing how "politics" or "power" managed to insert itself inappropriately into processes that should be concerned with "justice." As I develop below, I would argue that, while this is an important part of the story, much more is at stake in this contest than a violation of the boundary between law and politics, and if we accept this as bounding the issues at stake we are in danger of reproducing the violences of sovereignty in particular ways.
12 See especially Cassidy (1992b), Monet and Skanu'u (1992) and Culhane (1998).
13 In his introduction to the Decision, Chief Justice McEachern firmly asserts that "the law" must provide the boundaries within which he operates. Thus the (temporary) sovereign shifts responsibility to the larger processes of sovereignty.
14 I don't pursue an evaluation of the logic or validity of the legal argument. This has been taken up elsewhere, not least in the two subsequent Appeal decisions, but see also Cassidy (1992b) and Borrows (2002). An understanding of the ways in

which sovereignty discourse authorizes the decision provides useful context for an evaluation of these analyses. Three of the articles (Tennant, Asch, Ridington) in Cassidy (1992b) critique Chief Justice McEachern's reassertions of "outdated" and "discredited" mythologies about Indigenous peoples. My argument is that the problem expressed by the reassertion of these ideas is more deeply embedded in our still-current imaginaries, discourses, and practices of politics, states, and selves than their readings emphasize. In order to understand why the judge is able to reassert these ideas, and under what conditions he would not be able to, these ideas must be located in this larger context.

15 See, for example, Tully (1993: 137–79), Arneil (1996), Kuehls (2003).

16 The distinction between "legal" and "cultural" principles is itself one the plaintiffs had clearly hoped to throw into question as they suggested that the legal principles themselves were expressions of a particular culture.

17 The role of anthropology in this case perfectly reproduces the dilemmas of anthropology discussed in relation to Gledhill in Chapter 3. It has been the subject of some excellent commentary. See, especially, Asch and Ridington in Cassidy (1992b), and Culhane (1998). On the dilemmas of being an expert witness in the case, see Ray (1990). For an earlier reflection on the relationship between law and anthropology in land claims cases, see Barsh (1986).

18 As he puts it in the introduction to the *Reasons*: "The Court is not free to do whatever it wishes. Judges, like everyone else, must follow the law as they understand it. . . . I am sure that the plaintiffs understand that although the aboriginal laws which they recognize could be relevant on some issues, I must decide this case only according to what they call 'the white man's law'" (*Delgamuukw v. B.C.*, 1991: 2). As an aside, this assertion is directly challenged by Brian Slattery (in Cassidy 1992b), who argues that the judge is bound by the law of Canada: "an amalgam of laws emanating from many sources and includes the customary laws of aboriginal Canadian nations. More to the point, it includes the common law of Canada, which, as the Supreme Court of Canada has recognized, is the source of the law of aboriginal rights" (Cassidy 1992b: 120).

19 This double bind is reinforced later in the decision, when the judge attributes the Indians' present situation to their "failure" to adapt to changing economic situations—their failure to "progress."

20 That the last sentence of the quotation would even be relevant indicates the strength of the "authenticity" problem.

21 This decision on the judge's part of course naturalizes a particular production of sovereignty.

22 Compare this application of law to his rejection of the validity of Gitksan and Wet'suwet'en legal systems as too flexible to be considered as proper legal systems: "It became obvious during the course of the trial that what the Gitksan and Wet'suwet'en witnesses describe as law is really a most uncertain and highly flexible set of customs which are frequently not followed by the Indians themselves" (*Delgamuukw*, 1991: 219; see also 221).

23 See Cassidy (1992b), Miller (1992), and Culhane (1998) for examples of these arguments.

24 For different evaluations of the legal strategies, see Kellock and Anderson, Slattery, Storrow and Bryant in Cassidy (1992b).

25 I do not do justice to legal arguments here, but there is extensive commentary on the case. See, for example, Borrows (2002: 77–110).

26 The opinion was written by Chief Justice Lamer. There was no dissenting opinion, although two Justices (La Forest and L'Heureux-Dubé J.J.) disagreed with some of Lamer C.J.'s reasons for judgment. I focus here exclusively on Chief Justice Lamer's reasons for judgment, as the dissenting reasons do not substantially differ on the points I am examining.

27 In the course of his reasons for judgment, he also identified what the subsequent step will probably be: the recognition, definition, and further clarification of the right to self-government (*Delgamuukw*, 1997: 93).
28 The principle of reconciliation is invoked at every stage of the decision in order to provide the underlying logic for each argument. For example, for an overview of the logic, see pp. 7–8; regarding criteria for proof of occupancy, see p. 82; regarding criteria for proof of exclusivity, see p. 85; regarding the test of justification for infringement, see pp. 88–91; regarding evaluation of validity of oral histories, see p. 53.
29 The principle of reconciliation thus reproduces the structure of Hobbes' treatment of the "Savages of America" in *Leviathan*. Sovereignty exists independently of the Savages; their status is determined from the perspective of the already sovereign.
30 To be clear, my emphasis here is on illustrating how the concept of Aboriginal title is functioning here as a practice of sovereignty, and what kinds of political terrains it thus produces. Others are in a far better place to evaluate the legal implications and potentials contained within and emerging from the decision.

7 Limits

1 Tully's choice to begin with Locke, and mine to begin with Hobbes, are not incidental. Although each theorist addressed questions of government and governance in similar historical circumstances, the contexts and questions that guide their analyses differ, and these differences echo through our respective analyses. Crucially, however, the governance questions pursued by Locke in the *Two Treatises* depend upon prior resolution of the problem of sovereignty. In this way Locke's work silently depends upon that of Hobbes, and Hobbes' resolution of sovereignty continues to exert its influence throughout Locke's work. In this way, Locke's work, like Tocqueville's, remains framed and constrained by the problem of sovereignty in ways their analyses cannot, or do not choose to, engage, and the influence of Hobbes, and the general political terrain shaped by his resolution of sovereignty, pervades.
2 In this respect, Tully is a great improvement on Habermas, who still seems to want to search for a "neutral" common ground. Tully relies heavily on language and possibility of communication, but he is careful never to assume that this is neutral territory for any speaker. Its value lies in its possibility for changing the ground (it is the ground), not in its possibility for pure communication or complete understanding.
3 For a critique of Tully that resonates with that I develop here, see Helliwell and Hindess (2002).
4 This is expressed in his insistence that the history of Western constitutional thought is adequate to deal appropriately with the problem of cultural difference because it contains a richer history of engagement with other cultures that has been acknowledged. While this is true, and the history of past engagements with cultural difference within this tradition is very revealing, the possibility that the problem of cultural difference might require drawing upon other cultures, even the cultures of those he seeks to recognize, to come up with a different way of responding to this problem is never considered, except within the process already structured, enabled, and framed by the history of constitutional thought.
5 My analysis of the implications of the assumptions and practices political theorists use to authorize their projects is indebted to that of McClure (1992).
6 Tully's assertion of "recognition" as the problem of the day relies on the work of Charles Taylor (Tully 1994). Perhaps the most powerful critique of "recognition" as a frame and trope within modern philosophy is articulated by Gilles Deleuze in *Difference and Repetition* (1994).

7 See, for example, Butler (1990, 1997), Braidotti (1991, 1994), Cadava *et al.* (1991), Haraway (1991), Rajchman (1995), Debrix and Weber (2003).

8 See pp. 45–53 of *Strange Multiplicity*.

9 It is worth noting that he selects an anthropological theorist rather than a political theorist to illustrate the political dangers of this position.

10 And, conversely, to the extent that one challenges the definition of the political one becomes a "postmodernist."

11 Just as for anthropologists the project of throwing the category of "culture" into question is deeply threatening, forcing a disciplinary crisis of authority (or "society" for sociology; "international" for international relations), political scientists also require the unquestioned assertion of resolutions of sovereignty insofar as they wish to be able to make prescriptive statements about "politics." This shows how resolutions of sovereignty are broadly constitutive of legitimate authority, and their disruption does require a reconstitution of authority.

12 The simplest explanation for this is that Tully's book is not—nor does it claim to be—about Indigenous politics. It is about constitutional theory, and the possibilities contained within it. Part of what I seek to question, though, are the implications of responding to a political movement such as Indigenous politics exclusively from within conventional disciplinary assumptions, rather than considering the challenges posed by such movements to these assumptions.

13 Both concerns, and my reading here, parallel the reading of anthropology and international relations in Chapter 3.

14 The recent renewal of the treaty-making process in British Columbia has spawned a debate about this problem, with many bands opting out of the process because they fear it will result in a drain on the human resources of the community (and offer very little guaranteed success) at a time when these resources are desperately needed within the communities. There is a significant amount of evidence that this is a legitimate concern. For a critical analysis of the Treaty process, see Alfred (1999: 119–25).

15 This danger is perhaps the central point of opposition in a heated struggle against approval of the first contemporary treaty in British Columbia: that to respond to the demands of Indigenous peoples (even as expressed by one of the most moderate First Nations in British Columbia) would place impossible strain on the resources of both provincial and federal governments, and is thus not in the best interests of "all Canadians." Unfortunately, of course, there is some truth to this, which gives it enormous rhetorical force.

16 Recent violent confrontations at Gustafson Lake in British Columbia and elsewhere provide excellent examples of this. The extreme military response to the protesters was justified by an argument—reinforced by many Indigenous leaders— that it wasn't a "legitimate" protest insofar as the protesters expressed demands at odds with ongoing processes and negotiations. See Miller (2004) for other examples.

17 It is not an exaggeration to say that each and every one of the terms Tully uses in his definition of "cultural feminism" is highly contested, even among the theorists he associates with the position. For example, is there a category of "woman" that would make "women's culture" an identifiable thing, something that could be "represented" and used as a basis for a "reworking of traditions"? This, after all, is the question that launched "second wave" feminism. See, for example, de Beauvoir (1952), as well as any number of representations of the origin and development of "second wave" feminism, such as Nicholson (1997).The resounding answer, after much debate, is that no such identity can be assumed, nor that it is even a desirable goal. The most active, vibrant and highly contested debates within the broad rubric of feminist theory over the past three decades have thrown the category of woman into question in a variety of different ways. For example, one

site at which this question has been pursued with some vigor is in the debates over epistemology and feminist methodology. See, for example, Hartsock (1983), Harding (1986), Benhabib and Cornell (1987), Trinh (1989, 1991), Collins (1991), di Leonardo (1991), Haraway (1991), Mohanty *et al.* (1991), Grant (1993). They have also thrown into question many of the other assumptions in Tully's summary. Are there traditions which are "masculine," and, if so, in what way? In language, concepts, style of argument, ethos, subject matter? What would reworking these traditions involve? What, indeed, is the status of "gender"? As analytical axis? Identity? Biological category? How does it relate to such other categories as "race," "class," "sexuality"? For a smattering of feminist positions on these questions, in addition to those cited above, see: Elshtain (1981), Moraga and Anzaldua (1981), Irigaray (1985), de Lauretis (1987), Brown (1988), Pateman (1988), Cocks (1989), Weed (1989), Braidotti (1991), Phillips (1991), Bock and James (1992), Frazer and Lacey (1993), Grosz (1994), Griffiths (1995), Butler (1997). The point here is that to *assume* these questions is to ignore precisely what feminist theory has most consistently expressed as a problem.

18 That is, if we raise these critiques, we will endanger the success of this promising project, a project that would allow at least some women's voices to participate in a constitutional conversation. The echoes in this position of how socialist movements have responded to concerns about gender, how some feminist projects have responded to accusations of racism, and so on, are abundantly clear. These are expressions of a very real and politically charged tension, one with a long history, one that is also an expression of how discourses of sovereignty structure politics.

19 Or reinscribing the assumption that political theory cannot accommodate feminist critiques and thus foreclosing feminist engagement with it. This tendency within feminist theory has led it into its own dead-ends, as it seeks to struggle with the problem of the political in the absence of an analysis of how this problem has come to be constituted and continues to be reconstituted in and through political science.

20 For an analysis of a parallel example of this practice in relation to feminist theory, see Shaw (2002).

21 These lines of analysis are developed, for example, by Spivak (1988a, 1988b), Trinh (1989), Butler (1990, 1993, 1997), Haraway (1991), Mohanty *et al.* (1991), Butler and Scott (1992). Similar lines of analysis have also been developed in a range of other contexts and traditions.

22 For a small sample of different arguments to this effect, see: Walker (1993 and forthcoming), Albrow (1996), Appadurai (1996), Magnusson (1996), Archibugi *et al.* (1998), Bauman (1998), Cheah and Robbins (1998), Linklater (1998).

23 Thus, in Tully's argument, Clifford is not considered a political theorist, and his insights are read and constrained by another version of the political, although Tully calls on his "anthropological" expertise to provide a definition of "culture" for his own purposes, using it to support an argument about the representation of "culture" that I think Clifford would find untenable.

24 This is a point made by conventional structural theorists of international relations like Hedley Bull or—in an extreme form—Kenneth Waltz, who examine the systemic determinations of state action, by critical theorists of international relations such as Ashley and Walker, who insist on the mutually constitutive character of individual states and collective subjectivities internally and externally, and by a vast array of political economists from Marx onwards, who analyze state actions in the context of a globalizing capitalism.

25 This is a point that has been taken up especially by post-colonial commentators on nationalism as a co-opted discourse, for example Chatterjee (1986, 1993), Spivak (1988b), Bhabha (1990), Nandy (1994).

26 The 20th century is littered with the violences of nationalist projects. For an

analysis that is attentive to these violences as violences of sovereignty/subjectivity in relation to Bosnia, see Campbell (1998). The broader literature on these violences is extensive; I would single out Chatterjee (1986, 1989); but see also previously cited post-colonial literatures.

8 Rethinking sovereignty

1 *A Thousand Plateaus* is the second of a pair of works they encourage readers to engage together. The first is *Anti-Oedipus* (Deleuze and Guattari, 1983).

2 Brian Massumi (1992) sketches some potential entrances to and deviations from their texts, as have a number of other authors. Two authors who have taken up Deleuze and Guattari's work specifically in relation to challenges posed by Indigenous politics are Paul Patton (1996a, 1996b) and Peter Kulchyski (1992). My analysis deviates from theirs significantly, both in terms of the elements of Deleuze and Guattari's work that we draw on, and in how we apply their work to the issues at stake in Indigenous politics, although their work has enriched my own. The differences amongst our uses and readings of Deleuze and Guattari illustrate the richness of their work in relation to contemporary political challenges.

3 Another caveat: I write about Deleuze and Guattari in this context because it is partly through their writing that I rethought and rearticulated the terrain of the political developed in this book. However, I am somewhat uncomfortable with their role in this text in part because so much of what they write speaks very precisely to very different theoretical contexts. Thus, it is important to remember two things: my encounter with them is also rhizomatic, and there are many other theorists or contexts through which to effect the kind of critical work I rely on them for here.

4 It is here that they draw from Clastres' argument that primitive socieites are not pre-political, but have structures of power that resist the production of resonance on the part of state societies. However, they disagree with Clastres' claim that non-state societies become state societies when they are unable to control population growth. Deleuze and Guattari argue that this still reproduces the linear temporal logic they wish to resist, in that it assumes that state and non-state societies are in a relation of succession, rather than being mutually constituted and always coexisting. See Deleuze and Guattari (1987: 429).

5 For this will never work. On the contrary, it will only produce more minorities. See Deleuze and Guattari (1987: 472). This strategy was, to some extent, pursued in the United States, alternating and coexisting with a "civilizing" policy more similar to that of Canada. The result of this combination has been a "hardening" or formalization of the relationship between Indigenous peoples and the state in the United States, as compared to the situation in Canada, where this relationship is still very much under negotiation.

6 See Knobloch (1996) for an excellent analysis of agriculture as a process of colonization in the American West.

7 Deleuze and Guattari are particularly critical of modern philosophy in this regard, which they consider to be state thought par excellence: "In so-called modern philosophy, and in the so-called modern or rational State, everything revolves around the legislator and the subject. The State must realize the distinction between the legislator and the subject under formal conditions permitting thought, for its part, to conceptualize their identity. Always obey. The more you obey, the more you will be master, for you will only be obeying pure reason, in other words yourself . . . Ever since philosophy assigned itself the role of ground it has been giving the established powers its blessing, and tracing its doctrine of faculties onto the organs of State power. Common sense, the unity of all the

faculties at the center constituted by the Cogito, is the State consensus raised to the absolute" (Deleuze and Guattari, 1987: 376). The philosophers they point to as exemplary of this are Kant and Hegel.

8 This raises the question of whether all thought is state thought. Their answer to this lies in their earlier discussion of tree thought versus rhizomatic thought: there are always rhizomes in trees and vice versa. To ask whether all thought is state thought is to presume that thought could ever only be one thing, to assume that there might be an "outside" to give definition to "state thought." This also raises the tension between the meaning of these identities/categories and the multiple, complex subjectivities/agencies who at times inhabit them. To say the categories only have meaning in relation to state thought is not to assert that these subjects are defined only by these categories.

9 This, of course, is no less true of the majority, whose identities are no less dependent upon the subjectification of minorities. However, their capacity or at least their sense of their capacity to presume that their identities are natural, liberating, expressions of their "selves" means that the experience of the identity might be enabling rather than constraining. The identity of "colonizer," and the tendency of the majority to evade its constraints as much as possible, is very revealing in this regard.

10 I take Deleuze and Guattari to mean this in a very broad sense. For example, I would read Foucault's analysis of governmentality as an example of how the state becomes organized in relation to capital: the flip side of moving towards the care of the citizens is that the state must enable their health. This requires that they not only function within and resonate with capital, but also benefit from it. It requires the production of subjects who desire and receive the benefits of the capitalist axiomatic. For an analysis of this aspect of Foucault in relation to Indigenous peoples, see Kuehls (1998) and Higgins (2004).

11 For their characterization of different forms of the state, see p. 459; for their characterization of the question of the relative isomorphism of states, see pp. 445–46.

12 They spend a lot of time playing with these details throughout *A Thousand Plateaus*, illustrating the ways in which they are crucial, configuring and reconfiguring their political relevance. Unfortunately, the scope of my analysis doesn't provide the necessary space to delve into this, and precisely because the details are so crucial it is impossible to summarize.

13 Again, as the axiomatic is not necessarily predetermined, this would not necessarily be a uni-directional activity. Perhaps the most obvious example of the ways in which such a struggle for recognition can effect a change in the axiomatic is evidenced by some strains of contemporary environmental politics, in particular the ways in which these political movements have had some (albeit limited) success changing the operation of capital in relation to the environment. The extent of the change effected may ultimately not be terribly significant, however (as the logic and structure of the marketplace so far seem to remain largely intact). For one examination of this problem, see Luke (1997).

14 This recommendation is embedded in their analysis in another plateau of the politics of "becoming," so the content and implications of this suggestion are not immediately obvious. Some feminists have expressed concern about this prescription; see especially Braidotti (1991: 108–23) and, to some extent, Spivak (1988a). Below I discuss some of my own concerns in relation to Indigenous politics, though it is deserving of much closer attention.

15 Though, of course, access to resources at all requires a certain amount of engagement with Canadian political institutions.

16 This is not only an abstract question, of course; it is the question posed by those who take up arms in defense of their communities. This is a live, simmering, debate

in Canada, as evidenced by the violent confrontations that continue to haunt the state. See, for example: Hornung (1991), Wadden (1991), York (1991), Johansen (1993), Blomley (1996), Edwards (2003), Miller (2004). In relation to the Mexican context, see Higgins (2004). For a rethinking of indigeneity, violence and the state, see Shapiro (1997).

17 And thus also dependent upon the exploitation of resources claimed by Indigenous peoples.

18 This is a point deserving of much more elaboration. In fact, it suggests where an analysis of Indigenous politics might begin, if one accepts the argument presented thus far. The next few pages are an attempt to gesture to the kinds of questions such an analysis would engage.

19 This explains, in part, why strategies of Indigenous peoples that involved publicizing their concerns internationally have generally been quite successful at attracting the attention of the Canadian government, as discussed in Chapter 5.

20 This perspective also reveals the misleading nature of the claim that "sovereignty" can exist independently from its recognition by a larger states system. Canada is a particularly obvious case of the fragility of such a claim, in that its sovereignty has always hinged on an interplay between "internal" and "external" claims of legitimacy, as exemplified by the ways in which its "identity crisis" is often assuaged by the assertion of what a good "international citizen" Canada is. In this sense it is not only because of the capitalist axiomatic that Canadian sovereignty cannot be analyzed in isolation from or as independent from a range of other forces, but also because of Canada's location within discourses of international politics, discourses that produce and maintain the authority and viability of states system, and thus any given sovereignty claim.

21 Again indicating the interplay amongst international discourses of the states system, specific claims of sovereignty and legitimacy, and the operation of the capitalist axiomatic.

22 Obvious sites for such an examination include the terms of the creation and governance of Nunavut, ongoing treaty-making and treaty renewal negotiations, and the extensive and rich debates over the role of traditional knowledge and cultural difference in governance and environmental management. On the latter, see, for example: Kawharu (1989), Berkes (1999), Smith (1999), Battiste and Henderson (2000),Dei *et al.* (2000), Borrows (2002), Nadasdy (2003), Pottier *et al.* (2003), G.C. Shaw (2003).

9 Rethinking Indigeneity

1 I draw on the work of several Indigenous scholars below, mostly those who work in and from Canada, as that is the primary context from which I have been speaking. However, I want to emphasize that this is a wide-ranging and blossoming field, and there are many, many other Indigenous scholars making important contributions to it. Serious engagement with their work is vital and rewarding: their work is bringing a distinctive and nuanced conversation into being. There is no need to speculate about the challenges posed by Indigenous peoples: they are articulated clearly and powerfully, and have received far too little attention to date.

2 See, for example, Chatterjee (1986).

3 Although the dynamism is somewhat new, there is a range of older work forwarding Indigenous perspectives on their situations. A few important earlier works include: Cardinal (1969), Akwesasne Notes (1978), Barsh and Henderson (1980), Deloria (1988), Adams (1989).

4 Some of the ideas contained within the essay are developed in more depth in T. Alfred (2005).

5 If we extend this to include those who benefit from the colonization of

Indigenous land, responsibility extends much more widely, not least to many European countries.

6 For a very small sample of this work, see Posey and Dutfield (1996), Stabinsky and Brush (1996), Shiva (1997, 2001), Battiste (2000), Battiste and Henderson (2000), Dei *et al.* (2000), Sell (2003), Gibson (2005).

7 It also shares characteristics of hybridity, the political import of which has been explored not least by Haraway (1991), but see also analyses of the political implications of hybrid management regimes combining modern scientific knowledge with traditional ecological knowledge. See, for example: Berkes (1999), Borrows (2002), Nadasdy (2003), Pottier *et al.* (2003), G.C. Shaw (2003).

8 See, for example, Henderson (2000b, 2000c).

9 See also Sharp (1990), Ivison *et al.* (2000), Ivison (2002).

10 Some of the most lively debate about these dangers takes place in the literature on the potential of, and dangers for, the integration of traditional ecological knowledge into resource management. See citations in note 7.

11 As Smith notes, these are questions which have been raised and engaged also by feminist researchers such as Harding (1986) and Haraway (1991).

12 This is not, of course, to say that there are not important standards of quality and "objectivity" to be applied to the evaluation of Kaupapa Maori research: quite the contrary. It is only to say that these standards themselves must be understood and engaged in and as part of their social and political context. See especially L.T. Smith (1999: 163–79).

13 For some of my own efforts in this regard, see K. Shaw (2003, 2004).

14 For specific examples, see: Hornung (1991), Wadden (1991), York (1991), Johansen (1993), Blomley (1996), Edwards (2003), Miller (2004).

10 Conclusions

1 This is an element of Hobbes' analysis elaborated on most productively by Flathman (1993).

2 For example, I see no basis in Hobbes' writing for a support of colonial processes in North America, as one finds in Locke (as Tully illustrates) or Mill. On the contrary, I find in Hobbes considerable ground for resistance to such violences.

3 This is also true of the other "Others" of modern subjectivity/sovereignty: the structures of the modern state and capital could and would not have developed as they have without the unpaid productive and reproductive labor of women, for example, or slaves.

4 Again, they are not alone in this role, and are only privileged at some sites. Women, the "Orient," immigrants, the mad, the criminal, Jews, animals—the list of the "others" of Western thought is long and its procedures and effects are complex.

5 See especially Tully (1989). Many other political theorists, of course, engage in and encourage such a conversation about the political stakes of political theory. The contrasting position is illustrated by the two strains of political theory that might be considered dominant in the United States, however—"Straussian" and "public choice"—both of which by and large refuse to engage in this conversation.

References

Ackerman, Lillian (2003) *A Necessary Balance: Gender and Power among Indians of the Columbia Plateau*. Norman: University of Oklahoma Press.

Adams, Harold (1989) *Prisons of Grass: Canada from a Native Point of View*. Saskatoon: Fifth House.

Akwesasne Notes (ed.) (1978) *A Basic Call to Consciousness*. Summertown, TN: Book Publishing Company.

Albrow, Martin (1996) *The Global Age: State and Society Beyond Modernity*. Cambridge: Polity Press.

Alfred, Gerald R. (1995) *Heeding the Voices of our Ancestors*. Toronto: Oxford University Press.

Alfred, Taiaiake (1999) *Peace Power Righteousness: An Indigenous Manifesto*. Toronto: Oxford University Press.

—— (2005) *Wasáse: Indigenous Pathways to Action and Freedom*. Peterborough, ON: Broadview Press.

Alfred, Taiaiake and Jeff Corntassel (2005) "Being Indigenous: Resurgences against Contemporary Colonialism." In *Government and Opposition, Ltd*, pp. 597–614.

Allen, Paula Gunn (1986) *The Sacred Hoop: Recovering the Feminine in American Indian Traditions*. Boston: Beacon Press.

Anaya, S. James (1996) *Indigenous Peoples in International Law*. Oxford: Oxford University Press.

Anderson, Karen L. (1991) *Chain Her by One Foot: The Subjugation of Native Women in 17th Century New France*. London and New York: Routledge.

Anderson, Kim (2000) *A Recognition of Being: Reconstructing Native Womanhood*. Toronto: Sumach Press.

Anderson, Kim and Bonita Lawrence (eds.) (2003) *Strong Women Stories: Native Vision and Community Survival*. Toronto: Sumach Press.

Appadurai, Arjun (1996) *Modernity at Large: Cultural Dimensions of Globalization*. Minneapolis: University of Minnesota Press.

Archibugi, Daniele, David Held, and Martin Kohler (eds.) (1998) *Re-imagining Political Community: Studies in Cosmopolitan Democracy*. Cambridge: Polity Press.

Arneil, Barbara (1996) *John Locke and America: The Defence of English Colonialism*. Oxford: Oxford University Press.

Asad, Talal (ed.) (1973) *Anthropology and the Colonial Encounter*. London: Ithaca Press.

Asch, Michael (1984) *Home and Native Land: Aboriginal Rights and the Constitution.* Toronto: Methuen.

—— (ed.) (1997) *Aboriginal and Treaty Rights in Canada: Essays on Law, Equality, and Respect for Difference.* Vancouver: University of British Columbia Press.

Ashley, Richard K. and R.B.J. Walker (1990a) "Speaking the Language of Exile: Dissident Thought in International Studies." *International Studies Quarterly* 34:3, pp. 259–68.

—— (1990b) "Reading Dissidence/Writing the Discipline: Crisis and the Question of Sovereignty in International Studies." *International Studies Quarterly* 34:3, pp. 367–416.

Balandier, Georges (1970) *Political Anthropology.* London: Penguin Press.

Barkan, Elazor and Ronald Bush (eds.) (1995) *Prehistories of the Future: The Primitivist Project and the Culture of Modernism.* Stanford, CA: Stanford University Press.

Barsh, R.L. (1986) "Behind Land Claims: Rationalizing Dispossession in Anglo-American Law." *Law and Anthropology* 1, pp. 15–50.

Barsh, R.L. and J.Y. Henderson (1980) *The Road: Indian Tribes and Political Liberty.* Berkeley: University of California Press.

Bartelson, Jens (1995) *A Genealogy of Sovereignty.* Cambridge: Cambridge University Press.

—— (2001) *The Critique of the State.* Cambridge: Cambridge University Press.

Battiste, Marie (ed.) (2000) *Reclaiming Indigenous Voice and Vision.* Vancouver: University of British Columbia Press.

Battiste, Marie and James (Sa'ke'j) Youngblood Henderson (2000) *Protecting Indigenous Knowledge and Heritage: A Global Challenge.* Saskatoon: Purich Publishing.

Bauman, Zygmunt (1998) *Globalization: The Human Consequences.* Cambridge: Polity Press.

Bedford, David and Thom Workman (1997) "The Great Law of Peace: Alternative Inter-Nation(al) Practices and the Iroquoian Confederacy." *Alternatives* 22:1, pp. 87–111.

Benhabib, Seyla (ed.) (1995) *Democracy and Difference.* Princeton: Princeton University Press.

—— (2002) *The Claims of Culture: Equality and Diversity in the Global Era.* Princeton: Princeton University Press.

—— (2004) *The Rights of Others: Aliens, Residents and Citizens.* Cambridge: Cambridge University Press.

Benhabib, Seyla and Drucilla Cornell (eds.) (1987) *Feminism as Critique.* Minneapolis: University of Minnesota Press.

Berger, Thomas R. (1991) *A Long and Terrible Shadow: White Values, Native Rights in the Americas, 1492–1992.* Seattle: University of Washington Press.

Berkes, Fikret (1999) *Sacred Ecology: Traditional Ecological Knowledge and Resource Management.* Philadelphia and London: Taylor and Francis.

Berkhofer, R.F. (1979) *The White Man's Indian.* New York: Vintage Books.

Bhabha, Homi (ed.) (1990) *Nation and Narration.* New York: Routledge.

Blomley, Nicholas (1996) "'Shut the Province Down': First Nations Blockades in British Columbia, 1984–95." *BC Studies*, vol. 111, pp. 5–36.

Bock, Gisela and Susan James (eds.) (1992) *Beyond Equality and Difference: Citizenship, Feminist Politics, Female Subjectivity.* New York: Routledge.

Boldt, Menno (1993) *Surviving as Indians: The Challenge of Self-Government.* Toronto: University of Toronto Press.

Boldt, Menno and J. Anthony Long (eds.) (1985) *The Quest for Justice: Aboriginal Peoples and Aboriginal Rights.* Toronto: University of Toronto Press.

Borrows, John (2002) *Recovering Canada: The Resurgence of Indigenous Law.* Toronto: University of Toronto Press.

Braidotti, Rosi (1991) *Patterns of Dissonance.* New York: Routledge.

—— (1994) *Nomadic Subjects: Embodiment and Sexual Difference in Contemporary Feminist Theory.* New York: Columbia University Press.

Brody, Hugh (1981) *Maps and Dreams.* Vancouver: Douglas & McIntyre.

Brown, G. and R. Maguire (1979) *Indian Treaties in Historical Perspective.* Ottawa: Indian and Northern Affairs.

Brown, Jennifer S.H. and Elizabeth Vibert (eds.) (1996) *Reading Beyond Words: Contexts for Native History.* Peterborough, ON: Broadview Press.

Brown, Wendy (1988) *Manhood and Politics.* Totowa, N.J.: Rowman & Littlefield.

Brysk, Alison (2000) *From Tribal Village to Global Village.* Stanford: Stanford University Press.

Bull, Hedley (1977) *The Anarchical Society: A Study of Order in World Politics.* New York: Columbia University Press.

Butler, Judith (1990) *Gender Trouble: Feminism and the Subversion of Identity.* New York: Routledge.

—— (1993) *Bodies that Matter: On the Discursive Limits of "Sex."* New York: Routledge.

—— (1997) *The Psychic Life of Power: Theories in Subjection.* Stanford, CA: Stanford University Press.

Butler, Judith and Joan C. Scott (eds.) (1992) *Feminists Theorize the Political.* New York: Routledge.

Butler, Judith, Ernesto Laclau, and Slavoj Žižek (2000) *Contingency, Hegemony, Universality.* London and New York: Verso.

Cadava, Eduardo, Peter Connor, and Jean-Luc Nancy (eds.) (1991) *Who Comes after the Subject?* New York: Routledge.

Cairns, Alan C. (2000) *Citizens Plus, Aboriginal Peoples and the Canadian State.* Vancouver: UBC Press.

Campbell, David (1992) *Writing Security: United States Foreign Policy and the Politics of Identity.* Minneapolis: University of Minnesota Press.

—— (1998) *National Deconstruction: Violence, Identity and Justice in Bosnia.* Minneapolis: University of Minnesota Press..

Cardinal, Harold (1969) *The Unjust Society: The Tragedy of Canada's Indians.* Edmonton: Hurtig.

Carter, Sarah (1999) *Aboriginal Peoples and Colonizers of Western Canada to 1900.* Toronto: University of Toronto Press.

Cassidy, Frank (ed.) (1992a) *Aboriginal Self-Determination.* Lantzville, BC: Oolichan Books and the Institute for Research on Public Policy.

—— (1992b) *Aboriginal Title in British Columbia: Delgamuukw v. The Queen.* Lantzville, BC: Oolichan Books and the Institute for Research on Public Policy.

Césaire, Aimé (1972) *Discourse on Colonialism.* New York: Monthly Review Press.

Chatterjee, Partha (1986) *Nationalist Thought and the Colonial World: A Derivative Discourse?* London: Zed Books.

—— (1989) "Colonialism, Nationalism, and Colonialized Women: The Contest in India." *American Ethnologist* 16:4, pp. 622–33.

—— (1993) *The Nation and its Fragments: Colonial and Postcolonial Histories.* Princeton, N.J.: Princeton University Press.

Cheah, Pheng and Bruce Robbins (eds.) (1998) *Cosmopolitics: Thinking and Feeling Beyond the Nation.* Minneapolis: University of Minnesota Press.

Chiste, Katherine Beaty (1994) "Aboriginal Women and Self-Government: Challenging Leviathan." *American Indian Culture and Research Journal* 18:3, pp. 19–43.

Chow, Rey (1990) *Women and Chinese Modernity: The Politics of Reading Between West and East.* Minneapolis: University of Minnesota Press.

Churchill, Ward (1994) *Indians Are Us? Culture and Genocide in Native North America.* Toronto: Between the Lines.

—— (1995) *Since Predator Came: Notes from the Struggle for American Indian Liberation.* Littleton, CO: Aigis Publications.

—— (1997) *A Little Matter of Genocide: Holocaust and Denial in the Americas, 1492 to the Present.* San Francisco: City Lights Publishers.

—— (2002) *Acts of Rebellion: A Ward Churchill Reader.* New York: Routledge.

—— (2004) *Kill the Indian, Save the Man.* San Francisco: City Lights Publishers.

Clark, Bruce (1990) *Native Liberty, Crown Sovereignty.* Kingston: McGill-Queen's University Press.

Clastres, Pierre (1977) *Society Against the State.* Translated by Robert Hurley. New York: Urizen Press.

Clifford, James (1988) *The Predicament of Culture: Twentieth-Century Ethnography, Literature, and Art.* Cambridge, MA: Harvard University Press.

Clifford, James and George Marcus (eds.) (1986) *Writing Culture: The Poetics and Politics of Ethnography.* Berkeley: University of California Press.

Cocks, Joan (1989) *The Oppositional Imagination.* New York: Routledge.

Collins, Patricia Hill (1991) *Black Feminist Thought.* New York: Routledge.

Connolly, William E. (1991) *Identity/Difference.* Ithaca: Cornell University Press.

—— (1995) *The Ethos of Pluralization.* Minneapolis: University of Minnesota Press.

—— (2005) *Pluralism.* Durham, NC: Duke University Press.

Coole, Diana H. (1988) *Women in Political Theory: From Ancient Mysogyny to Contemporary Feminism.* New York: Harvester Wheatsheaf.

Crawford, Neta (1994) "A Security Regime among Democracies: Cooperation among Iroquois Nations." *International Organization* 48:3, pp. 345–85.

Culhane, Dara (1998) *The Pleasure of the Crown: Anthropology, Law and First Nations.* Vancouver: Talonbooks.

de Beauvoir, Simone (1952) *The Second Sex.* Translated and edited by H.M. Parshley. New York: Bantam.

de Lauretis, Teresa (1987) *Technologies of Gender.* Bloomington and Indianapolis: Indiana University Press.

Debrix, François and Cynthia Weber (eds.) (2003) *Rituals of Mediation: International Politics and Social Meaning.* Minneapolis: University of Minnesota Press.

Dei, George J. Sefa, Budd L. Hall, and Dorothy Goldin Rosenberg (eds.) (2000) *Indigenous Knowledges in Global Contexts: Multiple Readings of Our World.* Toronto: University of Toronto Press.

Deleuze, Gilles (1994 [1968]) *Difference and Repetition.* Translated by Paul Patton. New York: Columbia University Press.

Deleuze, Gilles and Félix Guattari (1983 [1972]) *Anti-Oedipus: Capitalism and Schizophrenia*. Translated by Helen R. Lane and Robert Hurley. Minneapolis: University of Minnesota Press.

—— (1987 [1980]) *A Thousand Plateaus: Capitalism and Schizophrenia*. Translated by Brian Massumi. Minneapolis: University of Minnesota Press.

Deloria, Vine (1988) *Custer Died for Your Sins*. Norman, Oklahoma: University of Oklahoma Press.

Deloria, Vine, Jr. and Clifford Lytle (1984) *The Nations Within: The Past and Future of American Indian Sovereignty*. New York: Pantheon Books.

Denis, Claude (1997) *We Are Not You: First Nations and Canadian Modernity*. Peterborough, ON: Broadview Press.

di Leonardo, Michaela (ed.) (1991) *Gender at the Crossroads of Knowledge*. Berkeley: University of California Press.

Dickason, Olive Patricia (1992) *Canada's First Nations: A History of Founding Peoples from Earliest Times*. Toronto: McClelland & Stewart.

Dyck, Noel (ed.) (1985) *Indigenous Peoples and the Nation-State: 'Fourth World' Politics in Canada, Australia and Norway*. St. Johns: Institute of Social and Economic Research, Memorial University of Newfoundland.

Dyck, Noel and James B. Waldram (eds.) (1993) *Anthropology, Public Policy and Native Peoples in Canada*. Montreal: McGill-Queen's University Press.

Edwards, Peter (2003) *One Dead Indian: The Premier, the Police, and the Ipperwash Crisis*. Toronto: McClelland and Stewart.

Elshtain, Jean (1981) *Public Man/Private Woman*. Princeton: Princeton University Press.

Escobar, Arturo (1995) *Encountering Development: The Making and Unmaking of the Third World*. Princeton, NJ: Princeton University Press.

Fabian, Johannes (1983) *Time and the Other: How Anthropology Makes Its Object*. New York: Columbia University Press.

Fanon, Frantz (1963) *Wretched of the Earth*. New York: Grove Press.

—— (1967) *Black Skin White Masks*. New York: Grove Weidenfeld.

Fischer, Robin (1977) *Contact and Conflict: Indian–European Relations in British Columbia, 1774–1890*. Vancouver: University of British Columbia Press.

Fiske, Jo-Anne (1993) "Child of the State, Mother of the Nation: Aboriginal Women and the Ideology of Motherhood." *Culture* 13:1, pp. 17–35.

Flathman, Richard E. (1992) *Willful Liberalism: Voluntarism and Individuality in Political Theory and Practice*. Ithaca: Cornell University Press.

—— (1993) *Thomas Hobbes: Skepticism, Individuality and Chastened Politics*. Newbury Park: Sage Publications.

—— (1998) *Reflections of a Would-Be Anarchist*. Minneapolis: University of Minnesota Press.

Foucault, Michel (1980) "Two Lectures." In Colin Gordon (ed.) *Power/Knowledge*. pp. 78–108 New York: Pantheon.

—— (1990) "Governmentality." In Graham Burchell, Colin Gordon, and Peter Miller (eds.) *The Foucault Effect: Studies in Governmentality*. pp. 87–104 Hemel Hempstead: Harvester Wheatsheaf.

Francis, Daniel (1992) *The Imaginary Indian*. Vancouver: Arsenal Pulp Press.

Frazer, Elizabeth and Nicola Lacey (1993) *The Politics of Community: A Feminist Critique of the Liberal–Communitarian Debate*. Toronto: University of Toronto Press.

Fumoleau, Rene (1973) *As Long as this Land Shall Last*. Toronto: McClelland and Stewart.

Gellner, Ernest (1995) *Anthropology and Politics: Revolutions in the Sacred Grove*. Oxford: Blackwell.

Gibson, Johanna (2005) *Community Resources: Intellectual Property, International Trade and the Protection of Traditional Knowledge*. Aldershot, UK: Ashgate Publishing.

Glavin, Terry (1990) *A Death Feast in Dimlahamid*. Vancouver, BC: New Star Books.

Gledhill, John (1994) *Power and Its Disguises: Anthropological Perspectives on Politics*. London: Pluto Press.

Grant, Judith (1993) *Fundamental Feminism*. New York: Routledge.

Green, Joyce (1985) "Sexual Equality and Indian Government: An Analysis of Bill C-31 Amendments to the Indian Act." *Native Studies Review* 1:2, pp. 81–95.

Green, L.C. and O.P. Dickason (1989) *The Law of the Nations and the New World*. Edmonton: University of Alberta Press.

Grewal, Inderpal and Caren Kaplan (eds.) (1994) *Scattered Hegemonies: Postmodernity and Transnational Feminist Practices*. Minneapolis: University of Minnesota Press.

Griffiths, Morwenna (1995) *Feminisms and the Self: The Web of Identity*. New York: Routledge.

Grosz, Elizabeth (1994) *Volatile Bodies: Toward a Corporeal Feminism*. Bloomington and Indianapolis: Indiana University Press.

Hanke, Lewis (1959) *Aristotle and the American Indians*. Bloomington: Indiana University Press.

Haraway, Donna (1989) *Primate Visions: Gender, Race and Nature in the World of Modern Science*. New York: Routledge Press.

—— (1991) *Simians, Cyborgs, and Women: The Reinvention of Nature*. New York: Routledge.

Harding, Sandra (1986) *The Science Question in Feminism*. Ithaca: Cornell University Press.

Harris, Cole (2002) *Making Native Space: Colonialism, Resistance, and Reserves in British Columbia*. Vancouver: University of British Columbia Press.

Hartsock, Nancy (1983) *Money, Sex and Power*. New York: Longman.

Helliwell, Christine and Barry Hindess (2002) "The 'Empire of Uniformity' and the Government of Subject Peoples." *Cultural Values* 6:1&2, pp. 139–52.

Henderson, James (Sa'ke'j) Youngblood (2000a) "*Ayukpachi*: Empowering Aboriginal Thought." In Marie Battiste (ed.) *Reclaiming Indigenous Voice and Vision*. Vancouver: University of British Columbia Press. Oxford: Blackwell, pp. 248–78.

—— (2000b) "The Context of the State of Nature." In Marie Battiste (ed.) *Reclaiming Indigenous Voice and Vision*. Vancouver: University of British Columbia Press. Oxford: Blackwell, pp. 11–38.

—— (2000c) *Aboriginal Tenure in the Canadian Constitution*. Toronto: Carswell.

Henige, David (1998) *Numbers from Nowhere: The American Indian Contact Population Debate*. Norman: University of Oklahoma Press.

Higgins, Nicholas P. (2004) *Understanding the Chiapas Rebellion: Modernist Visions and the Invisible Indian*. Austin, TX: University of Texas Press.

Hindess, Barry (1996) *Discourses of Power: From Hobbes to Foucault*. Oxford: Blackwell.

Hirschmann, Nancy J. and Christine Di Stefano (eds.) (1996) *Revisioning the Political: Feminist Reconstructions of Traditional Concepts in Western Political Theory*. Boulder, CO: Westview Press.

Hobbes, Thomas (1968 [1651]) *Leviathan*. C.B. MacPherson (ed.) New York: Penguin Classics.

Hornung, Rick (1991) *One Nation under the Gun: Inside the Mohawk Civil War*. Toronto: Stoddart.

Human Rights and Equal Opportunity Commission (1997) *Bringing them Home: Report of National Inquiry into the Separation of Aboriginal and Torres Straight Islander Children from their Families*. Canberra: Commonwealth of Australia.

Ingram, David (ed.) (2002) *The Political*. Oxford: Blackwell.

International Centre for Human Rights and Democratic Development (1996) *People or Peoples; Equality, Autonomy and Self-Determination: The Issues at Stake of the International Decade of the World's Indigenous People*. Montreal.

Irigaray, Luce (1985) *Speculum of the Other Woman*. Ithaca: Cornell University Press.

Ivison, Duncan (2002) *Postcolonial Liberalism*. Cambridge: Cambridge University Press.

Ivison, Duncan, Paul Patton, and Will Sanders (eds.) (2000) *Political Theory and the Rights of Indigenous Peoples*. Cambridge: Cambridge University Press.

Jaimes, M. Annette (ed.) (1992) *The State of Native America: Genocide, Colonization, and Resistance*. Boston: South End Press.

Jamieson, Kathleen (1978) *Indian Women and the Law in Canada: Citizens Minus*. Ottawa: Minister of Supply and Services.

—— (1986) "Sex Discrimination and the Indian Act." In J. Rick Ponting, (ed.) *The Arduous Journey: Canadian Indians and Decolonization*. pp. 112–136 Toronto: McClelland and Stewart.

Johansen, Bruce E. (1993) *Life and Death in Mohawk Country*. Golden, CO: North American Press.

Jones, Dorothy V. (1982) *License for Empire: Colonialism by Treaty in Early America*. Chicago: University of Chicago Press.

Jung, Courtney (2003) "The Politics of Indigenous Identity: Neoliberalism, Cultural Rights, and the Mexican Zapatistas" *Social Research* 70:2, pp. 433–62.

Kawharu, I.H. (ed.) (1989) *Waitangi: Maori and Pakeha Perspectives of the Treaty of Waitangi*. Auckland: Oxford University Press.

Keal, Paul (2003) *European Conquest and the Rights of Indigenous Peoples*. Cambridge: Cambridge University Press.

Knight, David B. (1988) "Self-Determination for Indigenous Peoples: The Context for Change." In R.J. Johnson, David Knight, and Eleonore Kofman (eds.) *Nationalism, Self-Determination and Political Geography*. pp. 117–134 New York: Croom Helm.

Knobloch, Frieda (1996) *The Culture of Wilderness: Agriculture as Colonization in the American West*. Chapel Hill and London: University of North Carolina Press.

Kreober, Karl (ed.) (1994) *American Indian Persistence and Resurgence*. Durham, NC: Duke University Pres.

Kuehls, Thom (1998) "Between Sovereignty and Environment: A Reading of the Discourse of Government." In Karen Liftin (ed.) *The Greening of Sovereignty in World Politics*. Cambridge, MA: MIT Press.

—— (2003) "The Environment of Sovereignty." In Warren Magnusson and Karena Shaw (eds.) *A Political Space: Reading the Global through Clayoquot Sound*. Minneapolis: University of Minnesota Press, pp. 179–97.

Kulchyski, Peter (1992) "Primitive Subversions: Totalization and Resistance in Native Canadian Politics." *Cultural Critique* (spring), pp. 171–95.

—— (ed.) (1994) *Unjust Relations: Aboriginal Rights in Canadian Courts*. Toronto: Oxford University Press.

Kymlicka, Will (1989) *Liberalism, Community and Culture*. New York: Oxford University Press.

—— (1995) *Multicultural Citizenship*. New York: Oxford University Press.

—— (1998) *Finding Our Way: Rethinking Ethnocultural Relations in Canada*. Toronto: Oxford University Press.

Laclau, Ernesto (1996) *Emancipation(s)*. London: Verso.

Laclau, Ernesto and Chantal Mouffe (1985) *Hegemony and Socialist Strategy: Towards a Radical Democratic Politics*. London: Verso.

Lawrence, Bonita (2003) "Gender, Race, and the Regulation of Native Identity in Canada and the United States: An Overview." *Hypatia* 18, pp. 3–31.

Lefort, Claude (1988) *Democracy and Political Theory*. Minneapolis: University of Minnesota Press.

Leslie, J. and R. Maguire (eds.) (1983 [1975]). *The Historical Development of the Indian Act*, 2nd edn. Ottawa: Indian Affairs and Northern Development.

Linklater, Andrew (1998) *The Transformation of Political Community*. Cambridge: Polity Press.

Luke, Timothy W. (1997) *Ecocritique: Contesting the Politics of Nature, Economy, and Culture*. Minneapolis: University of Minnesota Press.

McClure, Kirstie (1992) "The Issue of Foundations." In Judith Butler and Joan C. Scott (eds.) *Feminists Theorize the Political*. New York: Routledge.

McGrane, Bernard (1989) *Beyond Anthropology: Society and the Other*. New York: Columbia University Press.

Macklem, Patrick (2001) *Indigenous Difference and the Constitution of Canada*. Toronto: University of Toronto Press.

Magnusson, Warren (1996) *The Search for Political Space*. Toronto: University of Toronto Press.

Manganaro, Marc (ed.) (1990) *Modernist Anthropology: From Fieldwork to Text*. Princeton: Princeton University Press.

Marcus, George E. (ed.) (1992) *Rereading Cultural Anthropology*. Durham, NC: Duke University Press.

Marcus, George E. and Michael J. Fischer (1986) *Anthropology as Cultural Critique: An Experimental Moment in the Human Sciences*. Chicago: University of Chicago Press.

Martin, Calvin (ed.) (1987) *The American Indian and the Problem of History*. New York: Oxford University Press.

Massumi, Brian (1992) *A User's Guide to Capitalism and Schizophrenia*. Cambridge, MA: The MIT Press.

Memmi, Albert (1957) *The Colonizer and the Colonized*. Boston: Beacon Press.

Mercredi, Ovide and Mary Ellen Turpel (1993) *In the Rapids: Navigating the Future of First Nations*. Toronto: Viking.

Mihesuah, Devon (2003) *Indigenous American Women: Decolonization, Empowerment, Activism*. Lincoln, NE: University of Nebraska Press.

Miller, Bruce (ed.) (1992) *Anthropology and History in the Courts*. Special Issue of *BC Studies* 95 (autumn).

Miller, J.R. (1991) *Skyscrapers Hide the Heavens: A History of Indian–White Relations in Canada*, revised edn. Toronto: University of Toronto Press.

—— (2004) *Lethal Legacies: Current Native Controversies in Canada*. Toronto: McClelland and Stewart.

Mohanty, Chandra, Ann Russo, and Lourdes Torres (eds.) (1991) *Third World Women and the Politics of Feminism*. Bloomington, IN: Indiana University Press.

Monet, Don and Skanu'u (1992) *Colonialism on Trial: Indigenous Land Rights and the Gitskan and Wet-suwet-en Sovereignty Case*. Gabriola, BC: New Society Press.

Monture-Angus, Patricia (1995) *Thunder in My Soul: A Mohawk Woman Speaks*. Halifax, NS: Fernwood Publishing.

Moore, Gail Stacey (1992) "Statement on the 'Canada Package.'" Ottawa: Native Women's Association of Canada (February 2).

Moraga, Cherrie and Gloria Anzaldua (eds.) (1981) *This Bridge Called My Back: Writings by Radical Women of Color*. New York: Kitchen Table Press.

Moss, Wendy (1997) "The Canadian State and Indian Women: The Struggle for Sex Equality under the Indian Act." In Caroline Andrew and Sanda Rodgers (eds.) *Women and the Canadian State/Les Femmes et l'Etat Canadien*. pp. 79–88 Montreal and Kingston: McGill-Queen's University Press.

Nadasdy, Paul (2003) *Hunters and Bureaucrats: Power, Knowledge, and Aboriginal–State Relations in the Southwest Yukon*. Vancouver: University of British Columbia Press.

Nahanee, Teressa Anne (1997) "Indian Women, Sex Equality and the Charter." In Caroline Andrew and Sanda Rodgers (eds.) *Women and the Canadian State/Les Femmes et l'Etat Canadien*. pp. 89–103 Montreal and Kingston: McGill-Queen's University Press.

Nandy, Ashis (1983) *The Intimate Enemy: Loss and Recovery of Self under Colonialism*. Delhi: Oxford University Press.

—— (1994) *The Illegitimacy of Nationalism*. Delhi: Oxford University Press.

Nicholson, Linda (ed.) (1997) *The Second Wave*. New York: Routledge.

Niezen, Ronald (2003) *The Origins of Indigenism: Human Rights and the Politics of Identity*. Berkeley: University of California Press.

Okin, Susan Moller (1979) *Women in Western Political Thought*. Princeton, NJ: Princeton University Press.

Pagden, Anthony (1993) *European Encounters with the New World*. New Haven: Yale University Press.

Palonen, Kari and R.B.J. Walker (eds.) (2003) *Politics Revisited*. Special Issue of *Alternatives: Global, Local, Political* 28.

Parker, Andrew, Mary Russo, Doris Sommer, and Patricia Yaeger (eds.) (1992) *Nationalisms and Sexualities*. New York: Routledge.

Pateman, Carole (1988) *The Sexual Contract*. Stanford: Stanford University Press.

Patton, Paul (1996a) "Sovereignty, Law, and Difference in Australia after the Mabo Case." *Alternatives* 21:2, pp. 149–70.

—— (1996b) "Mabo, Difference and the Body of the Law." In Pheng Cheah, David Fraser, and Judy Grbich (eds.) *Thinking through the Body of the Law*. Sydney: Allen & Unwin.

Pearce, Roy Harvey (1967) *Savagism and Civilization: A Study of the Indian and the American Mind*. Baltimore: Johns Hopkins University Press.

Phillips, Anne (1991) *Engendering Democracy*. Cambridge: Polity Press.

Posey, Darrell A. and Graham Dutfield (1996) *Beyond Intellectual Property: Toward*

Traditional Resource Rights for Indigenous Peoples and Local Communities.
Ottawa: The International Development Research Centre.

Pottier, Johan, Alan Bicker, and Paul Sillitoe (ed.) (2003) *Negotiating Local Knowledge: Power and Identity in Development.* London: Pluto Press.

Rajchman, John (ed.) (1995) *The Identity in Question.* New York: Routledge.

Rancière, Jacques (1999) *Disagreement: Politics and Philosophy.* Translated by Julie Rose. Minneapolis: University of Minnesota Press.

Rawls, John (1971) *A Theory of Justice.* Oxford: Oxford University Press.

—— (1993) *Political Liberalism.* New York: Columbia University Press.

Ray, Arthur J. (1990) "Creating the Image of the Savage in Defence of the Crown: The Ethnohistorian in Court." *Native Studies Review* 6:2, pp. 13–29.

Reynolds, Henry (1996) *Aboriginal Sovereignty: Three Nations, One Australia?* St. Leonards, NSW: Allen & Unwin.

Richardson, Boyce (1994) *People of Terra Nullius: Betrayal and Rebirth in Aboriginal Canada.* Vancouver: Douglas & McIntyre.

Rogin, Michael Paul (1987) *Ronald Reagan, the Movie and Other Episodes in Political Demonology.* Berkeley: University of California Press.

Rowse, Tim (1993) *After Mabo: Interpreting Indigenous Traditions.* Melbourne: Melbourne University Press.

Sachs, Wolfgang (ed.) (1992) *The Development Dictionary: A Guide to Knowledge as Power.* London: Zed Books.

Said, Edward W. (1979) *Orientalism.* New York: Vintage Books.

—— (1993) *Culture and Imperialism.* New York: Alfred Knopf.

Sandel, Michael J. (1982) *Liberalism and the Limits of Justice.* Cambridge: Cambridge University Press.

Sanders, Douglas E. (1985) "The Indian Lobby and the Canadian Constitution, 1978–82." In Noel Dyck (ed.) *Indigenous Peoples and the Nation-State: 'Fourth World' Politics in Canada, Australia and Norway.* pp. 151–189 St. Johns: Institute of Social and Economic Research, Memorial University of Newfoundland.

Sangari, Kumkum and Sudesh Vaid (eds.) (1990) *Recasting Women: Essays in Indian Colonial History.* New Brunswick: Rutgers University Press.

Scott, Joan W., Cora Kaplan, and Debra Keates (eds.) (1997) *Transitions, Environments, Translations: Feminisms in International Politics.* New York: Routledge.

Sell, Susan K. (2003) *Private Power, Public Law: The Globalization of Intellectual Property Rights.* Cambridge: Cambridge University Press.

Shanley, Mary Lyndon and Uma Narayan (eds.) (1997) *Reconstructing Political Theory: Feminist Perspectives.* Cambridge: Polity Press.

Shanley, Mary Lyndon and Carole Pateman (eds.) (1991) *Feminist Interpretations and Political Theory.* Cambridge: Polity Press.

Shapiro, Michael J. (1997) *Violent Cartographies: Mapping Cultures of War.* Minneapolis: University of Minnesota Press.

Sharp, Andrew (1990) *Justice and the Maori: Maori Claims in New Zealand Political Argument in the 1980s.* Auckland: Oxford University Press.

Sharp, Nonie (1996) *No Ordinary Judgment.* Canberra: Aboriginal Studies Press.

Shaw, Gary C. (2003) "Clearcut Identities: Tracking Shapeshifters in Clayoquot Sound." In Warren Magnusson and Karena Shaw (eds.) *A Political Space: Reading the Global through Clayoquot Sound.* pp. 199–221 Minneapolis: University of Minnesota Press.

Shaw, Karena (2002) "Feminist Futures: Contesting the Political." In Richard Falk,

Lester Ruiz, and R.B.J. Walker (eds.) *Reframing the International: Law, Culture, Politics.* New York and London: Routledge, pp. 218–47.

—— (2003) "Whose Knowledge for What Politics?" *Review of International Studies* 29, pp. 199–221.

—— (2004) "Knowledge, Foundations, Politics." *International Studies Review* 6, pp. 7–20

Shiva, Vandana (1997) *Biopiracy: The Plunder of Nature and Knowledge.* Boston, MA: South End Press.

—— (2001) *Protect or Plunder? Understanding Intellectual Property Rights.* Halifax, NS: Fernwood Press.

Silman, Janet (ed.) (1987) *Enough is Enough: Aboriginal Women Speak Out.* Toronto: The Women's Press.

Skinner, Quentin (1996) *Reason and Rhetoric in the Philosophy of Hobbes.* Cambridge: Cambridge University Press.

Smith, Dan (1993) *The Seventh Fire: The Struggle for Aboriginal Government.* Toronto: Key Porter Books.

Smith, Linda Tuhiwai (1999) *Decolonizing Methodologies: Research and Indigenous Peoples.* London and New York: Zed Books.

Snow, Alpheus H. (1921) *The Question of Aborigines in the Law and Practice of Nations.* New York: Putnam.

Spivak, Gayatri C. (1988a) "Can the Subaltern Speak?" In Cary Nelson and Lawrence Grossberg (eds.) *Marxism and the Interpretation of Culture.* pp. 271–313 Chicago: University of Illinois Press.

—— (1988b) *In Other Worlds: Essays in Cultural Politics.* New York: Routledge.

Stabinsky, Doreen and Stephen P. Brush (eds.) (1996) *Valuing Local Knowledge: Indigenous Peoples and Intellectual Property Rights.* Washington, DC: Island Press.

Supreme Court of British Columbia (1991) *Delgamuukw et al v. British Columbia: Reasons for Judgment of the Honourable Chief Justice Allan McEachern.* March 8, 1991. No. 0843, Smithers Registry.

Supreme Court of Canada (1997) *Judgment and Reasons for Judgment in Delgamuukw v. British Columbia.* December 11, 1997. File No. 23799, Ottawa.

Takaki, Ronald (1990) *Iron Cages: Race and Culture in 19th Century America.* New York: Oxford University Press.

Taylor, Charles (1993) *Reconciling the Solitudes: Essays on Canadian Federalism and Nationalism.* Guy Laforest (ed.) Montreal: McGill-Queen's University Press.

—— (1994) "The Politics of Recognition." In Amy Gutmann (ed.) *Multiculturalism and the Politics of Recognition.* Princeton: Princeton University Press.

Tennant, Paul (1990) *Aboriginal Peoples and Politics.* Vancouver: University of British Columbia Press.

Thomas, Nicholus (1994) *Colonialism's Culture: Anthropology, Travel and Government.* Princeton, NJ: Princeton University Press.

Thornberry, Patrick (2002) *Indigenous Peoples and the Discourses of Human Rights.* Manchester: Manchester University Press.

Tobias, John L. (1976) "Protection, Civilization, Assimilation: An Outline History of Canada's Indian Policy." *Western Canadian Journal of Anthropology* 6:2 pp. 39–55.

Tocqueville, Alexis de (1990) *Democracy in America: Volume I.* New York: Vintage Books. First edition: 1835; first English edition: 1945.

Todorov, Tzvetan (1982) *The Conquest of America.* New York: Harper & Row.

Trigger, Bruce G. (1985) *Natives and Newcomers: Canada's 'Heroic Age' Reconsidered.* Kingston: McGill-Queen's University Press.

Trinh T. Minh-ha (1989) *Woman Native Other: Writing Postcoloniality and Feminism.* Bloomington, IN: Indiana University Press.

—— (1991) *When the Moon Waxes Red: Representation, Gender and Cultural Politics.* New York: Routledge.

Tucker, Vincent (1999) "The Myth of Development: A Critique of Eurocentric Discourse." In Ronaldo Munck and Denis O'Hearn (eds.) *Critical Development Theory: Contributions to a New Paradigm.* London: Zed Books, pp. 1–26.

Tully, James (ed.) (1988) *Meaning and Context: Quentin Skinner and His Critics.* Princeton: Princeton University Press.

—— (1989) "Wittgenstein and Political Philosophy." *Political Theory* 17:2, pp. 172–204.

—— (1993) *An Approach to Political Philosophy: Locke in Contexts.* Cambridge: Cambridge University Press.

—— (1994) *Philosophy in an Age of Pluralism.* Cambridge: Cambridge University Press.

—— (1995) *Strange Multiplicity: Constitutionalism in an Age of Diversity.* Cambridge: Cambridge University Press.

Turpel, Ellen (1989) "Aboriginal Peoples and the Canadian Charter of Rights and Freedom." *Canadian Womens Studies/Les Cahiers de la femme* 10:2&3, pp. 149–57.

Turpel-Lafond, Mary Ellen (1997) "Patriarchy and Paternalism: The Legacy of the Canadian State for First Nations Women." In Caroline Andrew and Sanda Rodgers (eds.) *Women and the Canadian State/Les Femmes et l'Etat Canadien.* pp. 64–78 Montreal and Kingston: McGill-Queen's University Press.

Upton, L.F.S. (1973) "The Origins of Canadian Indian Policy." *Journal of Canadian Indian Studies* 8:4 pp. 51–61.

Venne, Sharon (1998) *Our Elders Understand Our Rights: Evolving International Law Regarding Indigenous Rights.* Penticton, BC: Theytus Books.

Vincent, Joan (1990) *Anthropology and Politics: Visions, Traditions and Trends.* Tuscon: University of Arizona Press.

Wa, Gisday and Delgam Uukw (1989) *The Spirit in the Land: The Opening Statement of the Gitksan and Wet'suwet'en Hereditary Chiefs in the Supreme Court of British Columbia.* Gabriola, BC: Reflections.

Wadden, Marie (1991) *Nitassinan: The Innu Struggle to Reclaim Their Homeland.* Toronto and Vancouver: Douglas & McIntyre.

Walker, R.B.J. (1993) *Inside/Outside: International Relations as Political Theory.* Cambridge: Cambridge University Press.

—— (forthcoming) *After the Globe, Before the World.*

Walzer, Michael (1983) *Spheres of Justice: A Defense of Pluralism and Equality.* New York: Basic Books.

—— (1987) *Interpretation and Social Criticism.* Cambridge, MA: Harvard University Press.

Weatherford, Jack (1988) *Indian Givers: How the Indians of America Transformed the World.* New York: Crown.

Weed, Elizabeth (ed.) (1989) *Coming to Terms: Feminism Theory, Politics.* New York: Routledge.

Williams, Robert A., Jr. (1990) *The American Indian in Western Legal Thought: The Discourses of Conquest.* New York: Oxford University Press.

Wilmer, Franke (1993) *The Indigenous Voice in World Politics*. Newbury Park, CA: Sage Publications.

Wittgenstein, Ludwig (1969) *On Certainty*. New York: Harper & Row.

Wright, Ronald (1992) *Stolen Continents: The "New World" through Indian Eyes Since 1492*. New York: Houghton Mifflin Company.

York, Geoffrey (1991) *People of the Pines: The Warriors and the Legacy of Oka*. Boston and Toronto: Little, Brown.

—— (1999) *The Dispossessed: Life and Death in Native Canada*. Toronto: McArthur & Company.

Young, Iris Marion (1990) *Justice and the Politics of Difference*. Princeton: Princeton University Press.

—— (2000) *Inclusion and Democracy*. New York and Oxford: Oxford University Press.

Index